THE MEMOIRS OF
CHARLES HENRY VEIL

THE MEMOIRS OF
CHARLES HENRY VEIL

A Soldier's Recollections of the Civil War and the Arizona Territory

Edited and with an Introduction by
Herman J. Viola

The Library of the American West

Orion Books
New York

HOUSTON PUBLIC LIBRARY

Published by Orion Books, A division of Crown Publishers, Inc., 201 East 50th Street, New York, New York 10022. Member of the Crown Publishing Group.

Random House, Inc. New York, Toronto, London, Sydney, Auckland
ORION and colophon are trademarks of Crown Publishers, Inc.
Manufactured in the United States of America

Library of Congress Cataloging-in-Publication Data

Veil, Charles Henry, 1842–1910.
    The memoirs of Charles Henry Veil : a soldier's recollections
of the Civil War and the Arizona Territory / edited by Herman J.
Viola.—1st ed.
        p.   cm.—(Library of the American West)
    Includes index.
    1. Veil, Charles Henry, 1842–1910. 2. United States—History—
Civil War, 1861–1865—Personal narratives. 3. Gettysburg (Pa.),
Battle of, 1863. 4. Arizona—History—To 1912. 5. Frontier and
pioneer life—Arizona. 6. Apache Indians—Wars. 7. Indians of
North America—Wars—1866–1895. I. Viola, Herman J. II. Title.
III. Series.
E601.V45   1993
973.8'092—dc20   93-14733
                                                                            CIP

ISBN 0-517-59463-3
10 9 8 7 6 5 4 3 2 1
First Edition

Contents

Acknowledgments

Two individuals were essential to the successful preparation of Charles Veil's memoirs for publication. One is Anne Hoffman Cleaver, a descendant of General John Fulton Reynolds who has long been involved in the study of her family's history. Years ago Anne told me of the Reynolds-Hewitt love affair that distracted her grieving family after the death of her great-great-uncle at Gettysburg, and it was the opportunity to publish Veil's version of the story that encouraged me to recommend publication of his memoirs. Anne provided considerable assistance by combing family correspondence for references to General Reynolds and his orderly Veil and by providing copies of pertinent photographs that remain in family custody.

The other person I must acknowledge is David P. Perrine, a retired U.S. Army colonel who goes by the nickname "Skip." As a labor of love for a great military story, Skip undertook the tedious task of checking the facts in the Veil memoirs and did a marvelous job. He not only documented Veil's military life virtually day by day, but he also provided biographical information on his many comrades-in-arms, both during the Civil War and later in Arizona Territory. Skip accomplished this by sifting through an immense number of documents in the National Archives and then by pestering librarians and archivists in Pennyslvania and Arizona. Three of these individuals deserve recognition and a thank you: Susan Peters of the Arizona Historical Society, Kris Darnall of the Arizona Historical Foundation, and Scott P. Gitchell of the Tioga County Historical Society.

Introduction

As editor of the Library of the American West, I invite you to enjoy with me the memoirs of Charles Henry Veil, a Pennsylvania farm boy who left home in 1861 to save the Union and "see the elephant" and returned to his home state in 1891 having seen enough "elephants" and experienced enough adventures to put Indiana Jones to shame.

Were Veil's memoirs a work of fiction, they would be delightful and entertaining reading in their own right, but they are not fiction. Indeed, a novelist would be hard pressed to create the adventures Veil experienced during the Civil War and then afterward in Arizona Territory, first as a cavalry officer chasing Apaches and then as one of the region's early pioneers. Impossible as it might seem, his tales are true except for a few embellishments and mistakes regarding details, which are inevitable when describing events that occurred up to half a century earlier. Veil was not only an eyewitness to history, he helped make it, beginning with his enlistment in a Pennyslvania volunteer regiment a few months after the firing on Fort Sumter.

At once awful and awesome, no other event in American history has so deeply affected our nation's soul and so compellingly kept our interest as the Civil War. Even today, more than 125 years after Robert E. Lee and the remnant of his loyal but starving army bowed to the inevitable at Appomattox, the Civil War continues to fascinate people the world over. What draws us to that terrible conflict is not the struggle over slavery or states' rights, but the human drama that unfolded on fields of glory—the incredible bravery and remarkable spirit of Johnny Reb and Billy Yank.

Even those who marched and fought could not resist the war's color and pageantry. Perhaps Lee himself said it best, after routing the Federals at Fredericksburg: "It is well that war is so terrible—we should grow too fond of it."

Often overlooked in the romance and pageantry—the surging armies, prancing horses, and flashing sabers—is the war's dark side. Few families North or South escaped the war years without the loss of a friend, relative, or loved one. Imagine the anguish of the Prentiss family of Maryland. Clifton Prentiss fought for the North, his brother William for the South. Their regiments met at Petersburg on April 2, 1865, just seven days before Appomattox, where both brothers were mortally wounded. After a separation of four years, the brothers were reunited on their deathbeds in a hospital in Washington, D.C.

The war knew no age limit. Men in their sixties and seventies fought alongside boys in their teens. For the most part, however, it was a young man's war. Of the 2.3 million soldiers in blue, fully 1.6 million were under twenty-three years of age. Of these more than 200,000 were sixteen or younger, 300 were under thirteen, and at least 25 were ten or younger. Perhaps the youngest was musician Edward Black who joined the 21st Indiana at age nine.

Age was certainly no barrier to combat as evidenced by the 247 Virginia Military Institute cadets—sixteen years old and younger—who helped carry the day for the Confederacy at New Market and by thirteen-year-old John Mather Sloan, a private in the Ninth Texas, who lost a leg early in the war. His only regret, Sloan insisted, was that "I shall not soon be able to get at the enemy." Veil, nineteen when he enlisted, was typical of those teenagers touched by fire.

The patriotic young man doubtless would have remained one of those thousands of nameless youngsters in the ranks were it not for the fact that he happened to be next to Major General John Fulton Reynolds, commander of the Union Army's First Corps, at the moment of his death on the first day of the battle of Gettysburg. Veil was his orderly. Instead of taking to his heels in the face of onrushing rebels and humming minnie balls, he helped drag Reynolds's body over the brow of a hill and saved it from capture.

At the time, the exploit marked a turning point in the young man's life. Today, more than a century later, thanks to these memoirs and various letters and documents still extant, it provides some insights into one Civil War family's grief.

Veil's account of the death of General Reynolds was widely circulated at the time and he never tired of retelling the tale in later years. As he grew older, the basic facts remained the same but some embellishments crept in.

According to Veil, the reason Reynolds pressed forward that day so energetically—some said so recklessly—was to prevent the Confederates from entering the town of Gettysburg. Once inside the city, Reynolds knew, only artillery fire would dislodge them. Hoping to prevent needless loss of civilian life and property, he urged the lead division of the First Corps to come forward on the run and blunt the advance of Confederate General A. P. Hill's division led by General James J. Archer's brigade, which was threatening to seize a key plot of land known as McPherson's farm. The Confederates were sweeping through a grove of trees and moving up a ridge toward Reynolds, who was on the flat of the ridge at a point where the woods ended and about two hundred yards from the McPherson barn.

The Union forces responding to Reynolds's urgent call were units of the famed Iron Brigade—five midwestern regiments noted for their jaunty black hats and ironlike valor. Their reputation was not tarnished at Gettysburg: only one in three were left to answer muster after the carnage. But at this moment they were not moving fast enough to suit Reynolds. As the Second Wisconsin swept over the crest of the hill, Archer's men stopped them with a well-placed musket volley. The Second Wisconsin faltered and fell back. Upon witnessing this, Reynolds galloped along behind their line, shouting, "Forward, forward, men! Drive those fellows out of there. Forward! For God's sake forward!" Then, turning in his saddle as if to see what had become of the other regiments in the Iron Brigade rushing forward at the moment to buttress the Union line, Reynolds suddenly sagged and fell off his horse, pitching face first onto the ground.

A Confederate sharpshooter standing in the loft of McPherson's barn had made the shot of a lifetime. The minnie ball entered below Reynolds's right ear, exited through the left side of his head, and lodged in his chest. "I have seen many men killed in action," Veil later informed D. M. McConaughy of Gettysburg, "but never saw a ball do its work so *instantly* as did the ball which struck General Reynolds. He never spoke a word, or moved a muscle after he was struck."

Although Veil in his memoirs gives the impression that he alone dragged Reynolds's body to safety—a claim he repeatedly made after the war—he related a different version on April 7, 1864, in his letter to McConaughy. "When the General fell," Veil writes, "the only persons who were with him was Capt. Mitchell & Baird and myself. When he fell we sprang from our horses. The Genl fell on his left side. I turned him on his back, glanced over him but could see no wound except a slight bruise above his left eye. We were under the impression that he was only stunned, this was all done at a glance. I caught the Genl under the arms while each of the Capts took hold of his legs, and we commenced to carry him out of the woods toward the Seminary. Between the woods where he was killed & the Sem[inar]y, he gasped a little and I thought he was coming to his senses. We stopped a moment & I gave him a drop of water from a canteen but he would not drink, it was his last struggle." In this letter, Veil also declares he did not discover the death wound until much later, after he and other orderlies had carried Reynolds from the battlefield to the Emmitsburg Road where they hoped to find an ambulance. Except for these discrepancies, however, the account of Reynolds's death in the memoirs and its effect on Veil's life are supported by historical records in the National Archives and documents, photographs, and correspondence in the custody of Reynolds family descendants.

John Reynolds was one of thirteen children—six boys and seven girls—of whom nine survived infancy. John and a younger brother, William, were the only members of their family to venture far from their Lancaster home. Both entered military service. William went into the navy, where he enjoyed an illustrious career. As an ensign he accompanied the U.S. Exploring Expedition of 1838–41, a round-the-world naval exercise that discovered Antarctica (among other accomplishments). William Reynods eventually rose in the ranks to rear admiral and twice served as acting secretary of the navy.

The career of John Reynolds was equally distinguished. He entered West Point in 1837, was brevetted for outstanding service in the Mexican War, twice crossed the continent during the troubles with Indians and Mormons in the 1850s, and was offered—but declined—command of the Army of the Potomac prior to the battle of Gettysburg.

Reynolds was liked and respected by all who knew him. Some considered him the best officer in the Union Army. Typical of the tributes to the fallen warrior was one penned by Captain Joseph G. Rosengarten, his adjutant: "Impetuous without rashness, rapid without haste, ready without heedlessness, he liked better to be at the head of a compact corps than to command a scattered army."

Upon hearing of his death, a Confederate prisoner at Gettysburg compared the loss of Reynolds to that of Stonewall Jackson, but claimed the North got the worse end of the exchange. That Reynolds enjoyed Confederate respect and admiration is supported by a petition sent to the Confederate secretary of war by the mayor and twenty-six citizens of Fredericksburg, Virginia, upon hearing the news that he had been captured by the Confederacy. The petitioners urged the Confederate government to show Reynolds the utmost clemency by arranging an early parole for him, if it would not jeopardize the Southern war effort, because "we do feel inasmuch as when we were prisoners in the hands of General Reynolds we received from him a treatment distinguished by a marked and considerate respect for our opinions and feelings, it becomes us to use our feeble influence in invoking for him now a prisoner of our Government a treatment as kind and considerate as was extended by him to us."

Reynolds was captured on June 28, 1862, and held prisoner in Richmond until August 8 of that year, when he was exchanged for Confederate General William Barksdale. Paroled together, they died together. Barksdale was struck down at

Gettysburg leading his Mississippians in an assault on the Peach Orchard the day after Reynolds fell

Fortunately for Veil, Reynolds came from a large and loving family overcome with gratitude for saving his remains from the enemy. "It never entered my mind until this moment that they would not be saved, which was a merciful thing," wrote Eleanor—Ellie—Reynolds on July 5 to her brother William, then at sea on board the U.S.S. *Vermont* performing blockade duty off the South Carolina coast. "Our first intimation of [John's death] . . . was Ms. Reynolds coming up while we were at breakfast table & she told us most kindly. The papers came in a moment & it was there, but we had to wait a long time for confirmation. It came at last & sad it was, but a good comfort to know that the remains were coming to us."

William also heard the news from another sister, Jennie, in a letter written the same day. "Before this reaches you the papers will have told you that John's life has been given to his country," Jennie wrote. "His orderly (an intelligent man and devoted to John), was nearest to him as he fell from his horse and caught him, but he never spoke and when asked if he suffered only slightly smiled. As they were only 50 yards from the rebs, they had to make haste to get the body off."

Although Reynolds was killed within fifty miles of his home, his body went first to Baltimore for embalming. From there it went to Philadelphia, where Reynolds lay in state in the home of his sister Katherine, and then, on the morning of July 4, to Lancaster for burial in the family plot. "When we arrived at 11½ o.c.," Jennie wrote, "the whole street was filled with people, flags at half mast, draped with crepe where ever one could see. Went direct to the cemetery where several clergy made short address. 8 or 9 of the old Reserves begged to act as pall bearers; of course, twas granted."

With Reynolds until his internment were six of his personal staff, including Veil. "Everything," Eleanor declared, "was quietly & unostentatiously done & his staff each & all said they thought it was just what his wish would have been & was most gratifying to them. They feel it as keenly as we can. I cannot even *tell*, much less *write*, you of theirs or my own feelings." Major Riddle, for example, "threw himself on the precious remains & wept uncontrollably. When he & Col. Kingsbury met they wept like children & the rest left them to comfort each other."

As Veil confirms, the Reynolds family, staunch Protestants all, received two shocks at once: news of the general's death and that he was engaged to be married—to a Catholic, at that. "I need not tell you what a thunder clap it was to us all," Jennie announced in her letter to William. His family believed that the forty-two-year-old bachelor did not have a romantic bone in his body. The mystery began to unfold when Veil loosened the general's collar to inspect the wound and found around his neck a silver chain with a Catholic religious medal and a gold ring in the form of clasped hands inscribed with the words DEAR KATE. When Veil delivered Reynolds's personal effects to the family, his valise contained several photographs of an attractive woman and two letters from Eden Hall, Torresdale, Pennsylvania, and signed "Kate." The family also noticed that Reynolds's West Point ring, which was missing from his hand, had been used to imprint the wax seals on the two letters.

The identity of the mysterious Kate became known almost immediately. Friday morning in Philadelphia, as the family sat around General Reynolds's open coffin—"It was such a comfort to have the body so soon and to have it look so natural," wrote Jennie—someone brought a note upstairs announcing a Miss Hewitt at the door who wished to see the remains if agreeable to the family. "Is she Kate?" asked Ellie. Indeed so.

It was the morning of July 3. Less than a hundred miles away Union and Confederate forces were still smashing at one another with a fury unprecedented in the history of warfare. Before the last musket was fired in that terrible battle thousands of northern and southern households would be sharing the grief felt by the Reynolds family that, for a brief moment, was distracted by the appearance of the mysterious Kate, who entered the room, knelt next to the coffin, and wept unabashedly.

Kate, the family soon discovered, was Catherine Mary Hewitt. She had met John Reynolds in San Francisco in 1860 while working as the governess to a wealthy family. Upon returning to the East, she had entered the Academy of the

Sacred Heart in Torresdale, Pennyslvania, where she became a convert to Catholicism. During the war John had also converted to Catholicism and they became engaged, planning to marry after the war. As Jennie wrote to William, Kate had explained to the hushed family that "she had given him first to God, then to his country, then to herself. She had his consent to enter a religious life should she lose him and now she intends to do it as the world has no interest for her now. You would be so pleased with her letters; they show such a delicate, refined mind, so far above the ordinary love epistle. We felt so sorry for her, 'tis like crushing the life out of her. They would have been such a happy couple."

"Poor girl," echoed Ellie, "she has been a heroic woman & most worthy of our dear one. I cannot tell you all she said of him, but she was in his heart & from her I have learned much of him, of his feelings & inner life than I ever knew before. She had not shed a tear till she entered the parlor, and then she wept copiously on her knees beside him, but before she saw his face."

Eight days after John Reynolds was laid to rest, Kate Hewitt entered the Saint Joseph Central House of the Sisters of Charity in Emmitsburg, Maryland. John Reynolds and his troops had passed the convent en route to Gettysburg only ten miles away and, according to tradition, the nuns and students had knelt in prayer alongside the road as the Union troops trudged past. It was there, as Veil describes, that he later shared a few moments with Reynolds's grief-stricken fiancée and received the embroidered handkerchief intended for her beloved.

Although Veil makes no mention of it in his memoirs, he remained in touch with both Kate and the Reynolds family for several years through Ellie. "Miss Hewitt sends you her kindest regards and says she is much pleased at your selection of active duty—your late commander having always taken the active part. She is very well and is much happier looking then when you saw her," Ellie informed Veil in August 1865. "Her position is a settled one and she feels at home in her duties."

Through Ellie's letters to Veil, which continued until 1870, it is learned that Kate left their lives as suddenly as she had appeared. Miss Hewitt, "now Sister Hildegardis" (a name selected in consultation with Ellie and Jennie Reynolds), had been quite ill but had recovered, Veil learned in October 1865. Three months later Sister Hildegardis went to Albany to teach in a large school the Sisters of Charity had recently opened. Kate remained there until September 1868, when she abruptly left the religious order and severed contact with the Reynolds family. A possible explanation for her unexpected departure is found in a letter from Ellie to Veil, written a month earlier: "Miss Hewitt is still at Albany. She says she is happier as a 'sister' than she would be 'in the world'—I hope we shall visit her in October . . . [but] she is not strong and has a cough that is almost constant."

The final part of Veil's account, besides meeting Kate Hewitt at the convent, that is verified by Reynolds family correspondence concerns his visit to the Gettysburg battlefield to mark the spot where the general was killed. Indeed, Lee's forces had scarcely left the area before Reynolds's staff and the family began making plans for a suitable monument in his memory. Ellie, who seems to have been an indefatigable correspondent, firmly established the family position with respect to the placement of the monument in February 1864. "The family feels the necessity of marking the spot upon which the Genl. fell," she informed Captain C. McLure, "& since you have so delicately referred the matter to them for decision—would prefer the Corps to erect the monument on that spot rendered sacred by reason of his death & where they so bravely confronted the rebels for the last time under his command. When at Gettysburg in Nov. we were unable to ascertain its precise location but that it will be identified there can be no doubt, Orderly Veil being very decided in his recollection of it, & all its surroundings."

Since recovering Reynolds's body and marking the precise spot where he fell obviously loomed so large in his family's grief, it is not surprising that Veil became a person of such importance to them. The family could not do enough to express its gratitude to the teenager from Scalp Level. Besides giving him a gold watch, the family managed to get him a promotion as well. Nor is it surprising, considering the shock at Reynolds's death—the highest ranking Union officer to die in combat during the Civil War—that the federal government would attempt to do anything within reason to pacify his family.

The person directly responsible for Veil's promotion, of course, was Ellie. On December 23, 1863, she met personally with President Abraham Lincoln to urge Veil's appointment as a second lieutenant in a regular army regiment and came away with the following handwritten note to Secretary of War Edwin M. Stanton: "Please see this lady who is a sister to our gallant and brave friend Gen. Reynolds who fell at Gettysburg. Please oblige her if you can."

Oblige her Stanton did. Veil went from private in the Ninth Pennsylvania Reserves to a second lieutenant in the First U.S. Cavalry. Obviously better educated than the majority of youngsters who fought on both sides in the Civil War, Veil sent three letters to the Reynolds family expressing his gratitude for their kindnesses to him and informing them of the outcome of their efforts.[1] In the first letter, dated November 10, 1863, Veil thanked the family for the gold watch. In the second letter, dated January 5, 1864, he thanked them for his commission. The third letter, which bears the same date, he wrote at the request of Secretary of War Stanton, who wanted Veil to explain to the family the circumstances delaying his appointment to the regular army.

Immediately upon hearing the welcome news from Veil, Ellie rushed a heartfelt thank-you letter, bordered in mourning black, to Lincoln. "Let me now assure you," Ellie wrote on January 11, 1864, "we *are most* grateful for the assistance, so graciously afforded us, in procuring a position for one, who is every way worthy of it, & well able to discharge its duties. His devotion to my brother, during his life, and his heroic conduct in rescuing his precious remains, in the face of terrific fire, from the rebels, at the battle of Gettysburg, has endeared him to us, and emboldened me to solicit your Excellency's aid, in giving him some permanent, and suitable mark of our high appreciation of his services."

Veil did nothing to change the opinion the Reynolds family held for him. As luck would have it, he joined a regiment that achieved a distinguished war record. The First Cavalry, which was attached to the Army of the Potomac throughout the war, fought in forty-seven engagements and suffered the heaviest losses of all Union regiments of cavalry. Only nine officers and seventy-three enlisted men died on the battlefield, but the regiment's wounded numbered in the hundreds. At the Wilderness alone, in just three days of fighting—May 5 to 7, 1864—the First Cavalry lost forty-five men, eight of them battlefield fatalities. It was there, at the battle of Todd's Tavern on May 6, that Veil, after only three weeks with the regiment, was brevetted first lieutenant for gallantry. According to the regimental returns, ten of the fifteen officers—seven of them company commanders—were wounded in that month alone.

Regimental returns tell the tale. The First Cavalry opened the 1864 campaign with a total complement of seven hundred officers and enlisted men. It went into winter quarters at Winchester with only two hundred men present for duty. The regiment recovered some strength during the winter as a number of officers and enlisted men returned from convalescence, so that there were three hundred men in the ranks when the First Cavalry took to the field again in early 1865. Its last raid began on February 27, reaching the Army of Virginia a month later. On April 1 the regiment had a sharp fight at Dinwiddie Courthouse, followed two days later by the hard-fought engagement at Five Forks, where Veil was brevetted captain for conspicuous bravery and major for meritorious service. A week later, on April 9, Lee surrendered.

Here is where most memoirs of Civil War veterans normally end, but not Veil's. Having obtained a commission in the regular army thanks to the Reynolds family, he chose to make a career of military service. He remained in the army another six years, until February 19, 1871, when he reluctantly accepted an honorable discharge during a period when the army was undergoing a reduction in force. Much of that time was spent in Arizona Territory, which was as "wild and woolly" as the Wild West ever got. Veil's story, which is corroborated by military records, reads like a Ned Buntline dime novel.

Besides regaling the reader with tales of fighting Apaches and tracking deserters, however, Veil's memoirs also provide a compelling glimpse into life as it was on this turbulent and cosmopolitan frontier. Here was a potpourri of Mexicans, Indians, Chinese, soldiers, prospectors, ranchers, migrants, and immigrants, each hoping to strike it rich in an environment that

Arizona Territory

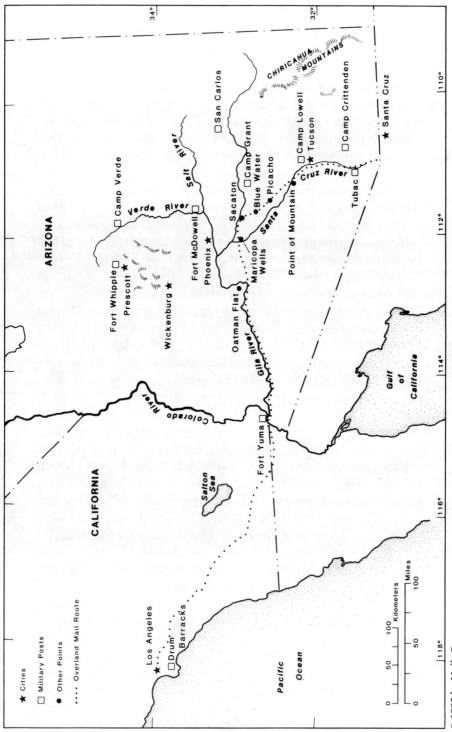

© 1993 by Molly Ryan

was largely isolated and lawless. Arizona Territory in the 1860s and 1870s is the stuff of which today's western novels and movies are made but without their glamour and romance.

Indeed not, especially for the officers and enlisted men assigned to Arizona's godforsaken military posts and charged with attempting to keep order. Camps Crittenden, Tubac, Grant, Lowell, and McDowell—Veil's duty stations—were isolated, dirty, and unpleasant. Like most western forts, these consisted of clusters of ramshackle buildings as vulnerable to the elements as they were to hostile Indians. Typical of their condition is the description of Camp Bayard in New Mexico Territory, written by a newly arrived recruit in 1871: "The locality was all that could be desired; the post everything undesirable. Huts of logs and round stone, with flat dirt roofs that in summer leaked rivulets of liquid mud: in the winter the hiding place of the tarantula and centipede, with ceilings of condemned canvas; windows of four to six panes, swinging door-like on hinges . . . : low, dark, and uncomfortable. Six hundred miles from the railroad."

Barracks were hot in summer, cold in winter. Bathing was done in rivers and ponds. Sometimes one metal bathtub serviced an entire company. Spit and polish had no place on this frontier, where the men spent most of their time on monotonous patrols or fatigue duty, such as making roads, building houses, digging latrines, all for $13 a month. Little wonder that Veil and his fellow officers had to contend with men drawn largely from the ranks of the desperately poor or simply desperate, not ideal military material and far removed from the citizen soldiers of the Civil War.

There was one similarity to the Civil War. Veil again got to see death up close. This was a time when the Apaches, especially the Chiricahuas under Cochise, were making their final desperate attempt to remain a free and independent people. The roads through their territory—as are the pages of Veil's memoirs—were littered with the charred remains of wagons and the bodies of those who chose to risk their lives in search of homesteads or gold. Veil even got to meet Cochise and his fabled friend Tom Jeffords after he left the army and entered the milling business. Veil's experiences with the Apaches were typical of the frontier army—constant pursuit and little contact, but when it occurred no quarter was given or expected.

Equally graphic are Veil's encounters with deserters. Veil was in the army when desertion was an everyday affair, when those who remained went mad from boredom or drink, and when suicide was an ordinary event. "It would appear to me," Veil writes, "judging from the large number of men who resided in the territory in the early days and who I was acquainted with, who ended their life by their own hands, that the effect of the climate and the excitement incident to their early life must have had some demoralizing effect on their minds."

One was Veil's companion-in-arms, First Lieutenant John F. Small, who had joined the First Cavalry a month after Veil, who survived the war, and who also accompanied the regiment to Arizona. Small inexplicably took his life while on leave in San Francisco. According to the account printed in the *Army and Navy Journal* on April 10, 1869, the thirty-year-old officer dressed himself in his finest uniform, lay down on the bed in his hotel room, placed a chloroform-soaked handkerchief over his face, and died. No reason was ever found, although Lieutenant Small left a number of notes and letters regarding the disposition of his personal effects. To his brother he wrote: "I cannot endure life longer. Go to the Fort and get everything that belongs to me. Should any one ever speak of me in your presence in terms that reflect upon my honor as a gentleman or my integrity as a man, *shoot* him upon the spot. Good-by dear brother; live and be happy, if possible, and when you die, die game."

Desertion by the men in ranks was so frequent, Veil recalls, that some officers would have been left without a command if steps were not taken to prevent it. As a result, company commanders seemed to spend as much time chasing their deserters as they did Apaches. In one such episode, Veil killed two deserters with one pistol shot. The incident, which has all the trappings of a tall tale, is verified by official records. Like Veil's description of recovering the body of General Reynolds, however, the story is slightly embellished in the memoirs. He declares that one of the deserters shot at him first, prompting his shot. This claim was never made at the court of inquiry. Other than that, the story as written is borne out by army records.

The court of inquiry was convened at Veil's request at Camp McDowell, Arizona Territory, on November 9, 1869. The witnesses were three troopers and Pasa Salazar, the scout Veil had sent in pursuit of the two deserters. According to their testimony, the deserters—privates Charles Brown and Julius Arnold of C Troop, First Cavalry—were found hiding in tall reeds along the bank of Gila River about two miles from Maricopa Wells. As soon as the deserters realized they had been discovered, both raised up on one knee with carbines in their hands. Private Brown leveled his at Veil as if intending to shoot. The sudden movement caused Veil's horse to shy and spin around, forcing Brown to hold his fire. Veil, meanwhile, yelled at the two men to drop their guns. Since it appeared Brown had no intention of doing so, Veil fired one shot from his pistol, killing him instantly. At the shot Arnold, still clutching his carbine, rose to his feet and began backing up. As he did so, Veil repeatedly yelled at him to drop his weapon. "It's not loaded," Arnold finally replied and then came forward. As he dropped his carbine and pistol to the ground, Arnold then said, "Lieutenant, I am wounded." Veil's shot, it was discovered, had passed completely through Brown and gravely wounded Arnold, who died about an hour later.

The main concern of the court of inquiry was to determine whether Veil had been justified in shooting at them. Each of the witnesses testified to the violent nature of Trooper Brown, whose carbine when examined was found to be loaded and cocked. According to Trumpeter John Keesy of C Troop, Brown had frequently boasted among the men that he would never be taken alive: "If brought back, it would be his carcass, and that, if followed, he would shoot the leader of the party, and try to get the others to turn back." Private William Henry of C Troop knew nothing about such a boast but confirmed that Brown was the sort to do so. "I never had much to say to him," Henry admitted. "He was considered a desperate man, and once since he has been in the troop, he attempted to or threatened to shoot his tentmate." Based on the evidence and testimony, the court ruled that Lieutenant Veil had "saved his life by his prompt action" and adjourned.

No matter who shot first, it was a good story that Veil

loved to relate to anyone who would listen. A neighbor who lived near Veil after his return to Pennsylvania recalled that his cavalry pistol hung from a loop on his bedroom doorknob where it was sure to catch attention and prompt a story from the old veteran.

That Veil was a great raconteur there can be no doubt. According to Major George W. Merrick of the 187th Pennsylvania Infantry retired, who wrote Veil's obituary for the Military Order of the Loyal Legion of the United States, "he was the ideal of good fellowship. His fund of war stories and anecdotes seemed inexhaustible, and his style and manner of relating them original and graphic."

All that may have been true of Veil, but he also had a less jovial side that is not reflected in his memoirs. While in New Hempstead, Texas, in October 1865, before proceeding to California to join his regiment, Veil witnessed a quarrel between Private Joseph B. Perry of the 29th Illinois Infantry and a black man named Virgil. According to the charges preferred against Veil, he stopped the quarrel with undue severity by cursing at the enlisted man and striking him about the head and face with his saber. The charges were based on the testimony of seven enlisted men who had witnessed the incident and claimed that Veil had continued to beat Perry even after he had agreed to accompany him to the office of the provost marshal. The case was never brought to court-martial and no further details are known, but one can imagine that Veil had intervened to protect a freedman who was being abused by a group of enlisted men.

Veil's post–Civil War military career is not quite as illustrious as his war record, although he did get mentioned favorably in one official report, with reference to the incident in his memoirs in which he led a charge on a band of hostile Apaches, killing one and recapturing stolen property: "Great credit is due here to Major Veil and his command, for the promptness of their charge," wrote his commanding officer.

Instead of commendations, however, his postwar record is sprinkled with misconduct charges. Most seem to stem from the petty bickering among officers that appears to have been a way of life in these isolated posts. In January 1869, for example, Veil was court-martialed on seven charges, six of which concerned alleged misuse of government funds. Essentially, Veil was being accused of the sort of sharp dealing in which he fancied himself quite proficient and which, as he states in his memoirs, led him to believe he could become quite wealthy in civilian life. One specification, for example, accused him of misrepresenting the amount of grain he was feeding to C Troop's mules and horses. He allegedly claimed one amount but fed the livestock a lesser amount and pocketed the difference. Another specification accused him of exchanging eleven thousand pounds of corn for eleven thousand pounds of wheat, by which he realized a profit of $190, "more or less, which he used himself."

Unrelated to the financial shenanigans was a seventh charge concerning alleged immoral conduct. It specified that Veil, while commanding officer of C Troop, "did keep a Mexican woman in said post, as mistress, she being publicly known as a prostitute, a woman of ill fame, and did live and cohabit with her. All of which was known to the enlisted men at Camp Tubac, AT, and the house in which said woman was kept was spoken of and known by the enlisted men as 'the house where Major Veil keeps his woman': This at Camp at Tubac, AT, during the months of July, August, September, and October, 1867." On all seven charges Veil was found not guilty and released from arrest.

Unfortunately for Veil, a year later he was again charged with conduct unbecoming an officer—that is, sexual misconduct. While in Tucson, he had evidently become infatuated with a laundress named Elizabeth Urton, who was not only married at the time but had a child. Nonetheless, he urged her to accompany him to Camp Crittenden as his mistress, telling her, "You shall never be in want of anything while I am there, although you will have to take in a little washing to avoid suspicion." He also advised her to leave her child behind as it would cause trouble for him at his post. To hide their relationship at Camp Crittenden, Veil allowed the post bugler to live openly with Mrs. Urton, "knowing that she was married and bringing scandal and disgrace to the military service." When confronted about this by military authorities, Mrs. Urton testified before a justice of the peace to the truth of the charges. She admitted receiving ten dollars from Veil on one occasion and "having carnal knowledge" of him three times. The court sustained all charges and specifications against Veil, concluding that he was not "a good officer to his men." Based on this verdict, the commandant of the Department of Arizona recommended that Veil be placed "on the list of undesirables to retain."

For Veil, this indiscretion could not have been more ill timed. At the very time of his court-martial the United States Army was undergoing a reduction in force mandated by the Act of July 15, 1870. This act established a board of five senior officers headed by General Winfield Scott Hancock—known as the Benzine Board—charged with involuntarily purging, or "benzining," from the rolls army officers identified as substandard or undesirable. The board eventually dismissed 151 officers, one of whom was Charles H. Veil.

Contrary to the impression Veil gives in his memoirs, he had to leave military service, like it or not, and he did not like it. In 1897, he managed to have a bill introduced in Congress (HR 3506, 55th Congress, First Session), authorizing the restoration of his name to the rolls of the army on the list of retired officers, "with rank and pay from the date of his discharge and muster out." Despite support from old friends in the military service and the suggestion that he merited special consideration for his heroism during the war and that Abraham Lincoln had taken a personal interest in his welfare, the army rejected his appeal. "In making the reduction," declared the adjutant general, "every effort was made to select for discharge the least worthy and efficient officers. Had Lieutenant Veil been retained, some other officer would have been discharged in his place—perhaps one not reported for any deficiency. It cannot be perceived that Mr. Veil has any better claim for a place on the retired list of the Army than have many others who were mustered out at the same time. There is nothing of record showing that he was, at the time of his discharge, or that he is now, eligible for a place on that list, under the laws providing for the retirement of officers."

Veil must have been about fifty-five years old when he began his memoirs. As he makes very clear, the time spent in Arizona after the military was actively engaged in various mercantile ventures by which he hoped to strike it rich, a goal that evidently eluded him.

According to a family history, Veil was one of eight children—four boys and four girls. He went into the milling business in Arizona with a fellow officer after his discharge from the army and prospered. In December 1874, he sold his shares in the business to his partner and returned to Pennsylvania, where he purchased a steam mill in Canton. Meanwhile, his former partner in Arizona went broke, forcing Veil to return in early 1876 and resume ownership of the mill. He left his brother Henry to manage the Canton Mills, but an inability to make the financial payments forced their sale and Veil and other investors lost heavily. The Arizona mill also failed, leaving Veil financially embarrassed.

Some things that do not appear in the memoirs are worth noting. He was elected a trustee of the Methodist Episcopal Church South in East Phoenix in 1873, he served as a member of the board of supervisors in Maricopa County in 1876, he was postmaster of East Phoenix for a month in 1876, and he was elected captain of the Phoenix Rangers in 1881.

Sometime following his departure from military service he got married, but his wife remains an elusive person. He never mentions her name in the memoirs and nothing is known of her from outside sources. She evidently had a daughter by a previous marriage, however, because after her death in 1891, he moved East with an adopted daughter to place her in school, intending to return to Arizona. He never did. Instead he lived for a time with a brother and sister in Williamsport, Pennsylvania, then with an uncle in Wellsboro. During the 1890s he worked as an insurance agent and as a deputy sheriff. It was evidently in that capacity that he served as the hangman in an execution in Wellsboro in 1898. Veil died of "congestion of the lungs" in Blackwell, Pennsylvania, on New Year's Day 1910, but is buried in Wellsboro.

Whether a saint or sinner, there can be no doubt that Veil was a colorful character rich in friends and memories. Among a number of tributes written about him after his death the most heartfelt was by a former comrade-in-arms, who wrote, "He was a manly man, a trusty friend, a good soldier, a loyal citizen, and deserves well of his country. His one creed was that the Great Republic is good enough for every man to live, and to fight, and to die for."

The original copy of Veil's memoirs is apparently no longer extant. This edition is based on a typescript in the possession of a Veil descendant. I presume that Veil originally wrote the memoirs in longhand and that someone used the original in preparing the typescript for this edition. Evidence for this supposition is based on the innumerable minor mistakes of grammar and spelling in the typescript that indicate the typist had difficulty in reading Veil's handwriting. Such mistakes have been corrected in this book.

Although Veil obviously could tell a good story, his written versions of them have serious stylistic problems. Since he evidently wrote his stories down as he tended to tell them, his text rambles and is somewhat wordy. Another problem was his failure to understand the basic principles of punctuation, especially the use of the period. In order to improve the readability of the typescript, I had to break his excessively long sentences into smaller and more manageable segments. Every effort was made, however, to retain the charm of Veil's literary style.

Although Veil's prose was improved, his ideas, expressions, and opinions were retained as expressed. Unfortunately, some of what he said about ethnic groups is considered offensive today. He had a low opinion of people of color, Catholics, and Jews. Nonetheless, what he says—and the way he says it—provides an unvarnished look at mainstream American attitudes regarding minorities at the time Veil wrote his memoirs at the turn of the twentieth century. Interestingly, the frequency with which Veil makes mention of Jews in Arizona Territory reveals that they were well represented on the American frontier.

H. J. V.

THE MEMOIRS OF

CHARLES HENRY VEIL

1. Personal Recollections and Reminiscences of the Civil War

I was born February 14, 1842, in a small village in the western part of Pennsylvania. The name of the place was Scalp Level, in the southern part of Cambria County and about seven miles south of Johnstown.

My father, Henry Veil, was a German, born in Schorndorf, Kingdom of Württemberg. He had traveled many years in Europe and emigrated to this country in 1834.

My mother, Mary, was born in Huntington, Pennsylvania. The only education I had was what I gained in the district school—three months a year—December, January, and February. Our school was distant from home, about a mile. It was an old log building, built of unhewn logs, rough slabs for seats, with holes bored in the sides and pins driven in for legs—no backs to the seats.

My first teacher was Mr. William Slick, lately deceased, whom I had the pleasure to call upon a few months since. I was particularly pleased to find that he still remembered me and called to mind an incident I well recollect. In returning from school one evening (it was then the custom for the teachers to board around with the residents of the district—one week here and another week there—at this time he was at our house) the wild pigeons were flying over us so thick that we could not see the sky, which was often the case in those years. Mr. Slick ran for the shop where my father had an old single-barrel gun. I followed and as I passed through the garden I pulled up a tall

1

bean pole that had been left standing and armed myself with that. As the birds commenced lighting in some tall hemlock trees, the teacher opened fire and, as the birds had been getting low down, I opened with my bean pole. The result was that I got more birds than did the teacher.

Children in those days did not have the opportunities of being educated as they have at the present day. As soon as I was able to perform certain kinds of labor, I was put to work. In the morning we arose before daylight. I first had to feed the cow, horses, and pigs and then build a fire in the shop stove. By that time breakfast would be ready, and I then had to fill the wood box and bring in the coal for the day. When I returned from school, the first thing I had to do was to tackle the wood pile and fill the wood box again, get the coal, water, etc., and after that eat supper and then probably shell corn over an old tub with a spade or shovel for the corn sheller until time to go to bed.

When I was about fourteen years of age, being of a pretty good size for a boy of that age, Father thought I had education enough, and I was put to work in his tan yard, but the work was too heavy for me. I was perfectly willing, but could not stand the labor, so I went to work in a store in Davidsville for Mr. Walters, whom I remained with for a short time, and then went to Ashtola, where a lumber company was operating, and attended a planer.

When I was about sixteen years of age, Andy Kunkle, one of my chums, one day in the fall of the year, suggested that we go out to the Rachel Hill schoolhouse to attend a teacher's examination. As I had nothing in particular to do for the day, I went with him. After we arrived at the schoolhouse, we found quite a gathering of girls and boys and prospective teachers. It was at the time when the county superintendent went to the different school districts and held an examination for applicants to teach in the township. The superintendent soon arrived and invited the teachers into the schoolhouse. Andy Kunkle suggested that we go in and take the examination, and we went in with the balance. The superintendent passed around some blank paper and asked us to write our address and a short sentence he gave us, gave us a little simple sum in arithmetic, asked us a few questions, and then asked us to pass up our papers and excused us. We went out and were having a pretty good time generally, when he came to the door and called for a certain party to come in. The certain party soon emerged and informed us he had made a contract for a certain school, the trustees or school directors being present and ready for business. Soon a young lady was called in and soon returned, smiling, and said she had such and such a school. About that time the superintendent again came to the door and called out C. H. Veil and in I went, wondering what was wanted as I had not the slightest idea of getting a school, but as soon as I got in, one of the directors asked me if I wanted a school. I hardly knew what to say, but finally said yes. "Well," said he, "we have one number so and so over at South Fork Reservoir that we have concluded to give you. The salary is eighteen dollars per month." I accepted and made the contract then and there and was then excused and another called in, who went through the same process, until all the schools in the township were supplied.

When I arrived home that evening, Father inquired where I had been. I, of course, told him, adding that I had a contract to teach the South Fork school. "What! You teach school? What do you know about teaching school? Why, boy, you must be crazy; you can't teach school, and especially the South Fork school. Why, don't you know they 'lick' and 'fire' every teacher who undertakes to teach that school?" The old gentleman was evidently better posted on the record of the South Fork school than I was, but when he said they "licked" and "fired" all the teachers, he made me a little "spunky." I replied that I had a contract, that I intended to teach the school, and that they wouldn't "lick" me, or "fire" me either, and so our interview ended for the time being. But I always thought Father was rather pleased with the spirit I exhibited on the occasion.

In the latter part of November, I went out to find my school. I found it situated on the banks of the South Fork Reservoir, the dam of which later gave way and was the cause of the destruction of Johnstown and the drowning of thousands of people and the loss of millions of dollars worth of property. The classroom was like the one I had attended at home—rough slab seats, holes bored into the rough sides and pins driven in for legs, and then the corners rounded off, no backs. The stove was an old box-wood affair that took wood about three feet in length. Altogether, it was not a very attractive place for a young schoolmaster to start in at—no house nearer than a mile, at one of which I engaged board for the winter, five dollars per month and washing in the bargain. I think it was at Johnny Stull's.

On Monday morning, December the first, I was on hand for business, as that was the opening day. I was on hand early, had cleaned out the school house as best I could, and had a good fire going. About nine o'clock or a little before, the scholars began to arrive—big and little, boys and girls, some much older than myself. I was particularly interested to see that there were several strapping big boys in the lot that I at once saw would be the cause of any trouble I might have. We got along all right for a day or two, but about the third day at noon, when I went to the door to enter, I found it locked and "high jinks" going on inside. To my repeated request to enter I was answered by loud yells: "Locked out! Locked out! "

There was a little brook that ran close by the schoolhouse that had a lot of beech trees growing on its banks with a lot of shoots, or suckers, growing out from them. I thought of the fine switches these would make and went down to the brook and commenced amusing myself by cutting a bunch of them, good stout ones too. I began trimming them up, at the same time keeping an eye on the schoolhouse. I could see the younger scholars were watching me, but the "doings" were still going on. But by and by they quieted down and I went back and was let in. When I got inside, I locked the door and put the key in my pocket. "Now," said I, "I want to know who locked the door. I am going to punish the party who did it." There was no answer, but I could see the smaller scholars looking at the two big boys (the ones who I had at first made up my mind would be the cause of any trouble I was to have). "Well," said I, "I am going to whip the boy that locked the door if I have to lick the whole school." I gave the order to "line up" on the boys' side. They all stood, backs to me, and I started in at one end, coming down toward where the two big boys were. As I got near and was about to commence "operations" on one of them, I noticed he doubled up his fists and was about to make a spring to "tackle" me, but the stove was just opposite me and we had a big green stick for a poker and quick as I saw what he was up to, I dropped my switch and grabbed the poker. With that he saw I had the best of him and as I suppose he was afraid I might use that, he again turned his back and I gave him an unmerciful thrashing. The dust flew out of his coat at every lick and when I thought he had what he deserved, I moved on down the line to the tail end. After I got there, I unlocked the door. "Now boys," said I, "I have whipped the boy that locked the door and I want you all to understand that I am going to teach this school and that I am going to have order. The reputation you have is that you run this school to suit yourselves, or run the teacher off, and I want you to distinctly understand you have one this year that you can't lick, or that won't be run off, for I have got a contract to teach this school and I am here to carry out my contract." From that time on, I had no trouble and the report was that I had as orderly a school as there was in the district; in fact, the children all took a liking to me and they wanted me to come and teach again the next year.

A few years ago I was in Gettysburg, where I met Senator Stineman, who received me very cordially. "Why, Charlie," said he, "do you remember when you taught the South Fork School?"

"Yes," said I, "but what do you know about the South Fork school?"

"Oh," said he, "I know," and he brought out his wife and introduced me to her as the schoolmaster who had whipped the whole South Fork school. (He did not say that he was one of the scholars, but I am half inclined to believe he was.)

Next year I taught our own Scalp Level school and the year following, the Civil War broke out. Fort Sumter was fired upon in April and war was declared. Seventy-five thousand troops were called for by President Lincoln to put down the Rebellion. Johnstown had a company of militia that filled our quota, so that no men were enlisted. How I envied the boys who belonged to the Company and had the privilege of going out and having a hand in defending the flag and restoring the Union.

From April to June no action had occurred, but still no other troops were called for. In the meantime, I felt that I could not remain at home but that it was my duty to at least make an effort to show that I was loyal and willing to lend a hand at such an important time. After brooding over the matter up to June 13, 1861, I concluded I would make an effort to find some place where I could enlist. When I had fully made up my mind to do so, after breakfast that morning I said to Father and Mother that I was going to Johnstown or to find some place where I could show that I was willing to sacrifice my life, if necessary, in the defense of the Union. I said good-bye and started to walk to Johnstown. I was the first boy to leave Scalp Level for the service.

When I arrived in Johnstown, I met a Baptist minister whom I was acquainted with, Mr. Pyatt. I inquired of him if he knew of any place where soldiers were being enlisted. He replied that Governor Curtin had commenced the organization of fifteen thousand Pennsylvania Reserves, that the governor had all they would accept at the time, but that Governor Curtin thought they would need more, and that he, the governor, of his own accord, had concluded to raise fifteen thousand men and have them ready, in case of need. And fortunate indeed was the country that Governor Curtin had the foresight to have the troops ready for action, as will appear later on. Mr. Pyatt told me they were enlisting some men in Pittsburgh and that he was taking a number of boys down that day and I could go with them if I desired. I was promptly on hand when the train left Johnstown and a few hours after we were in Pittsburgh. From there we took the Allegheny Valley Railroad out a short distance to what was then called Camp Wright, where a temporary camp had been established and where part of the Pennyslvania Reserves were being enlisted. My squad of boys, in the charge of the Baptist preacher, at once presented itself to the adjutant's quarters and our examination at once commenced. After the doctor had passed us and description rolls were made, the adjutant inquired of me what company I wanted to join. I told him it made no difference. "Why," said he, "haven't you any friends or acquaintances here?" I answered, "None." "Well," said he to Captain John Brookbank, who stood by, "Captain, you better take this boy down to your company." I followed him to his company quarters, some rough board sheds, where he turned me over to his First Sergeant, James Read, and instructed him to give me a uniform. Almost before I was aware of the change taking place, I had a soldier suit of blue on and was a full-fledged volunteer Union soldier. By this time it was getting on toward evening and I was getting real hungry. I began to look around for the boarding house, or something of that kind, but could not see anything in the shape of a hotel or anything of the kind. Soon after, the company drummer came out in the street with his drum and began to beat a "supper call" (I did not know, but it might be the "long roll") for the company at once tumbled out of their "shacks" and began to "fall in line" and I followed suit and fell in too. After we were all in line, Sergeant Read called the roll and then gave the order "Right face" and then "Forward" and so we marched up to the head of the street. As we did so, we passed a big empty store box that had a pile of tin cups and plates piled up on it, and I noticed as each man passed he took a plate and cup so I "followed suit." At the end of the street I found a couple of company cooks, one of whom handed each of us a very fat piece of pork and a piece of bread. The other dipped up and gave each of us a cup of black tea.

That was my first army ration. We then dispersed, each eating his fat pork and bread and drinking his black tea where ever he pleased. No knives or forks or spoons were furnished. We used our fingers for that, and so I ate my first army supper in Camp Wright. It was not as good a meal as I had on a former trip to Pittsburgh with Father a year or two before, but then I had enlisted and wanted to help put down the Rebellion and I was satisfied to put up with whatever was furnished us. When I was in Pittsburgh with Father, we went to what at that time appeared to me a very large hotel. When we went into the dining room and took our seats, one of the waiter girls came round for our order and ran off the bill of fare so fast that I could not follow her, so the only order I gave was "Yes." She looked at me awhile and finally said, "Well, what do you want?" "Why, dinner, of course" was my answer, so she left. At the entrance to the kitchen I remember she stopped and looked back. But as I gave no intimation of a change in my order, she went on and by and by returned with, I suppose, the entire bill of fare. It was all she could do to carry the tray in, but when she had served it to me it certainly was all that my heart could desire. Meats of different kinds and all kinds of vegetables to go with it. When it came to dessert, I "passed." I had cleaned up about all the good substantial fare she had brought, but had no room for dessert. After dinner "Dad" inquired how I had "made out." I told him all right, but I guessed I would have to "let out a button."

Along toward time to go to bed, I began to wonder where I was to sleep. As I had noticed that Sergeant Read, the Orderly Sergeant of the company, appeared to be the "Big Injin," or "boss" of the camp, I inquired of him where. "Why, did I not give you a blanket?" said he. "Yes," I answered. "Well, what do you expect? A feather bed? Sleep anywhere you please. Plenty of room round here." I noticed some shelves or board bunks built up around the "shacks," but there were no mattresses, or even straw, nothing but bare boards. As I saw some of the boys lying there, I selected a vacant place and tried to turn in. I first tried lying on the boards and spreading my blanket over one, but I could not stand that for long. Then I got up and doubled my blanket, trying to sleep on one half and cover myself with the other, but I had no pillow. I took off my shoes and tried to make one out of these, but then my feet got cold. In the meantime I thought my flesh would cut through onto the board. I got up and walked around awhile and then tried it all over again, but finally morning came and I was glad of it. When the company drummer got out and beat the drum for us to get up, we all fell into line and the sergeant called the roll to see that none of us had got lost during the night.

That was my first night in camp. Up to that time I had never slept outside of a fairly good bed and I thought it was pretty tough, but I had enlisted to help crush the Rebellion and was determined to take things as they came. Later on, I should have been delighted to have the same accommodations, but that was after we became hardened and accustomed to army life.

We were not given arms at Camp Wright and remained there until July 21 when the battle of Bull Run was fought and our army disastrously defeated. Then our corps was accepted by the general government and ordered to Washington. It was then that Governor Curtin's foresight and good judgment came in. Pennyslvania was the only state that had troops ready to take the field and I really believe that had such not been the case, the

Confederates would have followed up their success at Bull Run and have captured or taken Washington City. The wires were almost "burned" to get us out now. Trains of cars—no palace or Pullman cars were served us—but cattle, coal, and box cars, anything to get us aboard and off for Washington. I remember that I went through Johnstown on top of a box car and as we halted a moment there on our way, old man Englebach—with a basket of bread on his arm—discovered me and the first thing I knew he was throwing loaves of bread up at me and the rest of my comrades. We caught them. That night we got to Harrisburg. After we arrived, the adjutant came down to our company and detailed me to take charge of the officers' car on which were supplies of eatables and drink in the bargain. I do not know why he selected me, unless it was something that happened the day I enlisted. Captain Brookbank had been elected captain of the company and in return of the compliment had ordered several kegs of beer, cigars, etc., to treat the men. In the course of the evening, he and the adjutant and several other officers were in the company street, when the captain saw me and remarked, "Well, bub, did you have your beer?"

"No sir, I don't drink."

"Oh, well, then get a cigar."

"No, Captain, I don't smoke."

Nor did I, and I think it was because the officers knew that I did not smoke or drink that the adjutant detailed me to look out for their car supplies. He told me to help myself to anything I wanted, and I did to good ham sandwiches and cheese, etc., but to none of the drinkables.

In Harrisburg we were furnished arms, old Harper's Ferry muskets that fired a big ounce ball and three buckshot. In the bargain, if you could not hit anything with that, you were not of much account. Of one thing you were certain, you would know when your piece was discharged, for the recoil was so great that the chances were you would be facing to the rear after you had fired.

That same night we took the train for Baltimore and next morning before we entered the city, which we marched through, the regiment loaded their pieces—ball, buckshot, and all. It was fortunate for the inhabitants that no trouble arose and that none of our guns were discharged, for certainly someone would have been killed. This was but a day or two after the Sixth Massachusetts Regiment had been fired on while marching through the city (April 19, 1861) and we did not know but that we might have the same experience.

After marching through the city we again embarked in a train and were carried through to Washington where, on arrival, we were hailed with delight by all. After a few days camping in the immediate vicinity of the city, we were marched out through Georgetown to Finnallytown, where we established camp and were engaged in drilling, building forts, etc., until about October, I think, when we broke camp and were marched across the chain bridge into Virginia. We now were in the enemy's country and soldiering in earnest commenced.

Our first real duty was to put out not only a camp guard, but an outer line of pickets. That meant a line of guards facing the enemy, one that the safety of the army depended upon. I was put on picket duty the first night after crossing the Potomac into Virginia and I well remember how trying and important the duty appeared to me. My impression was that the safety of the entire army depended upon my vigilance. When—after being on post for the night—toward morning I became so sleepy that it appeared impossible for me to keep awake, I got a pin and pricked myself in the leg to wake me up and keep me awake. Next morning I discovered a lot of Union soldiers out in front of our line. How they got through our line I don't know, but after I was relieved from duty, about noon and still seeing the men out in front around a large house, or mansion, I thought I would try and get out and see what was "going on." I watched for my chance and managed to slip out through the guards and got up to the large house I had seen, where I saw a lot of boys in blue had been marauding. They had carried a fine piano out of the house onto the lawn. One was playing the piano and the balance were having a regular "hoedown," dancing, singing, and raising regular "Cain." I looked on a bit and then took a look into the big house. Everything had been destroyed. Large mirrors, the height of the wall, had been smashed. In fact, beds, bedding, and everything was torn to pieces and scattered over the floors. At one of the basement entrances I saw an old darky, of whom I inquired where the owners were. He said they had "refugeed," which meant they had gone South. I then inquired if there was anything to eat about the premises. He said no; everything had been carried off by the "Yanks." "Well, I see a big garden down there," I said. "Is not there anything left in the garden?" He said there might be some potatoes, so I went down to see. I saw there were a lot that had not been dug, so I went back, "borrowed" a pail, and went to digging potatoes. I had my pail about filled when I heard someone call "Patrol." The next moment I heard "Fall in here, you damned thieves" and, looking up, saw an officer and a squad of men. He gobbled up the whole "shooting match" and me along with the rest. He ordered us all to fall in line and then assorted us. Those of the First Regiment were put in one squad, those of the Second another, until finally he came to me and mine was the Ninth Regiment. There were two of us belonging to the Ninth. After he had us all assorted, he detailed a guard from his squad and ordered the one commissioned officer in charge to take us to our several regiments and turn us over to our regimental commanders. When my squad of two arrived at camp, a big crowd of boys gathered around us, near the colonel's tent, to see what was going on. They got so close that I thought I saw a chance of slipping into the crowd surrounding us and making my escape. The idea no sooner suggested itself than I put it into execution and the first I knew I was making my way out through the surrounding crowd and striking a "bee line" for the picket line where I had left my musket and tricks. About the time I reached there, our relief had arrived and the detail was about to start back for camp. I fell in with the balance and got back all right. The other fellow of the Ninth, the one arrested with me but who had not taken the chance of escaping through the crowd, was packing a rail in front of the camp guardhouse when we got back to camp. That was the first time I was arrested; the next—and last—time, a little later. But of that, by and by.

The camp we established at the time was named Camp Pierpont. The entire division of Pennsylvania Reserves, commanded by General George A. McCall, was encamped there. The division consisted of three brigades: General John F. Reynolds in command of the first; General George G. Meade of the second;

and General E. O. C. Ord of the third, to which my regiment, the Ninth, belonged. All of the general officers afterward became prominent, especially Meade. He succeeded to the command of the Army of the Potomac and under his command the battle of Gettysburg was fought.

About that time, I was very unexpectedly detailed by our regimental adjutant, who had been present when I enlisted at Pittsburgh and whose attention I had evidently attracted, as an orderly for General Ord. I was informed where to find headquarters and was instructed to report to the general or the assistant adjutant general.

When I arrived at the headquarters I saw an ordinary-looking kind of an elderly man, in a common soldier's uniform with an overcoat and a very greasy cap, overseeing some work being done about the tents. I inquired of him as to where the general's tent was. He pointed to a certain one and I went to it and rapped, but had no reply. I then called out to the old gentleman and inquired where the assistant adjutant general's tent was, saying, "the general ain't here." In a very short and "snappy" way he indicated the one I was inquiring for. When I rapped on that, someone said, "Come in." I entered and found an officer at a desk in full uniform to whom I reported, saying Colonel Conrad Jackson of the Ninth had ordered me to report to General Ord for an orderly. "Oh, yes," said he, getting up and leading the way out and up to the old gentleman, saying, "Here, General, is the man Colonel Jackson has sent you for an orderly."

When he led me up to the old gentleman whom I had so unceremoniously accosted and addressed him as General, I felt like sinking into the ground. However, the general looked me over, asked if I had any relations, told me to take a certain tent for my quarters, and to make myself comfortable. He also told me how to fix a fireplace. I was to dig a trench through the tent, cover it with flat stones, build my chimney at the back end, and then put in a bunk, etc. When he got through, I inquired what he wanted me to do. "I will tell you when I want you," was his sharp answer. So I asked no more questions, but went to work fixing my tent and trying to make myself comfortable as he had instructed me. He came over several times to see how I was getting along and made several suggestions and appeared rather pleased to see how I was getting fixed up. I had no roll calls to attend, no drill, could go to bed when I pleased, get up the same, and began to think I had struck a pretty "soft snap." All I had to do was to cook, eat, and sleep.

About that time, horses were being provided by the Quartermaster's Department for the use of the different staff officers at our headquarters, and among the lot was one that was fractious and throwing everyone who undertook to ride him. I watched the boys being thrown for a while and then said to Captain William Painter, our brigade quartermaster, that I could ride him. "Well," said he, "if you can ride him you may have him." So I had a chance. I got hold of him, and after leading him around, petting and trying to get acquainted with him, I finally thought I would try and get on. When he was not particularly on the "lookout," I got my foot in the stirrup and quickly mounted. He gave me some pretty violent exercise for a spell, but I managed to keep my seat and by and by got him started. For an hour I gave him a pretty lively ride around the camp and by the time I got back to our headquarters he was pretty well tired out and "broken." Just as I got back the adjutant was inquiring for a mounted orderly on duty at the headquarters to carry orders to the different regiments of the brigade and as he was not present, I volunteered to carry them. They were given me, and I rode to the several regiments in our brigade and delivered my orders. From that time on to the close of the war, I had a horse to ride, not the same horse but others.

While we were in camp in Pierpont, the division was ordered out in the direction of Leesburg. After marching a certain distance we were halted and, while lying there, could hear firing on our right and front, but we took no part. The fact was the battle of Ball's Bluff was being fought and there again our troops were defeated. Colonel Edward Baker was killed. To this day I cannot understand why we were allowed to lie idle within sound of the guns. We were on the Virginia side of the Potomac River, the side occupied by the enemy, and General Charles Stone, who commanded our troops at Ball's Bluff, where he attempted to cross the run, was roughly handled. Yet we, near by and on the Virginia side, lay idly by and did nothing.

That same fall our brigade was ordered on a foraging expedition to Drainsville where, on November 26, we were attacked by a Confederate force, which we repulsed. General Ord, who was in command, handled the troops admirably and at once gained their confidence. Several were killed and wounded. That was the brigade's first engagement and introduction to battle.

We remained in the camp during the winter of 1861. In the spring General George B. McClellan moved the bulk of the Army of the Potomac to Yorktown by vessel. Our division, the Pennsylvania Reserves, was left with General Irwin McDowell's corps, as an army of protection for Washington, and moved out in the direction of Fredericksburg by way of Centerville and Manassas. After arriving at Fredericksburg, McClellan called for more troops and our division was ordered down the Rappahannock River by transport to join and reinforce him. McClellan in the meantime had advanced up the peninsula as far as the Chickahominy River.

While we were waiting for the arrival of the transports near Fredericksburg, we were encamped on the bank of the river below town. Our headquarters occupied a fine plantation mansion overlooking the river. It was a typical southern mansion, a large, fine, roomy house, with slave quarters, stable, fine garden, and, among other surroundings, a large number of hives of honey bees. A lot of the headquarters' officers got together one day and decided that we ought to have a little feast before we started down the river, so one or two of us were detailed to capture a pig and I was detailed to capture one of the bee hives. An old wench had been engaged to cook the pig and make the corn bread and coffee. Safeguards were posted in the garden, in which the bee hives were stationed. I engaged a comrade to get into conversation with the guard and, while he was so engaged, I managed to slip into the garden and pick up a bee hive. I got out all right and packed it down to one of the Negro cabins where the fight with the bees took place. They were about the sauciest lot of bees I ever got hold of. We finally got rid of them and got all the honey we wanted, but not until we had been stung in many places. I remember my hands were so swollen next morning that I could not close them. One eye was "bunged up" so I could not see out of it and my mouth was all swollen on one side. [While I was] in that shape the adjutant general called me up and said the d——d thieving boys had stolen a hive of bees the night before and that it was an infernal outrage. If he was giving me a lecture, I took it all right, but we had a good supper of fresh pork, corn bread, and honey.

After the boats, or transports, arrived we were at once embarked and had a fine trip down the river out into the Chesapeake Bay, round Fort Monroe, and up the Pamunkey river to White House Landing. We disembarked and marched up to the right of our army, occupying the Chickahominy, to Mechanicsville, where we went into camp and occupied a line of entrenchments already built. We remained there but a short time when, on June 26 in the afternoon, the enemy came out from Richmond and attacked us in large force. We had a severe engagement, but the advantage was all on our side as we fought from behind breastworks, while the enemy had to attack from the front and open. Their loss was very severe, while ours was comparatively small. We held our line at all points until after dark and were expecting a resumption of the battle on the same ground, but during the night we were withdrawn from our works and marched to the left, to Gaines Mill, where we arrived after daylight and were at once formed into line of battle. Here we joined other troops, infantry, and artillery. Being placed in position as they were, something important was about to take place, but no firing was heard. Our line of battle ran around on the crest of a ridge nearly in the shape of a half moon. In front of us was a ravine covered with timber, and in the ravine ran a little stream. About noon, without any warning, our batteries all opened, and the first I knew the enemy's infantry was in our front, firing and advancing on us. They had come down the bank and crossed the stream in front of us, and were then met by our men and driven back followed by our men, but they were again reinforced and pushed us back and up the side of our hill. Here we got more troops and had pushed them down and across the stream when both sides, apparently exhausted, halted. It was now "give and take" in the open without cover. I cannot remember how long this state of affairs lasted, but probably not long. The general rode along the line encouraging the men and, as he passed Colonel Samuel Black, commanding one of the Pennsylvania regiments sent in to reinforce us, he halted and made a few remarks to him and then passed on a short distance and halted. In doing so, as I was riding in his rear, he left me by the side of Colonel Black, whom he had just passed. I happened to be looking the colonel in the face when I saw a minnie ball strike him between the eyes and instantly kill him. He fell from his horse, and I passed on after the general, who a moment later gave me a message to carry to someone. As I turned my back on the firing, I got scared for the first time, as I recollect. I was trying to get up the hill as fast as I could with my horse, when all at once a lot of the enemy's guns opened from a new direction—on our right—and about the first round knocked off both my horse's forelegs and threw me over his head, but in the direction I wanted to go, so I kept going. At the very moment the general had given me the message to carry, Confederate General Thomas Jonathan "Stonewall" Jackson arrived from the Shenandoah Valley and was making his attack on our right flank. As we were not aware, prior to this, that there was any danger to look for in that quarter, it took our men by surprise and caused a bad stampede. When I gained the top of the ridge after my horse had been shot and could take a look over the field to our rear, the sight was frightful. Men, wagons, ambulances, and every individual that could move was in a run to the rear or toward Grapevine Bridge. Shot and shell were striking and exploding in their midst as they ran. (I might better say as we ran, for I was one of them.) Wounded men that had been carried to the rear when Jackson opened on our flank jumped to their feet and joined the party. Even one man, I recollect, who had lost one foot, jumped up and caught on to the step of an ambulance that was passing, loaded with a man hanging on to the step. He pulled him off and managed to get on himself and get away. It was one of the most demoralizing sights I ever saw.

When I came to get over my scare and pulled myself together again, I began to think of what was best for me to do to find my command and join the general. From the movements I saw take place, I soon guessed that another movement would be made that night, so I sat down by the side of the road with a little thicket of young pines at my back and concluded to wait awhile and see what would take place. Not long after I did so and soon after dusk, along came a column of troops from the direction of the front. To my great pleasure, I saw that it was my own brigade with the commander at its head. As they arrived directly in front of where I was sitting, the general and his staff dismounted and the men dropped down in the road and took a rest. My great annoyance, or worry, now was that I had lost my horse, and the probabilities were there might be a long march ahead and I afoot. But soon after the general halted, I noticed a stray cavalryman belonging to the Sixth Pennsylvania Cavalry, or "Rush Lancers," ride into the pine thicket, dismount and jab his lance into the ground, tie his horse to one of the scrub pines, sit down, and commence eating some hardtack. He had no sooner done so than I began to concoct some plan to get his horse. I noticed he was a good stout-looking young fellow, who I thought was as fully able to walk as I was, and the horse, I knew, belonged to the government. In short, I made up my mind to try and get him.

The cavalryman had no doubt been in some hard service, marching or in picket, and was worn out. I noticed he lay down, and soon after I heard him begin to snore. That was my chance. I quietly slipped around to the rear of his horse and worked my way up to where he was tied to the pine tree. As the man still continued to snore, I deliberately untied his horse and led him back into the pine grove. I then got out my pocket knife, roached his mane and tail, and then led him in a roundabout way onto the road where my general was. As I did so, the general got an order to move on and mounted his horse, as did the staff. I mounted the cavalryman's horse and rode off with the rest, taking his saddle and all. I never learned how the cavalryman got through, or made the march, but I rode his horse to Harrison's Landing. More than likely, the cavalryman had stolen some other fellow's horse.

That night the entire portion of McClellan's army, engaged that day on the north side of the Chickahominy, was crossed to the south, or Richmond, side. We marched to Savage Station, where I saw more government supplies burned and destroyed than I had ever seen before. Millions of dollars worth of provisions and forage were burned and whole train loads run off the bridge into the river, cars, locomotives, and all. General McClellan had become demoralized and had concluded to withdraw his army to the cover of the gun boats to the James River. As he could not carry the supplies with him, he destroyed them to keep them from falling into the hands of the enemy.

During the day our division was moved out to White Oak Swamp, or Charles City Cross Roads, and ordered to take position there at an intersection of the roads and to hold that point while the balance of the army was passing toward the James River. Toward evening the enemy attacked us in great force and we had a very severe engagement and met with heavy loss, but we held the ground as we had been ordered to do. General George McCall, the division commander, was wounded and taken prisoner that day. General Meade was shot through the lungs, and General Reynolds had been captured at the battle of Glendale the day before, so that the general I was with was the only general officer left with the division and assumed command. I neglected to say before now that General Ord, whom I had at first reported to for orderly duty, had been relieved and General Truman Seymour assigned in his place, and he continued me on the same duty.

As we moved to the rear again that night after the army had passed our point of battle, I shall never forget the sad sight we saw, of hundreds, yes, thousands of our wounded men who had been carried out and laid in rows alongside the road, all of whom we marched by and left to the mercy of the enemy. In such cases we, of course, left some surgeons of ours to look after our own wounded; but the idea of leaving men like that, lying on the open ground, no cover, no comforts or care, some dying, some dead, is a scene never to be forgotten. That is war, indeed. General William Tecumseh Sherman said, "War is Hell," and he was right.

That night we continued our march toward the James River and early in the morning of July 1 arrived at Malvern Hill. The army that had preceded us was formed in line, occupying a very advantageous position. As our division had been heavily engaged the day before, we were placed in reserve and were not severely engaged in the battle that followed that day.

The enemy, elated by the success they had had, pressed on

and attacked our position time and again but were always repulsed and met with very severe loss. I thought at the time, and have since been informed by Confederates who participated in the battle, that if we had attacked the Confederates after they had expended their firing, we would have had no trouble to rout the enemy and take Richmond at that time.

That night, after the battle ceased, we were again put on the march and next morning arrived at Harrison's Landing. Our division was halted for bivouac in a big wheat field, headed out and almost ripe, but as it had rained hard that night, it made anything but a nice pleasant place to take a nap in. By the time we had marched into our position it was like a mortar bed. But the boys were worn out and lay down in the mud.

While at Harrison's Landing, General Reynolds, who had been taken prisoner at the battle of Glendale and who had been exchanged for Confederate General William Barksdale, whom we had captured, returned and assumed command of the Pennsylvania Reserves on August 8, 1862. He continued me on duty at headquarters as his orderly and with him I remained from that time until his death at Gettysburg.

While riding the horse I had "captured" of the cavalryman at Gaines Mill through the camp at Harrison's Landing one day, I heard someone calling and, as I looked round, found an officer beckoning to me. When I rode over to where he was, he inquired where I had gotten my horse. I frankly told him not exactly how I had acquired him but that I had captured him at Gaines Mill. "Well," said he, "that horse belongs to my company." "Well," said I, "I am an orderly at General Reynolds's headquarters and am carrying dispatches." With that I saluted him and put spurs to my horse and rode off. When I got back I saw the officer talking to General Reynolds. When I dismounted, the general in a very mild way called me over. "Veil," said the general, "the captain says you have a horse that belongs to his company. Where did you get him?"

As the general had been captured himself at the same battle, I knew I had the best of him. I promptly answered, "At Gaines Mill." To prove or identify his property, the captain came over to where the horse was and raised up his front foot and called the general's attention to the letter *H* branded in the bottom of his hoof. That was the letter of his company and that settled the horse question for me at that time, but if I had discovered the letter before, I would have cut it out, and the captain would not have been able to identify his horse. The captain rode his horse away and I was left afoot, but I was soon furnished another horse.

Soon after, as General Robert E. Lee had stolen a march on McClellan, our army was put in motion for Washington. Our division took boats for Aquia Creek, near Fredericksburg. As soon as we landed we were put in motion to join Major General John Pope, who was now getting in trouble with Lee. We joined his army near Manassas, or rather Warrenton, and then marched to the second battle of Bull Run field, which began on August 30. There we had two days' heavy engagement and were again defeated and had to fall back toward Washington.

As we passed through Centerville on our retreat, I saw a sight I often think of. The surgeons were operating on the badly wounded as they were brought in from the field. Long rows of wounded men were lying around. Some had been operated on, while others were waiting to be. The surgeons were cutting off arms, feet, hands, and limbs of all kinds in what looked like a little country schoolhouse. As an arm or leg was cut off, it was thrown out an open window. The cut-off limbs had accumulated so that they blocked the window, and a detail of a few men were hauling away the limbs with a wheelbarrow. It was an awful sight and one I have never forgotten. It had the appearance of a human slaughterhouse.

Now I have another little horse story that I ought to tell of, as it occurred the very day I am writing about. During the day, the general's horse was nearly exhausted (he was a very hard rider) and as he saw the one I was riding was in much better condition, the general said, "Veil, let me have your horse and take mine back to the wagon train." While I did not like to leave the field yet, all I could do was obey, so he dismounted and mounted mine without changing saddles. I took his back until I found the wagon train and then turned it over to his man. I then borrowed a musket and cartridge box filled with ammunition off one of the wagon guards and started out front again to where I had left the general. As I arrived on the field, he was leading a brigade out to make a reconnaissance so I followed with them without getting in line or rather in ranks. I was going out on my own hook. We had marched but a few hundred yards when the Confederates discovered us and each side began forming a line of battle to our right and on the side I was marching at that moment. I saw a Rebel battery of artillery come out to the edge of a wood, take position, and open fire on us at close range for cannon. Between us was a field, and in the field were several large trees with stones piled up around the butt of the trees. I at once saw the advantage I would have behind the stone pile if I could reach it, and made up my mind to try. Off I went on a run and got behind my stone pile without getting hit. I then crept up all cocked and primed and ready to fire. As soon as I had my shot I would get down behind the pile and load again. In that way I had several good shots. As I was about to make another, I saw the battery officer fall off his horse, which started to run down toward our line. As he was coming in a direct line for me, I saw my chance to capture another horse. As he was about to pass my stone pile, I dropped my gun and went out to try and stop him, but as I did so I frightened him and he continued on down toward our infantry line with me after him, calling out, "Stop that horse! Stop that horse!" He ran on and into the line where one of the boys caught and held him until I caught up. I suppose he thought the horse had gotten away from me. At any rate he asked no questions. He was a fine bay with a fine officer's saddle and bridle, and I rode him many miles before he was shot.

During the evening and night we fell back on Alexandria and Washington. A terrific rain storm came on during the early evening and, during the rain, a severe engagement took place to our left at Chantilly. Major General Phil Kearney was killed in that. General Lee followed up his success at Bull Run, or Groveton, as the two days' battle was named, and the first thing our authorities knew he was across the Potomac in Maryland. Our army was at once put in motion to meet him. We made forced marches and, when the Pennsylvania Reserves arrived at Frederick, Maryland, General Reynolds was detached and ordered to Pennsylvania to assume command of a force of militia called into service by Governor Curtin. The general and a couple of his staff officers, I included, left Frederick that evening and rode to Baltimore that night. The distance I think is about forty miles. From there we took a train to Harrisburg, where the general reported to Governor Curtin. Soon after we continued by train up the Cumberland Valley to Chambersburg where the general found the militia assembling and at once commenced organizing them. As fast as an organization was effected they were ordered on to Hagerstown. In the meantime, there was great excitement in the valley and in Pennsylvania in general. One report had the Rebels in this, and another in that, place. No one apparently really knew where they were. When our militia were all organized and sent on to Hagerstown, the general and his staff followed. When we arrived at Hagerstown, the enemy were reported at the crossing of the Potomac and the militia army of defense was at once ordered to advance. As a matter of fact a Rebel force did occupy Williamsport and the crossing of the Potomac. The general selected a line of battle and occupied it with his force; but, outside of some slight skirmishing, no action was had, nor further advance made by our militia boys. I think it fortunate that none was, for one regiment of old troops would have demoralized the whole shooting match. While we occupied our line between Hagerstown and Williamsport, the battle of Antietam was fought and there was great excitement in the North, especially in our immediate vicinity. The governor of Maryland came to Hagerstown and made his headquarters there with his staff. Every four hours I was sent with a message from General Reynolds to the governor keeping him informed of what was taking place.

I think I had about as hard riding on this occasion as any I ever had. I was the only mounted man the general had to carry orders and messages and for forty-eight hours I was constantly on the move. In addition to that I had no rations nor, in fact, anything to eat for that length of time. The militia were about the worst lot of foragers or thieves I ever came in contact with. They had stolen and eaten everthing eatable in that vicinity, so that a decent-minded soldier was about starved, but I had my innings. When the battle was over and the Rebs withdrew, the general sent me with a message to the governor in Hagerstown advising him of the fact. The news I brought pleased him so much, having delivered it while he and his staff had about completed a very sumptuous lunch they were having, that some-one of the party inquired if I would not have some. I accepted the invitation; and, if you ever saw a hungry boy help himself, you will know about how I was getting along. I never had anything taste so good in all my life.

The general then rejoined his regular command of the Pennsylvania Reserves, which we found on the battlefield of Antietam. The battle had been a drawn one. Lee had retreated to the Virginia side again and, after considerable delay in follow-ing up or pressing a retiring army, for which McClellan was seriously censured, we finally got underway and followed him up. The retreat of Lee continued to the Rappahannock River. In the meantime, at Warrenton, Major General Ambrose Burnside succeeded to the command of the army. McClellan's slow move-ment in following Lee after the battle of Antietam brought about that result.

The rank and file of the army at that time were great admirers of McClellan. I well remember when the army was drawn up in review on his leaving. Many shed tears and I one of the lot. We thought a great mistake had been made by the authorities but later on thought differently, that is, when we understood the causes better.

After Burnside assumed command, our army was moved on to Fredericksburg, or rather Falmouth. Fredericksburg is on the opposite side of the Rappahannock River. There we went into temporary camp. In the meantime Lee, with the Con-federate Army, moved down and occupied Fredericksburg and the heights behind the town. In December, Burnside concluded to attack him, having first given Lee ample time to strengthen his works or position. On the 12th, our corps, with that of Major General William Franklin's, effected a crossing of the river some three miles below the town. On the 13th we advanced across the lowlands lying along the river and assaulted the Rebs occupying a low ridge running parallel to the river. Our assault was suc-cessful as we broke through their lines, driving them out and beyond, but at that very moment Stonewall Jackson again turned up on our right flank (he always had a habit of showing up when you did not want him) and drove us back, and we lost all the ground we had gained, more too, in fact, for they followed us down the slope of the ridge as far as the railroad crossing where we finally succeeded in halting their advance.

It was there the general galloped back to where he had about thirty cannon in line and ordered them double shotted with grape and canister. When the three Confederate lines came down the slope of the ridge, one line in the rear of the other, he opened on them with frightful effect, halting their advance.

We were always of the opinion that if we had been properly supported in our advance, the result of the battle of Fredericksburg would have been very different. That opinion has later been supported and confirmed in conversations I have had with Confederate soldiers who were there. They say nothing would have been in our way to advance on Richmond. We had open country and good roads ahead of us, but it appeared as though fate was against us.

Burnside, in the time that we were engaged, had effected a crossing of the river directly in front of Fredericksburg with the main portion of the army and assaulted the enemy lying under cover in his chosen position. The loss was terrible—some thirteen thousand killed, wounded, and missing. The result finally was that our army had again to retreat and recross the river. The wonder to me now is that we were allowed to do so. Had Lee known, he might have driven us all into the river or captured us all.

The night we withdrew, however, was favorable to us. It was a foggy, misty, rainy night and we had taken the precaution to put a lot of hay on the pontoon bridges to deaden the sound or rather muffle the bridges, so as not to make any noise. It was during the evening before the retreat commenced that I heard an officer from Burnside's headquarters give the order to General Reynolds to withdraw as soon as he could. As I had some acquaintances down in the front line, I thought it would be to their advantage to know what we were to do that night. I watched for my chance and slipped down to let them know of what they might expect.

That was all very kind of me, I admit, but when I think of what the result of my knowledge and the information I carried down to the line of battle might have resulted in, I almost shudder even at this late day. Suppose the enemy by some means had gained the information and General Lee had acted on it. Our whole army might have been destroyed. After we withdrew, we went into winter quarters, the same camps we had occupied before we made the crossing and had the battle.

You will now see that up to this time our success had been very discouraging. We had failed in almost every effort we had made. Our advance on Richmond was about where it had started the spring before. On the other hand, the Confederates were correspondingly elated. During the winter, Burnside concluded to make another advance. This was to the right, or up the river, evidently with a view of turning Lee's left. But the elements were against us. The first day out rain commenced falling in torrents and continued so for several days, so that the rivers rose very high and the roads we marched over became regular mortar beds. The result was we retraced our march, and again went into our same winter quarters where we remained until spring.

During that winter I made application for a ten-day furlough to go home and see my folks. The furlough was granted and I started for home. I arrived in Johnstown after dark, and concluded to walk out that night thinking I would surprise the folks. As I was coming down the hill into Scalp Level, I happened to think of an old black dog we had, "Fillmore" by name, and I knew he was cross at nights and I was afraid he might tackle me if I undertook to get in. I knew where he was in the habit of sleeping on the back porch, so I thought I would try and get in by the side gate, or opposite to where the old dog slept. It was probably nine o'clock when I arrived, and all was dark. As I quietly stole up to the side gate and was about to raise the latch, there stood old Fillmore on the opposite side. For a moment I did not know how to proceed, but the next instant I snapped my fingers. As I did that old Fillmore recognized me and was out over the gate with a bound, jumping up and yow-yowing so that he woke up the whole family. In fact, I doubt if anyone expressed any more pleasure on seeing me than did the old dog. The next I knew "Dad" raised a window hearing the commotion of the old dog going on and I heard him say, "Why, I believe it's Charlie." About that time the Veil family was getting up, and there was no more sleep that night.

That was a very enjoyable week to me. I had the best of everything that was to be had—chicken, turkey, and mince pies—everything that was good. The fathers and mothers, sisters and brothers of the boys who had enlisted in the meantime came to see me and to inquire about them. I had to tell about this and that fight, etc., and repeat it over and over.

But finally the time came when I must start back. I dreaded the good-byes, so I had my brother smuggle my satchel out and, without saying anything to anyone, stole away. When I arrived at Aquia Creek, which was by boat from Washington, it was raining hard and I had about ten or twelve miles to march to camp, but I started out through mud almost knee deep. All the supplies for the army were hauled over that road by mule teams, so you can imagine the shape of the roads. After I got out about four miles, darkness came on and I was stuck in the mud and pretty heavily loaded too. The parents of the boys whom I knew in the front and who resided near our home had loaded me down with cakes, pies, fruit, and one thing or another, so that I not only had my own satchel, but two of them. In this way I stumbled across the ruins of an old deserted log hut that had a piece of tent over one corner. I took possession and managed to strike a fire, and in that passed the night. Next day I got back to camp. Then all the boys who knew I had been home came to see me and inquired how their folks were and I, in turn, distributed the goodies I had brought them.

Next spring General Joe Hooker, having in the meantime succeeded to the command of the army again, moved out on to Richmond. The main Union Army moved to the right toward Chancellorsville while our corps under the command of General Reynolds made a feint movement to the same point at which we had crossed the river in December. When we came to laying the pontoon bridges across the river, we found the enemy occupying rifle pits on the opposite side. Their fire was so sharp and destructive and their cover so secure, that we had great difficulty in laying the bridges. After several efforts had been made and the pontooners driven off, General Reynolds finally gave Brigadier General James S. Wadsworth, the old governor of New York who commanded a division, an order to force the crossing. In doing so, he rushed down a regiment, loaded them in the boats, and pushed over under their fire. As they got started from the shore, the general jumped his horse off the bank and swam the river with the men. His son, Captain James Walcott Wadsworth, an aide on General Reynolds's staff, seeing what his father was doing, also put spurs to his horse and plunged him into the river and swam over after his father. I always thought that one of the most gallant acts I saw during the war. Once across, the men had no difficulty in capturing the rifle pits. Nearly all the Rebels surrendered and those who undertook to escape were shot down as they ran.

The same night General Hooker, having crossed the river higher up, sent us orders to join the main army and we made a forced march to get there, just as the Eleventh Corps was being driven from the field by Stonewall Jackson. We then took position on the right of the line, but did not become engaged. There we lay a day or so and then withdrew to the northern side of the river and another failure of the main army was recorded. General Lee, elated by his success at Chancellorsville—and he had reasons to be—had decided to invade the North again. The next definite news we had of him was that he was on his way into Pennsylvania. Our army was at once put into motion again over the same ground we had before passed over, and by forced marching we again found ourselves in Frederick, Maryland.

At that point, on June 28, 1863, General Hooker was relieved and General George G. Meade placed in command. General Meade was an old army officer and a particular friend of General Reynolds. He at once placed him in command of the left wing of the army, consisting of the First, Third, and Eleventh Corps. On the 29th we marched out toward Emmitsburg, and on the 30th to Marsh Creek with the First Corps, the Eleventh a short distance in the rear, and the Third Corps within supporting distance of the Eleventh.

Meanwhile, Brigadier General John Buford's division of cavalry, which was also under General Reynolds's command, had occupied Gettysburg. General Reynolds had no knowledge of where Lee was, but supposed, as reports were, that he was in the Cumberland Valley, heading for Harrisburg. Buford reported that evening that he was in Gettysburg and that all was quiet, that some Confederate troops had been in the town the day before but had gone out again. In that way we camped the night of June the 30th and next morning early started with the First Corps for Gettysburg, the general riding in ahead.

After proceeding about three miles we met one of General Buford's staff officers riding in great haste with the information that the enemy was advancing on Gettysburg by the Cashtown, or Chambersburg, Pike and that he was then sharply engaged. General Reynolds at once dismounted and sent staff officers to the different corps of his command with orders to press forward. He wrote a note to General Meade, giving him the information, which he dispatched by another officer, and then mounted his horse and rode rapidly into Gettysburg and to Seminary Ridge, where he found General Buford engaged.

When he met Buford, the Confederates were then in plain view advancing down the pike. The general held a short conversation with Buford, telling him to hold on as long as he could and that he would hurry his men forward to his assistance. In the meantime Reynolds had sent orders to the head of his column to cut across the country from the Emmitsburg Road toward the Lutheran Seminary and rode out in that direction himself until he met the head of his column coming on. He then led them out to where he had first met General Buford and indicated the position he desired them to occupy.

The regiments no sooner were in position than the action commenced. The general rode to the left, evidently with a view of selecting a position to occupy with his troops as they came up. When riding into the McPherson woods he discovered a column of Rebel infantry advancing through the woods and coming in such a direction as would take the troops the general had already placed in action on their left flank. He at once turned and rode toward the seminary, where he met the head of the brigade following the First, or one already in action, and with the leading regiment of that moved forward to the point at which he had discovered the Confederate infantry advancing through the McPherson woods.

As the regiment reached the brow of the little ridge, or incline ground, General Reynolds gave the word to charge, leading in person and riding considerably in advance of his troops. The regiment undertook to follow but met with such a hot fire from the Confederates that, instead of following him, it sheered off to the right or to where the leading brigade was in action, leaving the general and myself alone in front of the advancing Confederate line as he rode into the edge of the woods where the monument now stands marking the spot on which he fell. He turned in his saddle, looking toward the rear and the Lutheran Seminary, when he was struck by a minnie ball and fell from his horse.

General Reynolds fell upon his face, his arms outstretched toward the enemy. I at once sprang from my horse and ran to his side, gave one glance at his body and seeing no wound or blood, turned his body upon its back. I again glanced over it and, seeing no blood or wound, the suggestion struck me that he had probably been stunned by a spent ball. My next impression was to save him from falling into the hands of the enemy. Not having any assistance, not one of our men being near, I picked him up by taking hold under his arms and commenced pulling him backward toward our line or the direction in which we had come from. As I did so, the Confederates yelled, "Drop him! Drop him!" But I kept on backing off as fast as I could and finally got over the brow of the rise, where I found some men and where we were out of range of the enemy's fire.

As I laid him down there, I first discovered where he had been struck. The ball had entered the back of his neck, just over the coat collar, and passed downward in its course. The wound did not bleed externally and, as he fell, his coat collar had covered up the wound, which accounted for my not discovering it at first. With the assistance of the men I found, we carried the body across the fields over to the Emmitsburg Road, the one we had marched in on that morning.

This is an authentic account of the circumstances attending the death of the lamented General Reynolds and can be verified by no other living person than myself, having been the only person directly present when the general fell. The sad event impressed itself so indelibly upon my young mind that, after these forty-five years that have elapsed since it occurred, my recollections are as vivid as though it had occurred but a few days since.

The death of General Reynolds was a great loss to the

Union Cause deeply felt by all, but by no one person as much as myself. I had been with the general from the time he joined us at Harrison's Landing, in every move and march to the time of his death, and I am always pleased when I recall that I had won his confidence. I knew that on a number of occasions he had entrusted me with messages that ordinarily should have been carried by an officer.

After we carried his body to the little stone house on the Emmitsburg Road and laid it on the floor in the little sitting room, Major Adolph Rosengarten of his staff and I rode into town to try and find a casket, but the best we could do was to get a case that caskets are shipped in. We got one of these, which proved to be too short. One end was knocked out and in that the general's body was placed and started that evening for Westminster, Major Rosengarten and myself accompanying it. The major rode on the ambulance with the driver and I rode the general's horse, he having run into our lines after Reynolds fell. Mine was killed as I dismounted.

From Westminster, where we struck the railroad, we went to Baltimore. There the body was embalmed and from there we went to Philadelphia, the general's home. On the Fourth of July I accompanied the body with the general's family to Lancaster, where he was buried. I had never met any of the general's family before this, but they all appeared to know of me and paid me great attention. They appeared to feel themselves under great obligations from the fact of my preventing his body from falling into the hands of the enemy. When we were at Lancaster, so near my home, the general's brothers and sisters suggested that I should go on to my home for a day or two, and I did so. Father and Mother and all, of course, were very glad to see me. After remaining a day or two, I started back and rejoined the army before it had recrossed the river again, in pursuit of Lee.

By the general's death on the first day, I missed the battle of Gettysburg, save the opening of it, but the short experience I had has never been forgotten and led to a change in the whole course of my life, as subsequent events will show. When I got back to the army I found General John Newton in command of the corps, and I resumed my duties as orderly to the commanding officer.

While we were on the march following up Lee, who was again retreating into Virginia, I one day received an order to report in person to General Meade, the commander of the army. I first reported to General Williams, the adjutant general, as I knew was the proper thing to do, and he rode up to the front with me, where General Meade was riding at the head of his staff. "General," said he, "here is Veil." The general turned to me and said he had a package General Reynolds's sisters had sent him to give me. He then handed it to me, saying it gave him great pleasure to do so and that it was something I might be proud of. I thanked him without knowing what it contained, but when I fell back and opened the package I found a beautiful gold watch and chain with a nice letter from the general's sisters. There was an inscription inside the watch, saying "Presented to Orderly C. H. Veil by the Sisters of the Late General J. F. Reynolds, United States Army, Gettysburg, July 1, 1863." That I was, and am, proud of the watch you may be assured. I have it yet and always will as long as I live. There is not a farm in Tioga County that I would take in exchange for it. All I regret is that I have not a boy to hand it down to, who in years to come might say he had a watch General Reynolds's sisters gave his father and had it sent to him by the hand of General Meade, commanding the Army of the Potomac.

The winter of 1863 found us in camp in the vicinity of Culpeper Courthouse. Our headquarters were in the town. Before that, however, another attempt had been made to force General Lee out of his lines. We found him at Mine Run, south of the Rapidan, but the position appeared so strong that General Meade did not dare attack and the army went into quarters for the winter at Culpeper Courthouse as stated.

During the winter our corps made a reconnaissance out toward Orange Courthouse. The distance was some eighteen or twenty miles. After the corps had halted for the night, the adjutant general, Colonel Charles Kingsbury, called me and asked if I thought I could carry a dispatch back the way we had come and on to General Meade's headquarters, some twelve miles beyond Culpeper at Brandy Station. I volunteered to try and started about dark. The route was through Mosby's country and I was in danger of being picked up by his men, but I got through to our headquarters all right. There I changed horses and rode on to Brandy Station where I found the headquarters of the army. General Meade was absent, but Major General John Sedgwick was in command in Meade's absence.

General Sedgwick was very kind to me. He inquired how I had gotten through for so long a distance and then said it was necessary to have orders go back to our headquarters that night. As no one else knew the way, the only thing was for me to return at once and so I started over the same long route I had made that day and night. When I got back to Culpeper, I changed my horse again and by daylight next morning reached our headquarters which I had left the evening before. My trip and success pleased General Newton very much, and he congratulated me on having made it so successfully. The orders I carried were for the corps to return at once to Culpeper.

Our headquarters clerks and orderlies occupied a building that winter. When Christmas came, we decided that we ought to have a little blowout in the way of an extra dinner and began to make preparations for the occasion. The country had been gone over so often by both armies that there was no use in trying to forage, as our boys called it. Everything fit to eat had been stolen and a good many that were not, so we were put to our own resources for what we were to have. We found we could buy some fresh beef at the corps butchers, so we bought a good roast, also some potatoes and onions, but could get no bread or flour, so I said I would make the bread anyway. Soft bread, after having been on hardtack so long, was indispensable to our coming feast. I got a lot of hard bread which I pounded up as fine as flour, put in some pork fat for shortening, and mixed a good big loaf and thought I had solved the problem. My oven was what we called a Dutch oven. I put my loaf in and set the fire going top and bottom and, after I thought it was sufficiently baked, turned her out; but, as I did so, my loaf went to pieces. It would not stick together and the boys had a good laugh over me and my Dutch oven bread, but it was real good nonetheless and made a pleasant change. The only trouble was you wanted a spoon to eat it with.

Soon after, a telegram came to headquarters that said: "War Department, Washington D.C. Order Private C. H. Veil,

Company G, Ninth Regiment, Pennsylvania Reserves, to report in person to the Secretary of War for promotion. Signed L. Thomas, Adjutant General." On the strength of that I did not lose much time getting there. I arrived in Washington in the afternoon, and as soon as I had brushed myself up as best I could, I struck out for the War Department. When I arrived at Secretary Edwin Stanton's office, I found General James Hardie, to whom I showed my order. He informed me Mr. Stanton was not feeling well and had gone home for the day, and for me to call the next morning, saying as I left, "You are all right, young man."

Next morning about nine o'clock I again struck out for the War Department. As I drew near I saw a line of people ranged up along the sidewalk and leading into the building. I wondered what the cause might be, but followed up alongside to and into the building. As I followed up along the line into the building, I found the head of it in the Secretary of War's office and it then began to dawn on me what the trouble was. They were waiting for an audience with the Secretary. But I had gone so far and was so near his door that I kept going until I reached it and could look in. I saw the Secretary standing at his desk, his glasses up over his brow and talking to some general officer.

At the very moment I reached the door General Hardie, whom I had seen the evening before, saw and recognized me, and with his hand beckoned me to come in. It did not take me long to make up my mind to accept his invitation and in I went. He at once took me to Mr. Stanton and said, "Mr. Secretary, this is Private Veil, whom you ordered to report for promotion." The Secretary at once turned and took me by the hand and began to shake hands as though he was delighted to see me, at the same time saying how proud he was to hear of my brave act of saving General Reynolds's body from falling into the hands of the enemy. He told me that the general's sisters had told him and the president all about it and that the president had ordered that I should be made a commissioned officer. He wound up by asking me what branch of the service I preferred. While all this was going on, the general officer and all the others were staring at me and, I suppose, wishing I was out of the way so they could have their say with the Secretary again, but he still kept holding my hand. I finally pulled myself together and said I was used to riding. "Oh, well," said he, "we will make a cavalryman of you. Are there any vacancies in the cavalry regiments, General?" (this to General Hardie).

The general soon returned from an inner office and reported one in the First Cavalry and another in one of the other regiments. "Well, General," said he to Hardie, "nominate Mr. Veil for the vacancy in the First Cavalry and give him a certificate showing that he has been so nominated. I want him to have something he can show the general's sisters of what has been done." To me, he said, "Now, Mr. Veil (mind the Mister), do you think you could locate the spot on which the general fell? There are many different reports and the general's sisters and family are very anxious to know the exact spot." I told him I thought I could, that the surroundings were so impressed on my mind that I thought I would have no difficulty in doing so. "Well, now," said he, "Mr. Veil, you go to Baltimore tomorrow (to a certain number he gave me) and I will wire the general's sisters to meet you, and you go with them to Gettysburg and see if you can find and mark the place." All the time the Secretary held my hand. General Hardie finally thought this had gone on long enough and was pulling at my other coat sleeve to get me to break away and finally did, but that was one of the Secretary's hobbies—to make a lot of a private soldier and be gruff and austere with an officer.

When I finally got away, I followed General Hardie into the inner office, where he gave me a slip to take down to the adjutant general's office. The slip was for an order to be issued at once discharging me from the Ninth Regiment, which was done. I was then directed to another officer, who at once enlisted me into the General Service. As a matter of fact, I could not be appointed into the Regular Army from the Volunteers, but had to be appointed from the Regulars. My enlisting temporarily in the General Service turned out to my advantage, as subsequent events showed, and will probably be referred to later.

Next day I went to Baltimore and called at the address the Secretary had given me and found the general's sisters, and we went on to Gettysburg that afternoon. They were very anxious to locate the identical spot on which the general fell and were very particular in asking me to describe it, which I did as near as I could. I went over all the movements of the general after he had arrived on the field up to the moment he fell. Then I described the way I had taken the body. Among other things I told them of was a young oak tree having been cut off by a cannon ball about so high up from the ground, very close to where the general was killed, and of the top falling so some of the branches struck us.

After we had driven to the spot by the route we had taken that fatal day, which I had no trouble in locating as described, the ladies were perfectly satisfied that I was correct and we were about to leave, when one of them happened to think of the oak tree I had said had been cut off by the shot and inquired where it was. I had forgotten all about that and, for a moment, appeared to be all wrong. I knew I was right, but there was no tree there, cut off, as I had said. There was, however, a pile of cord wood. As I looked the wood over, I saw that the ends of some of the pieces had been shot off and not cut off with an ax. As a matter of fact, the trunk had been chopped down and that, and the top part, had been cut up into cord wood and piled up on the ground. That verified my statement. I have often, in thinking over the matter, been glad that it was settled then and there, for my circumstantial evidence fully corroborated all I had said to the sisters. I marked the spot at that time as directed by the Secretary and the monument now stands there.

While we were in Gettysburg the sisters informed me of what was [not known], or has not generally been known, that the general was engaged to be married to a Miss Catherine Hewitt of New York City. She was then in the Emmitsburg Convent, some ten or twelve miles from Gettysburg, and had expressed a desire to see me. They wished to know if I would go with them to call on her. I, of course, was glad to do so. The next day we drove over and, through the influence of the ladies, I was allowed to enter the convent and see the young lady. Miss Hewitt was very beautiful and highly educated. When she lost her sweetheart, she decided to give up the world and enter a convent and for some reason decided to enter the one at Emmitsburg. She made a great deal of me. I had to tell her all about the general, his last moments, and so forth. She wanted very particularly to know if he had left any last message. When we came to leave, she said, "Mr Veil, I have a little token here I had made for the general, some of my own work, and I want to give it to you as a token of remembrance of both of us." Taking from the folds of her dress a small package, she handed it to me. I thanked her for it and we left. After we had left the convent I told the sisters of what had taken place and, on opening the little package, which was nicely done up and tied with a ribbon, found a very beautiful embroidered handkerchief—the coat of arms of the United States, very beautifully done. I have the handkerchief and token to this day.

How I happen to have it yet, I may as well tell now as at some later time because it makes a pretty good little story. When I next returned to my home and showed my prizes to my mother, she said, "Now Charlie, let me keep this handkerchief for you. You will be apt to lose it." As a result, I gave it to her for safekeeping. In the course of time I got out West, where I remained many years. During that time my mother passed away. My elder sister, who was married and living in Johnstown, took it in charge to keep for me. She was there and had the handkerchief when that terrible flood came that washed away the city and took thousands of lives.

My brother-in-law was on the street in front of their home when he saw the wall of water coming down the street in the direction of their home, crushing every building in its course and carrying everything before it as it came on. He rushed into the house and up to the first story with my sister and her family of four children. As they gained the first floor, the water was there, too. My sister, like many other ladies, had a little casket with her valuable trinkets, jewelry, etc., and it contained, among other things, my handkerchief. In passing through the bedroom for the upper story, she picked that up on her way to the garret and out on the roof. By that time, the building had begun to turn on its foundation. Just then a large flat roof floated up alongside of their house and my brother-in-law, thinking that would make a more secure raft than the house they were on, pushed my sister off onto that and threw the children after, one after another, and then followed himself. They then floated off, first down toward the Stone Bridge, where a jam was formed, and then back up Stonycreek. They floated around during the greater portion of the night, among the drowned and drowning, until finally the roof drifted up to the John Thomas building, about the only building remaining on the main street, and they were handed up into that. There my brother John residing in our old home out at Scalp Level, having heard during the night of the destruction of Johnstown and having hurried in, found them. In order to reach them he had to build a raft and, after getting them to shore, took them out to our old home. During all this terrible night my sister had held on to her little casket containing, among other valuable things, my handkerchief.

On April 7, my commission as second lieutenant of the First United States Cavalry was issued and signed by the president. With it came orders for me to report to my regiment for duty. My regiment was then a part of Major General Philip Sheridan's command, he having about that time been assigned to the command of the cavalry corps of the Army of the Potomac. I never passed through a more trying ordeal than I did the day I rode from Culpeper Courthouse to report to my regiment. It was the idea of a mere uneducated country boy knowing nothing about cavalry tactics (all I knew was how to ride) going to join a regiment where the officers were educated West Point graduates and, of course, gentlemen. As I rode along, the more I thought of the situation the more trying it appeared to be. I finally came to the conclusion that the officers were educated and must, as a matter of fact, be gentlemen and that, when I reported, they would of course take for granted that I, too, must be a gentleman and that, if I acted as such, I should be treated in the same manner. When I came to that conclusion, I felt better and rode on. I found the regiment and reported to the commanding officer, Colonel George Alexander Hamilton Blake, who was an elderly man old enough to be my father. He saw and understood the situation at a glance and took pains to introduce me to all the officers, see that I was invited to mess and, in short, did everything to make me feel at home that he possibly could.

A few days after, we started out on the Wilderness Campaign (May 5 to 7, 1864) and it was but a few days before I was initiated into cavalry service in earnest. Our first day's engagement was at Todd's Tavern on the left of Grant's army. It is always a pleasure to me to know that I attracted my commander's attention in my first cavalry fight. He recommended me for a brevet of one file. I got it and was made first lieutenant. In the evening after having driven the Rebel cavalry from the ground, we withdrew a short distance and bivouacked for the night. Before daylight we were on the move again to occupy Spotsylvania, which was left uncovered the day before. General Meade had moved a division of cavalry that General Sheridan had posted to hold a certain road without Sheridan's knowledge. This had allowed General Lee to send troops in that night that got the ground we were to occupy, and fighting commenced long before daylight. All we had to shoot at was the flashes of the enemy's guns. A little after daylight the infantry came up. Brigadier General John C. Robinson's division was leading with him riding at the head. I had known him in the First Corps and had carried many messages and orders to him. As he rode by where I was, I heard him say to someone, "Oh, get your d——d cavalry out of the way. There is nothing ahead but a little cavalry. We will soon clean them out." I thought to myself, "Old man, you will find something more than a little cavalry on ahead." He went on and in, but less than fifteen minutes afterward I saw them carry my General Robinson back on a stretcher with a leg shot off.[1]

This was the opening of the battle of Spotsylvania Courthouse, which lasted from May 8 to 21. We then withdrew a short distance to give the infantry a show to go in. It was here that Sheridan rode over to Meade's headquarters and they had a regular row about Meade moving the division of calvalry without Sheridan's knowledge. Sheridan, so he said himself in his memoirs, told Meade that if he, Sheridan, was to command the cavalry corps he would give the orders and that, if he was not to do that, he would not give any more orders. He wound up by saying that if he, Meade, would let him alone, he would go out and lick hell out of the Rebel cavalry.

General Meade, who was a very crabbed and crusty old customer, as he acknowledged himself, felt badly about having had the row with General Sheridan, so he got onto his horse and rode over to General Grant's headquarters and reported what Sheridan had said about going out and licking Jeb Stuart.

"Well," said Grant, "you better let him go." Meade then rode back, sent for Sheridan, and told him to go ahead and lick Stuart.

Sheridan wasted no time. We got ready that day and early the next morning started out on our job. We rode to the left, going hard and continuously all day until late at night when we halted to feed and for a short rest. By daylight next morning we were on the march again, but before the command had got strung out on the road, the Confederates had found out what Sheridan was up to and were on his trail. Their advance had an opportunity to fire a few shots at us with a light battery, but Sheridan didn't stop to give battle. He simply held them back with a rear guard and pushed on with his advance.

That day while we were on the march a body of mounted Rebel skirmishers came openly out on our right flank and fired into our column. The adjutant of the regiment came back along the column to where I was and gave me an order to take so many men out of the regiment and drive them off, saying "I'll tell the men off." So there I was with an independent command, the first one I ever had. As to what order to give my men, I knew about as much as any other country boy would have known, but I did know what was expected of me. I rode out to the right, gave the command, "Forward, trot," and rode out in the direction of the Rebels. That was my only redeeming point. The men, all veterans, knew what was wanted. They followed and, as soon as we got in reach, deployed without my giving any order to do so and commenced firing. As I kept on going in the direction of the Johnnies, they kept on following and firing. The Rebels, however, seeing us continuing our advance, fell back. We drove them as far as I thought was necessary to secure the passage of the command unmolested and then rejoined my regiment.

About the first thing Sheridan did was to strike the railroad at Ashland, I think. There, on May 11, we captured immense supplies for Lee's army which, after supplying ourselves with what we wanted, we destroyed. We also recaptured a large number of Union prisoners. As soon as the supplies and railroad were destroyed, we pushed on. Major General James E. B. Stuart, commanding the Confederate cavalry, in the meantime was beginning to catch up with us and, at Yellow Tavern, within about twelve miles of Richmond, forced Sheridan to stop and fight.

The battle commenced about noon on May 11 and continued until after dark. We held our line at all points. Attacks had been made on us from all sides. Jeb Stuart had been killed. The losses on both sides had been considerable and, to cap the climax, it commenced raining about dark and the night itself was dark as pitch. Our horses were not unsaddled for the night; all stood in line ready for action or movement. I heard the old officers of the regiment talking while we lay in that way, wondering how we were to get out of the hole we were in, but all expressed confidence in the general being able to get us out. Probably ten o'clock that night the order came along quickly to mount and move out.

Yellow Tavern is on a main road leading directly to Richmond and one on which we had been advancing. Much to our surprise we continued on that and in the direction of Richmond. How it was that that should have been left uncovered, I am unable at this day to account for. Probably the death of General Stuart may have been the cause. We continued on that to about daylight, when we had passed through the outer lines of fortifications covering Richmond. We then turned sharp to the left and down the Chickahominy between the outer and inner line of Confederate works toward the Mechanicsville Road. The second line of fortifications in the meantime opened on us with big guns. General Gregg's cavalry division was given the duty of looking after these, while ours was to take the bridge crossing the Chickahominy on the road leading to Mechanicsville. That was our only outlet and the bridge was held by the Rebs. Brigadier General George Custer's brigade was first dismounted and sent down to make the attack but failed. Orders then came back to us to assist, and our orders were to take it at all hazards. That meant business, but we wanted a way to get out and went in with a will and cleared and took the bridge, enabling the entire command to cross and get on the north side of the river. We then had room to operate in.

At Mechanicsville we found an immense quantity of corn on the ear, enough to feed our whole command. As soon as we were all over, the entire command was fed. The animals were badly in need of it for they had not been fed for several days.

After feeding, the command moved out again. The First Cavalry, my regiment, had the advance. We had not gone a mile before we were into business again. We first drove in the pickets, or skirmishers, and then found a line of dismounted men lying behind a breastwork of rails running by a strip, or rather in front of a strip, of woods. That portion of the regiment I was serving with was ordered to dismount and fight on foot. The balance remained mounted for a charge. As soon as all was ready, the advance was sounded and business commenced. We made a rush for the fence rail barricade and got the enemy started. As soon as the mounted men saw that, they charged them into and through the strip of woods. We foot men followed as fast as we could, but had gone but a short distance when we saw our mounted men coming back fully as fast, if not a little faster, than they had gone in and a body of Confederates at their heels. If one had been off to one side, it might have been interesting to see the race, but I and my dismounted men were in the way. I called to the men to take to trees as I did and, after they had passed by us, I made a run to the left to try and get out of the way of the Confederates who had passed. I knew they would soon be coming back faster than they had followed our fellows, and they did. I had the run of my life to keep out of their way. At one time I was in their rear and inside their line, but they were too busy with others to pick us up.

That was the last effort they made to stop or bother us on our trip, and we continued by way of the White House, where we crossed the Pamunkey River and went on to Bermuda Hundred where we joined General Benjamin Butler's command on the James River. The raid had been a success in every way. Without any serious loss, we had first taken all the Confederate cavalry away from Grant's front in the Wilderness, had destroyed large quantities of stores and supplies needed by Lee's army, had defeated the Confederate cavalry in every engagement, and had besides killed one of the best Confederate cavalry commanders Lee ever had before reaching a base of supplies. It was a pretty good introduction to active cavalry service for a green country boy, but I believe I held my own. At any rate, Sheridan had made good.

* * *

While at camp we had a mail delivery and I had some letters from home. One was from a claim agency in Philadelphia saying there was a bounty of four hundred dollars due me from a certain ward in the city. If I would sign the enclosed voucher, they would send it to me or any address I might give them for a charge of ten dollars. I thought there must be some mistake and wrote them to that effect. At the same time I gave them my father's address and sent on the papers they had asked me to sign. Sometime after I had a letter from Father saying he had received a draft from the parties and asking me what to do with it. As a matter of fact, my enlistment at Washington at the time I got my promotion had been taken up and credited in a certain ward in Philadelphia where they wanted men and were paying bounties to get them. This was all without my knowledge, yet I got the $390. They might as well have kept the money. I would have never known anything about it.

Another incident occurred here that I must tell of. We had a lot of unserviceable horses in the regiment that had become broken down and unfit for use. They were all ordered to be turned into the depot quartermaster at Bermuda Hundred and I was detailed with a squad of men to take and turn them in. I had fifty-two, all told. When I turned them over to the quartermaster he simply told me where to put them. After I had turned them into the yard or corral, I supposed I ought to have something to take back and show that I had done so, but he didn't offer to give me anything, so I kept standing around waiting to see if he had anything to offer. Finally he said, "Well, young man, what are you waiting for?" I then picked up courage enough to tell him what I had on my mind. "Oh, well," said he, "write out what you want and I will sign it." I wrote out a memorandum receipt on a little strip of paper I had; he signed it and I left for camp.

No one asked me for it or what I had done with my horses. The incident appeared to be closed but I kept my receipt and many years afterward, long after I had left the service and closed my accounts with the different departments, I one day received a letter saying the record showed that I had failed to make returns to the department for a certain number of horses. As I knew I hadn't stolen any horses or sold any, either, I paid no attention to the letter. By and by I had another letter calling attention to the first, saying the record showed that I had failed to make returns for a certain lot of horses and that I must do so without delay. I paid no attention to that one either. By and by I got another one calling my attention to the two former letters. This was a rather sharp one, for it said that unless the horses were promptly accounted for proceedings would be brought against me and, further, that the price of the horses was $225 each. That woke me up. I began to wonder what the trouble could be and all at once I happened to think of the horses I had turned in on the James River. I remembered that I had the receipt, which if I could find it, would straighten my account. Where to look for it after all these years was the question. When I left the service I had all my retained papers (copies) boxed up, so I struck for the box. In a package of what I had labeled "Miscellaneous Papers," I found my memorandum receipt given by the quartermaster at Bermuda Hundred. I then went to town and before a Notary Public made a sworn copy and sent it to the Department. That settled the horse question. Had I not been able to find this receipt, it might have caused me much trouble and expense to clear myself of the charge. So better keep your receipts, boys; they don't cost much and may be of great service, as this one proved to be to me.

After resting our men and animals, General Sheridan started back to find General Grant's army. Grant, in the meantime, had been pounding away at Spotsylvania and in the Wilderness. Our course back was by way of the White House Crossing on the Pamunkey River. When we arrived there, we found that the enemy had partly burned the bridge over the river so the first thing the general did was to send out the command to tear down all the buildings we could find. In that way we secured sufficient timber to repair the bridge sufficiently to cross on. This delayed us a day or two, but we were not harassed by the Confederates and moved on again to find Grant and his army.

No sooner had we done so than we were again started off to the left to clear the way and lay some bridges for the infantry across a stream called Nottaway, if I mistake not, where we fought a very severe engagement. As soon as the infantry

43

reached the bridges and the ground we had uncovered, we were again put in motion to the left and at Cold Harbor had another heavy engagement. Here I lost one of my First Cavalry friends, Captain Samuel McKee, who had taken a fancy to me. Whenever we started out in a fight, Sam would say, "Come on, Veil." We had a habit of always humming some tune or another whenever an engagement was on and today, as he was doing so while we were fighting on foot, he was shot through the lungs.[2]

After the fight was over for the day, General Sheridan concluded we were too far advanced and our position too precarious to hold, so he withdrew some four or five miles to the rear. As soon as General Grant heard of the ground we had gained, however, he ordered Sheridan to go back and hold it at all hazards until the infantry, then on the march, could reach us, which meant we had to saddle up again and move back to the place we had left.

The first thing General Sheridan did was to dismount the command and send the horses to the rear. Then we occupied the line of breastworks the enemy had held, distributed boxes of ammunition along our line, and lay waiting for daylight. When daylight arrived, we could see the enemy's infantry in a piece of woods in front of us, but they made no movement looking toward an attack. We lay facing each other until sometime along near noon, when our infantry column arrived, filed in, and took our place. We were mighty glad to let them have it, for here some of the heaviest fighting of the whole campaign took place. It was here that General Grant ordered successive charges, or assaults, that many afterward thought were unnecessary sacrifices of life.

We had no sooner withdrawn and let our horses fill up on a large clover plantation and got some supplies for ourselves than we were again on the move, this time to the right. Our objective was to try and join Major General David Hunter's command somewhere at the head of the Shenandoah Valley and destroy the railroad on which the enemy was getting supplies. The enemy soon discovered our movement and at Trevilion Station, near Gordonsville, overtook us and we had to fight. The first day we were successful but lost heavily. The First Cavalry had two officers killed.

That day I was on the extreme right with dismounted men. As we pressed the enemy back, we came to a fence they had been occupying, and in one of the corners I saw one of the most gruesome sights I ever saw. A big Confederate cavalryman sat on the inside corner of the fence with his carbine in his hands, but he had been beheaded. A cannon ball had struck him, tearing his head clear off; the skin of his lower jaw was hanging down on his breast. He evidently had a long beard for that was hanging down almost covering his breast.

In the field stood a farmhouse in which I saw a lot of Confederates take refuge. As they had ceased firing on us, I concluded they wanted to surrender and we made a rush to the house, calling on them to surrender as we did so. When I got to the door one of the men partly opened it and commenced handing out the arms until I had a pile of them. When I inquired if that was all and he answered yes, I went in. I found the house floor covered with wounded men. In looking them over, I saw one young fellow lying in with the others who I thought looked pretty healthy for a wounded man and I stopped to inquire where he was wounded. As soon as I did that, I saw there was a "fox in the fence" somewhere, for there was an elderly lady and a young girl in the house who could not conceal their anxiety. The fact, as it turned out afterward, was that they had him lie down with the wounded thinking he might get away, that being his home. But I got the best of him and he had to go along.

Next day we attacked the Confederates again, but as they had had reinforcements come up by rail that night, we could not dislodge them. They occupied a railroad cut in our advance, which was on foot through thick brush. As we neared the cut, they opened upon us. As soon as we saw them, we dropped to the ground and their volley went over our heads, but to this day I can hardly see how we got away with our lives. We were at very close range, but as they were in the cut all we could see was their heads and did not have much of a mark to shoot at. We finally got out after dark and the general concluded to strike back and rejoin Grant.

The enemy were desperate and saucy by this time. They followed and skirmished with us all day. We had to keep out a strong rear guard and continual firing was going on. When we halted for the night we threw up barricades of fence rails, logs, and such.

Once, after we had halted for the night and my regiment was holding the road, I did not feel satisfied with the way things looked and rode to the right through a piece of woods where I discovered about a regiment of Rebel cavalry in a field. In riding back in great haste, I got too far to the front and when I reached the road we had been marching on I came out in plain view onto it between our and the enemy's line. The first thing I knew our fellows behind the barricades, not recognizing me in the dusk of the evening, opened fire upon me. Luckily for me, they missed. Why the Rebels didn't open too, I never could account for, but I got in all right and our right flank was looked after.

We continued our march back toward Grant's army, which we did not overtake until we got to the James River, he having in the meantime reached Petersburg. We crossed at Bermuda Hundred and marched to the left of the line.

About that time, word reached us that Lieutenant General Jubal Early was investing Washington, so Sheridan with two divisions of his cavalry was rushed to Washington by transport. We no sooner arrived there than we started up the Maryland side for Harpers Ferry. General Early fell back to the vicinity of Winchester and took up position there, setting the stage for Sheridan's campaign in the valley that ended at Waynesboro the following spring and resulted in the utter annihilation of Early's army. In addition to Sheridan's two divisions of cavalry he brought from the Army of the Potomac, he had the Sixth Corps, General Wright's cavalry, and the Eighth Corps (a small one) under Brigadier General George Crook.

As soon as his troops reached Harpers Ferry, he at once moved the cavalry to the front and we commenced reconnoitering and harassing the enemy by day and by night. Not a moment's rest was had or given the enemy. Finally, on September 19, the general thought the time had come to make an attack and everybody was moved forward. The cavalry to which I belonged was in the right and crossed the Opequon early in the morning and then pressed forward until we were before the works at Winchester close up, so near in fact that we could see the gunners looking out through the portholes in the parapets. There we waited for the final order to charge. It finally came and, with a rush and hurrah, the line moved forward and we took the works. Winchester was ours and the enemy in full flight up the valley. We captured many prisoners.

After following the noted Confederates some distance beyond, we went into bivouac for the night and the next day continued our pursuit to Strasburg just beyond. At Fisher's Hill, Early with his routed army had taken up another position, a very strong one, and Sheridan at once commenced operation looking toward its capture. General Crook's corps was ordered to the extreme right by night, following a mountain trail or road that would lead him to the right and rear of Fisher's Hill where, at daylight, he was to make an attack. At the same time the Sixth Corps was to attack in front.

Before this, however, the First Cavalry division, the one I served in, was ordered to make a detour to the left through Luray Valley and strike the pike at Newmarket in the rear of Early's position. Unfortunately, we met a considerable force of Confederates holding a narrow pass in the Luray Valley that we were unable to dislodge. After engaging them a day, General Alfred Torbett ordered a retreat. Our brigade was to lead the advance in following back, but before starting, the ambulance train, loaded with the wounded, was sent on ahead. They had driven but a few miles when it was captured by Mosby's guerrillas.

The word soon reached us and we started in hot pursuit. As we rode on, I remembered a back road I had noticed as we had marched up the valley, leading along the base of the mountain back of Front Royal. It occurred to me that Mosby would endeavor to escape through the mountain pass through which I knew a road led, so I received permission from the brigade commander to take a squadron of the Second Massachusetts Cavalry and try to cover the road. We moved at a gallop on this back road and, as we neared Front Royal, came in view of the captured ambulances, their horses at a full run and going in the very direction I had anticipated.

As Mosby's men saw we were about to cut them off from their line of retreat, we could see them firing into the ambulances containing the wounded, but it was too far off for us to do anything to prevent it. As we neared the point at which our road intercepted the one Mosby's men were on with the ambulances, they saw their retreat would be cut off by my men so they abandoned the ambulances and struck out for the woods. We saved the ambulances, but found many of the wounded men more seriously wounded and a number killed, among the latter Lieutenant Charles McMaster of the Second Cavalry.[3]

By me getting in ahead, some ten or twelve of Mosby's men were captured. General Custer's division, having been ordered to our assistance, came upon the scene in time to take a hand in the capture. I followed the retreating guerrillas a short distance up into the mountain pass and there left the squadron to hold the ground while I rode back for orders. When I got back to the command I found General Custer on the ground and nearby a large congregation of soldiers, who appeared considerably excited. When I rode up to see what the cause was, I found they were about to hang the captured guerrillas, which they did by putting a rope around their neck, throwing the other end over the limb of a tree, and then hauling up the victim, tying the end round the tree, and then letting him choke to death. In this way all were executed with the exception of a young man, a mere boy. Upon seeing what was being done to his comrades, he made a break for liberty, dodging around and through the mounted men and horses. He actually got through the crowd and out into an open field where he took to his heels, but our men were after him, shooting at him with their revolvers until finally down he went on his face, killed. The men who were hung all had a card pinned to their clothing saying, "Hung in retaliation for shooting and killing wounded officers and men after being captured."

After the men had been executed, the command mounted and marched back toward Strasburg and went into camp for the night. Soon after, the colonel of the Second Massachusetts Cavalry rode over to our headquarters to inquire of the commanding officer about his squadron I had detached on the back road. As a matter of fact, I had become so excited seeing the men executed that I had forgotten all about the men I had left up in the pass. The result was I had to take an escort and ride back over the same ground to bring them into camp. As we rode back, we passed where the men had been executed. They were still hanging there, a very gruesome sight.

Between there and the little town of Front Royal we met an old lady, a young lady, and a little girl coming out in our direction. The old lady inquired about her boy. She said he had joined Mosby's men but a day or two before and that she understood he had been captured and executed and wanted to know about it. I told her I did not think he had been hung, that they were all older men than she described, but that we were going out a short distance and would soon be back and that she had better wait until we returned. They then all sat down by the side of the road and waited until we went up into the pass and brought back the men I had left there. We then passed them and went on beyond where the men were hanging. Upon seeing the three women follow us, we dismounted and waited to see what would develop. When they arrived at where the men were hanging, they passed from one to the other looking them over. After examining them all, they withdrew a short distance and appeared to be in conversation when, by chance, the young lady appeared to notice the body of the boy lying out in the field and called attention to it. They then all walked over that way. As they neared it, all gave a scream and fell upon the body, and I had no doubt they found their boy.

We then joined the main army on the pike and started in pursuit. General Sheridan's plan, if successfully carried out, would have resulted in the capture of Early at Fisher's Hill. His plan was for the cavalry I was with to be in shape to strike them after Crook and the Sixth Corps started them, but results do not always come out as anticipated. Our failure to get through the Luray Valley and be on hand at Newmarket in this case was the cause of the failure. Sheridan was so disappointed that he sent the cavalry back through the same valley on the same route. After striking the pike at Newmarket, we continued on up the valley so that we got to see Luray Valley and Courthouse anyway.

Early's forces scattered to the mountains after the fight at Fisher's Hill, and we continued without any resistance up the valley through a number of little towns on the route. In passing through Harrisonburg, an incident occurred to me that I must relate. I had an aunt residing in the South somewhere that I had never seen, but had often heard my mother speak of—her only sister, who had married and gone South. As we passed through the town I noticed a lady standing in a door waving a handkerchief which of itself was enough to attract attention; ordinarily the doors and blinds would be closed. But this was not all. As I glanced at the lady, it struck me she resembled my mother. After I had ridden by, I kept thinking of the lady waving the handkerchief and the thought struck me that it might possibly be my aunt, so I received permission to ride back. When I got to the house, she was still there. I dismounted, stepped up, and, excusing myself for the intrusion, said, "You look so much like my mother that I could not pass without calling and inquiring." She exclaimed, "You are not Mary's boy, are you?" I was one and the same. It was my Aunt Patty. I not only had to come into the house, but also to wait until lunch or dinner or something of that kind was prepared. The command, in the meantime, had passed by, yet I had to remain. Aunt Patty sent her husband upstairs to watch out the gable window to see that no Mosby men or Johnnies were following so as to give me a chance to get away. And that is how I found my aunt.

We continued our march up the valley through Staunton. Our division went on as far as Waynesboro, where we arrived during the night and bivouacked on the commons outside of town. Early in the morning, a lady called at our headquarters asking for a safe guard, saying her husband owned a great deal of property there and that he was a Union man who had had to "refugee" and was then in Philadelphia, and she gave the name of the hotel he was stopping at. The general referred her to me as I was the provost marshal of the brigade and those kind of duties pertained to my office. She told me where they resided and I told her I would be down after breakfast and see what I could do. In the meantime she invited us all down to breakfast, but we of course declined. After we had ours, I took a man and rode down to find her place, a nice brick residence, and posted the guard with instructions not to allow any destruction of property or intrusion and rode back to headquarters. During the forenoon, I had instructions to destroy a large tannery and the contents of a flour mill in the town, both of which I found belonged to the lady or her husband to whom I had given the safeguard that morning. When I told her what my instructions were, she raised no objections and I proceeded to execute them. I found the tannery full of leather being tanned in the vats and a warehouse with probably a hundred barrels of unslaked lime. As I knew a little something about tanning, I had a barrel or two of lime emptied into the vats with leather in the liquor or tan and I am pretty well satisfied I "fixed that." The mill had probably five hundred barrels of flour. After the command had all that it could use and I had distributed all the Negroes could carry away, I had the balances rolled out and the heads of the barrels knocked in and scattered over the ground.

I had not much more than gotten through with my job when the enemy came down on us very unexpectedly from the side of the mountain and drove us out faster than we had come to town. During the day I had sent out a regiment under orders to cover a certain road and during the late afternoon or early evening I met General Torbett, who was in command, who instructed me to send out and have it come in at once. I did so by writing a note to the commanding officer and sending it out by an orderly. Later in the evening when General Torbett again met me, he inquired if I had sent for the regiment. I told him I had but that it had not yet reported. The fight at this time was going on pretty much all over the field and we were getting the worst of it. The general said, "Go out yourself and find the regiment. If you cannot get back here, cut across to the Staunton Road. I am going back by that."

Off I started on a gallop. I had two orderlies following me that evening, as they appeared to have no one else to follow. I rode out on a road by the side of a wood on my left and followed that some distance. It turned short to the right across open country toward another piece of woods. As we made the turn to the right, I saw before me the orderly I had sent out a short time before with the note to the commanding officer of the regiment. Just then a column of troops came out of the woods in my direction. I saw the orderly ride up and meet them and at the same time was near enough to see that they all had frock coats on. At that instant one of my orderlies said, "Lieutenant, they are Rebels." I wheeled my horse quick as I could and so did my men. Back we started on a jump with a lot of Rebs after us firing their pistols as they came. As we ran toward the angle of the road, where we had turned short to the right, I heard some men on ahead cry out, "Stop that firing, stop that firing. You are firing into your own men." By that time we had gained the edge of the timber, from which came the sound of the pursuing party still giving chase. My only hope was to plunge into the woods and take my chance in getting through whatever I might find, so in I went.

By that time it was early dusk and the woods made it more so. I had gained but a little distance when before me I saw a lot of men riding in my front and across my course, but before they were aware of what I was doing I was through and beyond. As soon as they recognized that I was a "Yankee," they joined in the chase. I was giving my horse the spur and making the best time I could, when as I gained the outer edge of the woods, I discovered a high fence in my front. I began to think it was about "up with my case," but still I had one chance and that was to ride for the fence. If I could clear that and get into the open field I might escape, so I gave my horse both spurs and over he went, even if he did knock the top rail off.

But now I had another trouble in front of me. Someone again commenced firing, but more at the horse and commotion we were creating than at what they could see. In an instant I thought I understood the situation, which, as it turned out, I did. I commenced calling out, "Don't shoot, don't shoot, you are firing into your own men." But I still kept on and the next minute was in among the rear guard, or skirmish line, of the very men I had gone out to bring in, they having withdrawn of their own accord. As a large Confederate force was advancing and had passed through the piece of woods I had first come through, they had thrown out a line of skirmishers while waiting for orders to move.

That was about as close a call to being captured as I ever had. The two orderlies I had with me must have been killed, for we never heard of them thereafter. I withdrew the regiment to the road General Torbett had instructed me to take and joined the command during the night on the way back to Staunton. The safeguard I had left at the house in Waynesboro relieved himself when he saw the Rebs coming and got away all right.

That day we started back down the valley with instructions from General Sheridan to lay the valley in waste and drive off every hoof of stock we could find, burn all grain and hay, and not spare barns or buildings housing grain. We stretched a line of men across the valley and started down carrying out the orders to the letter. Cornfields with the corn in shock were set on fire, hay and grain stacks were burned, barns that had hay or grain in them were set on fire so that the entire valley was ablaze and the smoke settled over it like a cloud. It was pretty severe medicine, but the valley, one of the finest in the land, was a granary for the Confederacy. Whenever winter came on and operations ceased, the Confederates in the army were allowed to go home and they usually found plenty to subsist on, but not that year.

I was in charge of a portion of the line that day and as I came to a fine barn and farm residence, I saw a venerable old gentleman standing at the gate. As he saw I was an officer, he beckoned me to come up and when I reached him, he said, "My dear sir, I see what you are doing. My barn is full of grain. I have a lot of women, children, and slaves here who will starve if you destroy my barn. Not only that, but you will burn my house. My men are all in the army. I have eighteen hundred dollars in gold in my cellar. Take my gold and spare my barn." My men were at the barn by that time. I sympathized with the old gentleman, but rode off and left his gold. The barn was burned and probably the house, too.

In that way we came on down the valley as far as Fisher's Hill where, toward evening, the command was massed for some reason, the general undoubtedly having heard through his scouts that the enemy was following us. While we lay there, probably an hour, a signal message was received from a high mountain peak on which we had established a signal station reporting that they had been fired upon. Sheridan then gave an order to the intermediate commanders, which finally came to our brigade, and the commanders instructed me to take the Second Massachusetts Cavalry and go out and learn what the trouble was. I at once mounted my horse and rode to the regiment and gave the colonel the order. The regiment mounted and we rode over to the left in the direction of the signal station. In marching along we went through a bolt of timber not more than a mile from where we had been massed and discovered a body of Rebel cavalry drawn up in line and facing the little mountain peak on which our signal station was located. We at once threw out a line of skirmishers and moved forward and, almost before we were aware of any trouble, were engaged in quite a brisk skirmish.

As soon as we had sufficiently involved the enemy's force, I rode back to where General Sheridan and the other general officers of the command were and reported what I had discovered. General Sheridan gave the order to the cavalry commanders to go in camp for the night and then go out in the morning and lick them, adding he would stay there until the job was accomplished.

The next morning bright and early we were in the saddle and started out for our day's work. We soon discovered the enemy and commenced business. For a while they gave a pretty sharp fight, but we finally got the best of them and got them started on the run. We kept them going for twenty-six miles before we gave up the chase. They had twelve cannon in the morning when the fight opened; in the evening they had but one left. We had the other eleven. This was what was known as the "Woodstock Races."

The command we defeated was General Thomas Rosser's, which had been sent by General Lee to try and retrieve General Early's losses, but they met the same fate Early had. By that time our cavalry, under Sheridan's superb generalship, had become invincible. All we needed was to meet the Confederates and they "were ours."

We then moved on down the valley to Cedar Creek where we went into camp. The impression was that Early would give us no further trouble so the authorities had in view the sending of a portion of Sheridan's army to join General Grant before Petersburg. Before doing so, Sheridan was called to Washington for consultation as to the best way of transporting part of his army to Grant. In going to Washington, he took a regiment of cavalry for an escort and started to ride across the country to the

Alexandria and Manassas railroad, where he expected to take a train for the city. Soon after Sheridan had left, a message was taken from a Confederate signal station saying, "Be prepared to crush Sheridan as soon as I arrive. Longstreet."

The message was at once wired to Sheridan, who had reported to the secretary of war and Mr. Lincoln upon his arrival in Washington. The Secretary immediately gave orders to have a special train ready to take Sheridan to Harpers Ferry and Winchester. As soon as the interview ended, Sheridan again started for the front, arriving at Winchester, where he remained that night.

In the meantime, the brigade in which I was serving as a staff officer was posted on the left of our line, picketing the banks of the Shenandoah River to the left of Strasburg, the position the army had occupied a day or two before the battle that followed. We were moved to the extreme right, over on what was called the "back road." In withdrawing my pickets on the left before we moved to the right, I noticed that we left quite a long space without pickets. I reported the fact to the brigade commander at the time, who replied that he supposed that would be looked after by the division commander who had ordered us away and who should have taken the precaution to fill the space we had left in our line.

On the morning of October 19, 1864, having been ordered to make a reconnaissance on the back road, we were up and ready to mount long before daylight. Before starting out, the brigade commander told me to ride to General Wesley Merritt, our division commander, and inquire if there were any further orders. I was making my way to the general's tent after reaching headquarters, when cannonading commenced on our left. The general sprang from his cot and inquired what the trouble was. I, of course, could tell him nothing further than it was firing on our left. He then told me to say to my commander that there were no further orders, but that if anything developed he would send him word, so I rode back to find my brigade.

When I found them, they were already engaged. The enemy, too, had been ordered out on the same road we had intended to take and had advanced so far that we almost believed we were engaged in a fight on the ground we had camped on the night before. When the fight began, or rather, as soon as I had reported back from General Merritt, the brigade commander instructed me to look out for a company we had on picket a mile or more to our right and rear at a crossing of Cedar Creek, telling me to get them back as best I could.

I rode rapidly to where the company was posted. By that time it was after daylight and I found a Rebel battery posted on the opposite bank of the creek shelling our position and a lot of our mounted men. It was not necessary to order the company to leave; they were already leaving "post haste" and without orders. I took a circuit and joined the command, which by that time had received orders to proceed to the left as rapidly as possible, the infantry having been routed from their camp in Cedar Creek and driven back in a most demoralized shape.

The sight as we rode across the open country to where we were ordered was frightful to behold. Everything on wheels that had not been captured in the early morning was being rushed to the rear. All over the open country there appeared to be no organization in sight, only a demoralized mob.

By the time our brigade and division reached the pike outside the town of Middletown, the bulk of the demoralized men had passed so we formed in line facing the enemy. The men who had been surprised and routed, upon seeing an organized line forming, soon regained their courage and began to fall into line again. The enemy, meanwhile, did not take advantage of their morning's success, as they should have done, but appeared to content themselves looting the camps they had captured. It is true they had a line facing us, but they did not push in as they should have done so they gave us time to organize our forces again.

In the meantime, it will be remembered, General Sheridan had arrived in Winchester. Upon hearing the firing he had started for the front. I was on the pike where our brigade was posted when he rode up, and I knew we would soon have "business on hand." The first thing he did was to order our brigade, or rather a portion of it, to charge and take some prisoners. He wanted to know if Longstreet was there. We made the charge and picked up a few dozen fellows, whom we rushed back to our line and to Sheridan's headquarters in the pike in our rear.

Through them he learned the report that Longstreet was there "was a fake."

Sheridan, in the meantime, had been gathering up all the stragglers and getting them to their organizations. When everything was ready, he ordered a charge of everything he had—Merritt with our cavalry division on the left, Custer with his on the right, and the infantry in the center. The first charge did not break the line but demoralized the enemy to some extent and before they could recover and prepare, Sheridan ordered another charge of our whole force. That broke their line and we got them started again and kept them on the run till midnight, not only capturing nearly everything they had but recapturing the thirty-odd guns they had taken from us that morning. Their loss in men and prisoners was large, ours not very great, but my brigade commander, Colonel Charles Russell Lowell of the Second Massachusetts Cavalry, a nephew of Charles R. Lowell, was among the mortally wounded and died that night. He was a young and gallant officer and had he lived would have made a record second to none. I never knew by what chance I became detailed as an officer in his staff, but soon after we arrived in the valley and the Second Massachusetts Cavalry was assigned to our brigade with Lowell in command, I was ordered on duty at headquarters as an aide at first and then as inspector and provost marshal. In fact, I remained in that position until the close of the war, and the troops were disbanded.

Turning the defeat of the morning into the brilliant success of the evening with the same troops made a great record for General Sheridan. Grant, as soon as he heard of our victory, ordered a salute of our hundred shotted guns. That was the last of Early or his army for that winter and we settled down into winter quarters.

The following spring, 1865, we moved up the valley without any molestation until we reached Waynesboro. There we found Early with the remainder of his army. General Custer, who had the advance, at once attacked and captured about seventeen hundred prisoners. Early and his staff escaped by swimming the Shenandoah River.

The roads in the early spring were in terrible condition.

Our brigade was left with the wagons. As a result we were some distance in the rear and did not get in on time, so Sheridan halted in Waynesboro for us to get there. When we got in, Sheridan sent a note to our headquarters, signed Mrs. Gallagher, asking the general if Lieutenant Veil was with the command. If so, would he please call. The general said, in finding it, "You had better call," and so I did. Mrs. Gallagher was the lady whom I had given the safeguard to on our former visit to Waynesboro, the fall before. When I rode down to the house, the little girl who had accompanied her mother to our camp the morning they asked me for the safeguard was in the doorway and saw me ride up. Recognizing me at once, she came running out to the gateway and met me and led me up the walk to the house where I met her mother and the young lady who had also been with her. The young lady was dressed in mourning, having from the time I had seen her the fall before been a bride, and was now a widow. As I soon learned, she had married an artillery officer in the Confederate Army before Petersburg who had been killed. They appeared pleased to have me call and insisted on my staying for tea, but I had other business to attend to, having been in the meantime instructed to assist with a detail of men in destroying a railroad bridge that crossed the Shenandoah at that point.

The engineer officer, with the assistance of the men I had, first built a caisson under the middle of the bridge out of railroad ties and timbers, which we filled with cannon powder we had captured. Using probably a hundred barrels, we laid a train of powder in boards, having no fuse to use, and then "touched her off." When it reached the powder chamber and exploded, it raised up the whole center of the bridge and then dropped it into the river.

Meanwhile, the command was fording the river above us. Being in the spring of the year, the river was high. If the men got a little below a certain point on which they were crossing, the horses were swept off their feet and quite a number of horses and men were drowned as a result. While we were at work, I noticed a man come down with the current. Sometimes I would see the man; then he would be out of sight and I would see his carbine' or saber flopping out as the current happened to be rolling him over. Finally, he caught on a snag sticking out of the water and there he hung, bobbing up and down in the water. After watching him hang there some time, I persuaded a man to strip and swim out and tow him to shore so that we might bury him, which he did. While we found the man dead, or drowned, I have always felt that if we had known how to resuscitate him, the man might have been brought to life again. His body was warm, yet perfectly limp, but not knowing the proper course to pursue in cases of that kind, the man was allowed to die. We buried him there on the bank of the river.

After we had blown up the railroad bridge, we crossed and followed the command up the mountain road through a pass in the mountain leading toward Charlottesville. Our brigade, as I stated, had been detailed to bring up the rear and wagon trains. Night overtook us, the wagons were stuck in the mud, and we could not tell where ours were to get provisions so General Alfred Gibbs, now in command, seeing a light off to the left of the road said, "Veil, ride down there where that light is and see if you can't find a place where we can quarter for the night." I rode down as directed and found a large home. When I got to the door and knocked, an elderly gentleman came to the door. I stated our case to him and inquired if he could accommodate us or would allow us to stay at his house. For an answer he slammed the door in my face, so I rode back and told the general I had found a first-rate place and we all rode down.

As I had selected the camping ground, I took it upon myself to be "master of ceremonies." I told the orderlies to take the horses to the barn, there being a large one on the premises, and we all entered the house and found a large sitting room or parlor with a big fireplace. I called some men who soon had a roaring fire going of fence picket for fuel. I then rapped on a side door and the old gent whom I had first met appeared. I told him we had nothing to eat and that he must furnish us something, that we were subsisting off the country, but were willing to pay for what we got. He disappeared and by and by showed up with a raw ham and about half a loaf of bread. "Well," said I, "that will do for a starter, now send us someone to cook the ham." Directly, an old, fat "Mammy" appeared, all smiles to see the Yankees. I gave her the ham and told her to cook it and to tell the old man I wanted to see him. He came back and I told him we did not have ham enough to go round and that we should have to trouble him for another. Back he went and soon appeared with another, but apologizing for the size, saying he had had to kill all his hogs before they were fit from the fact that all of them in the neighborhood had the hog cholera.

After we had our ham and bread I said to the old colored woman, "Now, auntie, bring in some bed clothes. We are going to sleep in the parlor." Soon she was back with loads of blankets, quilts, and pillows. I saw that all the officers had a shakedown, but after they were all fixed, there was nothing for me. As I had made friends with the old colored woman, I thought she would look out for me, so I told her I must have more bedding. "Good Lord, massa," said she, "I done gone bring all the bedding in the house, but Massa So and so, he done gone git married today and is coming." "Oh, well," said I, "he's not coming, bring down the bed," and so she did.

During the evening one of my men came to me and said, "Lieutenant, there is a lot of turkeys roosting on the trees out here." I asked him if they were high up and told him to look out that they did not bite any of the boys. I did not hear of any of them being bitten, but I did notice a lot of feathers next morning. This was an out of the way place or there would have been no turkeys at that stage of the war.

The following night found us in the same dilemma, our wagons stuck in the mud and no telling where ours were in the large train. Seeing a promising house to our right, we all went up and were met at the door by a couple of very nice ladies, both dressed in mourning. They invited us to enter, saying they were pleased to offer us any hospitality they had, but all they had in the house (a very nicely furnished one) was some corn and a very little bacon. They gave us all they had (and very pleasantly too).

Next morning when we found our wagons and could get at our provisions, we took pains to send them a fair supply of provisions to make up for what they had given us. Not only that, but while we were waiting for the wagons to get up, we had the band come over and give them a nice little serenade. I have often been sorry I did not inquire their names. Having met and treated us as gentlemen, we returned the compliment. The old fellow the night before having treated us like hogs, he received the same in return.

We finally caught up with General Sheridan and the command that day at Charlottesville. The next day we struck for the James River at Scottsville, intending to take in Lynchburg, but the Rebs burned the bridge across the river and it was very much swollen and we were unable to cross. In that vicinity we destroyed much property. The canal locks were given special attention. Large quantities of tobacco also were destroyed, and I remember we burned a woolen factory where cloth for Confederate uniforms was being made. The general then shaped his course for the James River, or City Point, where Grant was. We crossed the Pamunkey River at the White House again and finally reached Grant without having received any molestation from the time we had cleaned up the remainder of Early's army at Waynesboro to the James. Here we crossed the river and moved out to the extreme left of our line of works and went into camp for a few days to fit up for the final campaign to end in Lee's surrender at Appomattox.

About March 27, 1865, the cavalry moved out to the left toward Dinwiddie Courthouse. The very day we left camp it commenced raining. The country we marched over was low land, not much above sea level, and the road soon became extremely muddy. Still we pushed on and that night encamped near Dinwiddie Courthouse, which consisted of an old courthouse of antebellum days, a country hotel, and a few surrounding buildings. Next day we moved out toward what was known as the White Oak Road, but the roads were in such terrible condition we could make but little headway. Mule teams would sink into the quagmires so it was impossible to get them out. On several occasions I saw the mules shot in a bunch and another team rushed into place on top of their dead carcasses. The mud holes were finally filled in that way so as to make it possible to make a crossing. If one mule team did not make foundation enough, another was added.

When we moved out toward the White Oak Road, we first met the enemy's cavalry. Up to that time nothing had been seen of the enemy, but now they showed up and the day was put in skirmishing. It was at this time that General Grant suggested to

Sheridan that, owing to the conditions of the weather, operations had better cease until the rain let up, but Sheridan thought that as we were so far along we ought to continue and Grant finally acceded. That night we lay on the line; it rained steadily. I remember getting a couple of fence rails and laying one end of them on a log to keep me out of the mud. On the two rails I lay down and slept reasonably comfortably, as I was tired out.

Next day, near Five Forks, we again pressed the enemy, but in the afternoon General George Pickett's infantry division came to their cavalry's support and they pushed us back. As they came out in the open ground with three lines of Confederate infantry and our scattering dismounted cavalry trying to hold them in check, it looked as though we should be crushed. Our division was in the front, General John Irwin Gregg of our army in the left opposing their cavalry. Our dismounted men were throwing up little breastworks of rails, logs, and brush to try and hold them in check, when up rode Generals Sheridan and Custer, galloping along our line with battle flags flying in the breeze. Custer's cavalry division, which had been in the rear for the day guarding the wagon train, came in at a gallop and took position to help us stem the approach of Pickett's infantry. As it was getting late in the evening by that time and Pickett saw our reinforcements, he halted his advance and allowed us to remain for the night unmolested.

That night Sheridan asked Grant for the Sixth Corps, telling him of Pickett being outside of Lee's line of fortifications and that if the infantry came up by the White Oak Road the Rebels would be captured. Sheridan asked for the Sixth Corps because he said he knew how they liked to fight. The Sixth Corps could not be sent, however, owing to their station, so Grant ordered General Gouverneur Kemble Warren up with the Fifth.

Next morning Pickett was out of our sight, having withdrawn during the night. During the forenoon, I was sent out with the Fifth Cavalry, Captain Thomas Drummond in command, to reconnoiter and find where he had gone. As we moved out with a company or two, I skirmished in advance and noticed that Captain Drummond had on a fine, new, clean uniform, which was a little out of the regular order on an occasion of that kind with the weather as it was. When I mentioned to him that I thought he was wearing pretty good clothes, he replied, "These are the very best I've got. I am going to be killed." I thought he was only joking, but within ten minutes of the time he made the remark, riding by my side, the enemy opened on us and he fell dead from his horse, shot through the body. That certainly was a case of premonition (I had one once, later on, that I may speak of by and by). It was enemy skirmishers, occupying their extended line of breastworks out in front of the line, who had opened on us and killed Captain Drummond.[4]

In the meantime, General Warren, with the Fifth Corps, had arrived and General Sheridan at once made preparations for the attack. Warren was slow in getting his men up. In fact, he wanted to make coffee as they had made a hard march, but Sheridan, knowing the importance of prompt and decisive action, insisted on immediate assault. Warren was so slow in acting that Sheridan relieved him of command (which he was authorized to do by Grant in case Warren did not come up to his expectations) and led his leading division into action himself, all the cavalry cooperating, my command included. As a result the enemy's right was turned and we captured some six thousand prisoners and their works. The balance of those who escaped were in full retreat.

That night we bivouacked inside their works. After General Grant heard of our success, he ordered every gun on our line to open on the long line of Confederate works and, at four o'clock the next morning, the infantry made an assault. The cannonading was the most frightful I ever heard. The heavens were lit up as with lightning from the exploding of shells. The very earth we lay on that night trembled with the concussion.

The assault on that morning was successful. The enemy were driven out and started in retreat. Sheridan, in the early morning, had started down inside their works toward Petersburg but, finding they were retreating, undertook to cut in on their line and was repulsed. He then took to the left, trying to head off the retreat. Meade, in the meantine, followed in the rear. At Sailor's Creek, on April 6, we again struck their line of retreat and made an attack. Their resistance was so strong, however, that we could not break their lines until the Sixth

Corps came up and then we broke through, capturing a large lot of prisoners, many generals, wagons, and artillery. It was after dark that evening when the break occurred.

The First Cavalry had the advance in following the road they were on. After proceeding but a short distance, the advance ran into a barricade across the road and a flash of fire in their faces whereupon the commanding officer, Captain Richard Lord, gave the commands "Draw saber!" and "Charge!" In the darkness, on a gallop, forward went the regiment, over the breastworks and after the retreating enemy until about six guns posted on the opposite bank of a creek opened on us. That caused a halt.

Before morning Sheridan and his cavalry were again on the move, always south, trying to head off the retreating forces—no sleep, no rest, no forage for horses or feed for men. Everything appeared to be forgotten, save the one object of heading off Lee's army. Sheridan's scouts in the meantime had captured a Confederate messenger with a dispatch to be forwarded to the Confederate authorities from some point asking that supplies be sent Lee's famished army at Appomattox. Sheridan at once had the dispatch forwarded and then doubled his energies to get to Appomattox and the supplies when they arrived.

The evening of April 8 General Custer's command had the advance and arrived at Appomattox very shortly after the trains with the supplies had arrived. The first thing he did was to tear up the railroad track behind the trains so they could not back out. Then he not only captured the trains, but also a large lot of artillery that was just arriving and going into park for the night, expecting to get supplies there. By that time, Sheridan's entire command was up and we threw a line in front of Lee's retreat. The night was one of continual skirmishing as the enemy kept feeling our entire line trying to find some way to get through.

Sitting at a camp fire that night, as Lieutenant General John B. Gordon of the Confederate Army in his memoirs says, General Lee having called all his officers for a counsel of war, it was decided that their only hope was to cut through our line. General Gordon, having the best-organized lot of men left, was selected to make the effort when daylight came. I heard General

Gordon lecture on one occasion at Wellsboro and was sorry I did not meet him as I should have liked to have told him I was one of the boys that opposed him that morning when he undertook to comply with his orders of the night before.

When daylight came, they made the attack. Our orders were to hold on as best we could, that the infantry was nearby and would soon be to our assistance. As we were gradually being pressed back, I looked to the rear and saw the whole hillside covered with a line of Yankee infantry. As soon as the enemy saw them they stopped firing. Soon after the white flag of truce came into our lines. The moment firing ceased, our division of cavalry was mounted and galloped to our extreme right between the two lines, where we again were formed in a line and ready for another charge if necessary. I lately became acquainted with an old Confederate who was present that morning, who says that was one of the most beautiful movements of cavalry he ever saw.

The point we drew up on in the night overlooked a large park of Confederate wagons, a lot of artillery, and a battery of six brass pieces pointed in our direction, which if hostilities had not ceased we should soon have captured. The two armies lay in line facing each other while the terms of surrender were being negotiated. In front of our brigade, not more than three hundred yards distant, we faced the battery of six brass guns with their Rebel crews lounging around them. On our side the men dismounted and lounged around among the horses, some lying down, some asleep, all evidently feeling the end of the war had at last arrived and all feeling correspondingly happy. We had an officer on the staff, Lieutenant John Barry of the First Cavalry, who was a wonderful forager, especially when it came to foraging for anything that was good to drink, more especially so if it was stronger than water. I remember that day after hostilities had ceased, seeing Barry come galloping along down the line with a big demijohn. As soon as he found headquarters, he dismounted and inquired for a cup. Someone handed him one, and he commenced to turn out what he had. He first handed the cup to the general, who pronounced it all right. I had never taken anything strong till that time, but as it was an extraordinary occasion, I tried what he gave me when it came my turn. It turned out to be a homemade blackberry brandy or wine, very pleasant to the taste, but full of bees. Soon after I had taken mine I noticed the fence that we halted by commence to zigzag. Then I thought there were a couple of fences there. Finally, I wanted to take a nap and did so right there in front of the enemy. How long I slept I never knew, but when I woke up I saw all the rest of the staff, the general included, taking a nap too. The demijohn was still there with the tin cup on the neck. As everything was quiet, I took another little sniffle out of the demijohn and then lay down for another nap.

The surrender, or rather the terms of surrender, in the meantime having taken place, we bivouacked on the ground for the night. The men of both armies mixed up and rations were divided. To have seen us no one would have supposed that for four long years we had been involved in deadly war.

Next morning we started back toward Petersburg. After being several days on the road, Sheridan received an order to retrace his steps and go to the assistance of General Sherman in North Carolina. We marched back or South as far as Roanoke near where we received the news of General Joseph Johnston's surrender. We then retraced our march to Petersburg, Richmond, and on to Washington. There we lay until both armies arrived, when we participated in the big review. I am always proud when I can say that I was one of the boys who passed up Pennsylvania Avenue in that parade of the Army of the Potomac. For an entire day Pennsylvania Avenue was a solid mass of soldiers: cavalry first, our division at the very head, then infantry and artillery, corps after corps, an army the equal of which the world had never seen marching up that avenue all that day, both sides of the street lined with admiring spectators and then passing in review before the president, the cabinet, and General Grant. There was my friend, the secretary of war, looking on us with his smiling countenance, and I wondered if he ever thought of the big green boy he had made an officer and from whom he said he would expect to have good reports. The second day was a repetition of the first, only this time it was Sherman's army that had marched from Atlanta to the sea and then forced the surrender of General Johnston at Goldsboro, North Carolina. Sherman continued on to Washington to show

Charles Henry Veil, photographed
after his return to Pennsylvania from Arizona Territory.
(*Courtesy U.S. Army Military History Institute*)

General John Reynolds.
(*Courtesy Anne Hoffmann Cleaver*)

Katie Hewitt, fiancée of General Reynolds.
(*Courtesy Anne Hoffmann Cleaver*)

Sketch of General John Reynolds at the moment of his death, by battlefield artist Alfred Waud. Veil is evidently the enlisted man next to Reynolds. (*Courtesy Library of Congress*)

According to Reynolds family lore, this photograph was taken in November 1863 while searching for the spot where General Reynolds was killed. The person pointing the saber (*bottom right*) is believed to be Charles Veil. (*Courtesy Anne Hoffmann Cleaver*)

Civil War photographer Mathew Brady with one of his assistants, who is pointing toward the eastern edge of McPherson's Woods, indicating the spot where General Reynolds was felled by a sharpshooter during the first day's action at Gettysburg, July 1, 1863.(*Courtesy Library of Congress*)

Members of the First U.S. Regular Cavalry
photographed at Brandy Station, Virginia, in February 1864.
(*Courtesy Library of Congress*)

Noted Confederate guerilla leader John Singleton Mosby with
several of his men. Colonel Mosby is the jaunty person with the plume
in his hat seated in the center of the group. This photograph was
apparently taken a short time after the daring raid that captured
General E. H. Stoughton not more than a dozen miles from
Washington. (*Courtesy National Archives and Records Administration*)

The San Carlos Indian Reservation, from a photograph taken in March 1888 by A. Frank Randall of Los Angeles, California. (*Courtesy National Anthropological Archives, Smithsonian Institution*)

Apache camp scene, Arizona Territory, from a photograph by A. Frank Randall taken sometime between 1882 and 1886. The camp is of either San Carlos or White Mountain Apaches. (*Courtesy National Anthropological Archives, Smithsonian Institution*)

Geronimo's camp with one of his warriors on guard, taken by Tombstone photographer C.S. Fly at the time of Geronimo's meeting with General George Crook in March 1886 near Canyon de los Embudos in the Sierra Madre. (*Courtesy National Anthropological Archives, Smithsonian Institution*)

Geronimo and three of his followers. Photograph by C.S. Fly taken during Geronimo's conference with General Crook. Geronimo (*far right*) is accompanied by (*from left*) his brother-in-law Yanozha, his son Chappo, and Fun, his second cousin. Their rifles (*left to right*) are a Winchester model 1873 carbine; Springfield 1873 carbine, calibre .45-70; and Springfield 1873 rifle, calibre .45-70. (*Courtesy National Anthropological Archives, Smithsonian Institution*)

Apache scouts, Arizona Territory. Photographer and date not recorded. One scout wears an 1872 fatigue blouse with piping, while the one standing to the left has a corporal's chevrons on his five-button blouse. (*Courtesy National Anthropological Archives, Smithsonian Institution*)

Apache women and children taken prisoner by soldiers operating under the command of General George Crook. Credited to "Baker and Johnston, Photographers," this photograph was probably taken in 1882 or 1883. (*Courtesy National Anthropological Archives, Smithsonian Institution*)

Cochise's stronghold, Dragoon Mountains, Arizona. This rugged and forbidding terrain is typical of Apacheria, the heartland of the Chiricahua Apaches. Credited to C. S. Fly, the photograph is undated but was probably taken in the mid-1880s. (*Courtesy National Anthropological Archives, Smithsonian Institution*)

Captioned "Geronimo, the captured Apache chief," this photograph by A. Frank Randall appeared as a line cut in *Harper's Weekly*, September 18, 1886. The best known and certainly one of the most photographed Indian leaders of the late nineteenth century, the feared—and fearsome—Chiricahua raider seldom had more than a handful of followers, most of them members of his immediate family, yet at times he was pursued by thousands of U.S. and Mexican soldiers. Geronimo later learned to capitalize on his notoriety by selling his autograph and posing for his photograph for a fee. (*Courtesy National Anthropological Archives, Smithsonian Institution*)

his western boys the capital of the great Union they had fought for four years to preserve.

This about ends the old boy's recollections and remembrances of the Civil War. The war was over and the boys discharged and sent to their homes, those that survived, that is. Hundreds and thousands who left home to serve their country like the old boy are resting in southern soil and as many more are crippled and maimed for life. But the country has been saved, the Union preserved, and there is only one national flag. Long may it wave over the home of the free and the brave.

These remembrances are written almost fifty years since they occurred and entirely from memory. I used no notes or references of any kind, yet I have been surprised at the many little incidents they have brought to mind which had long been forgotten. No doubt many more are forgotten that might be of interest to my brothers and their boys, but if what I have written will afford any pleasure or kind remembrances of the old "boy," I shall be satisfied.

Before I close I want to say that General Sheridan, on arriving at Washington with his cavalry, was at once ordered to New Orleans to assume command of that department. General Kirby Smith had not yet surrendered and Sheridan suggested that the First United States Cavalry be ordered to New Orleans, and it was so ordered. Being on staff duty with the reserve brigade I was not returned in time to go with the regiment, but after the review was over and the brigade disbanded, I was returned by the following order:

Head Quarters Cavalry Reserve Brigade,
First Cavalry Division Sheridan's Army,
June 7, 1865.

General Orders}
No. 17}

Pursuant to instructions from Cavalry Corps headquarters of the 5th Inst., lst Lieut. C. H. Veil, Lt. United States Cavalry, Acting Inspector General of this brigade is hereby relieved from duty therewith and as soon as he has completed the present inspection required by existing orders will repair to New Orleans, Louisiana and report to the commanding officer of his regiment.

In parting with this officer, long connected with the brigade, the commanding officer desires not only to express his regrets at the separation, but to testify his full appreciation of the faithful devotion, to duty, uniform gallantry in action, entire disregard of self, cool consideration of what was best for the Public service, and unswerving devotion to the Cause for which we have fought and won.

The General commanding will always look back with pleasure to his service with Lieut. Veil and parts with him with earnest and cordial wishes for his future welfare and happiness, and the hope of meeting soon again.

> Alfred Gibbgs,
> Brevet Major General Commanding

2. Arizona Adventures, 1865–1871

My recollection of the Civil War closed with my orders to proceed to New Orleans and report to my regiment for duty. Since no particular route had been laid out by which I was to proceed to New Orleans, I selected my own. (I thought Philadelphia was on the route; at any rate I took a train for that city where I had a pleasant visit.) While there, General Meade commanded a review and parade of the returned Pennsylvania Volunteers then in the city and that was the last time I remember seeing the general. From Philadelphia I proceeded to Johnstown, my old home, where I remained for a few days. I then continued to Louisville, Kentucky, by rail and there took a steamer down the Ohio for Cairo. At Cairo I again took a steamer for New Orleans. The trip down the Mississippi was a delightful one. We laid up long enough at all the cities on the route to enable us to make a short visit and get a view of the different cities we passed.

Finally I arrived at New Orleans. Having been somewhat extravagant on my trip, I found I had but ten cents on hand upon looking over my "cash account" before leaving the steamer. As I was an entire stranger in the city and not knowing where my regiment was quartered, I began to think it about time to commence economizing. I inquired of a policeman on my disembarking where the First Cavalry was stationed. He thought they were down in what was known as the "Cotton Press." I then inquired how to get there. "Take the car," said he, "that passes the Press."

The street cars in New Orleans are what are known as "double deckers," that is, they are two stories in height. Thinking that it was time to commence economizing, I concluded to take the "upper story," as I supposed that probably was the cheapest. When the conductor came around, I handed him my last dime, received five cents in change, and ordered him to let me out at the "Cotton Press." After I rode a long distance, the conductor finally called out "Cotton Press" and I dismounted. Not seeing any signs of soldiers in the vicinity, I inquired of another policeman if he knew where the First Cavalry was stationed. He informed me they had been moved down to Jackson Barracks, some two or three miles below the city.

As it was raining by that time and I had but an officer's cap and uniform coat with white duck pants (and only five cents in cash), I began to calculate a little. I finally concluded to go to a hotel in order to gain time and have a chance to work my mathematical "calculation," so I inquired for the Saint Charles Hotel, the best one in the city at that time. The policeman told me to "take the car," and so I did, taking the upper story again, knowing what the rate was on that line.

We finally arrived on St. Charles Street and by and by the conductor called out "St. Charles Hotel." I entered, registered, and asked for a room. After brushing up a little, I went down to breakfast, though I must admit I felt a little prickling of conscience knowing that I was without a dollar on hand to pay my bill, yet knowing I had a month or two's salary due me. As I came out of the dining room, I met an officer of the First Cavalry—then Lieutenant (afterward Captain) Barry, the regimental quartermaster. I don't recollect ever meeting anyone with more pleasure than I did Barry. After shaking hands and inquiring about my friends, I inquired if he had any "loose change" about his clothes, telling him I was "broke." He replied by handing me a twenty-dollar bill and wanted to know if that would do. I now felt easier and, after chatting a while, inquired for the paymaster's and quartermaster's offices. Barry, being acquainted with all of the officers and offices in the city, soon put me on the way to replenishing my bank account. I have often thought of the incident, of how uncomfortable and trying it is for one to arrive "broke" in a strange city.

During the afternoon I went down to the barracks and reported for duty. Jackson Barracks is situated some three miles below New Orleans, on the banks of the Mississippi River. A few days after, I was ordered to report to General Sheridan's headquarters in the city. On reporting, the adjutant general inquired if I did not wish to go to Texas with a cavalry expedition then organizing at Alexandria on Red River, saying that General James W. Forsythe, commanding a brigade, was anxious to have me join his staff.[1] I was advised to accept the appointment, which I did, and a day or two later took a steamer for Alexandria where I arrived in due course of time and reported to General Forsythe. I was assigned to duty again as acting inspector general of the brigade, the same position I had occupied with the brigade in the Army of the Potomac during the latter part of the war.

This was in July of 1865 and the weather in that southern climate was very hot. The country and its customs were so very different to what I had been accustomed that I felt the change very materially. What I felt the want of most was water for drinking purposes. The only water there in use was cistern, or rainwater. Every residence had a large cistern built of cement and brick in which rainwater was caught; and I remember that in many cases great large worms were in the cistern, yet it was claimed to be the best and purest drinking water.

While our command was being organized at that point, one of the Volunteer Regiments mutinied and two of the ringleaders were tried by court-martial and sentenced to be shot.[2] On the day of the execution, the entire command was formed on three sides of the square. The graves were dug and the condemned men brought out and placed at the head of their respective graves, sitting on their coffins. The executioners, some ten or twelve in number, were drawn up in front with arms loaded except for one piece, which is customary in cases of that kind. The arms are loaded by an officer, who leaves one blank. This always leaves the doubt in each executioner's mind as to who may have had the blank cartridge. The division commander, General Custer, and staff were all present. The men then were blindfolded and ordered to stand up.

At that very moment, General Custer directed that the sentence of one of the men should be commuted; I carried his order to the executing officer, who took the man by the arm and led him to one side (but without removing the blindfold). As he did so, the executioner gave the command to "Fire" and both men fell to the ground, the one pierced with a number of balls and the other unhurt. The one who fainted, of course, soon recovered; but I have always thought he suffered death to all intents and purposes and probably would have been better off had he been executed, for he was sentenced to the Dry Tortugas for life.

This was after the war was over, but it was one of those cases where, in order to maintain military discipline, an example had to be made. That put a stop to all mutinous conduct in the command.

Red River, on which we were at that time encamped, was full of alligators, and large ones, too. One day one of the Negro camp cooks, after dinner was over, went down to the bank of the river, where large cottonwood trees grew, to have an afternoon "nap" in the shade. He had been lying there some time, when one of the camp guards on post close by saw an immense alligator stealing on to the sleeping Negro, who was snoring away all unconscious of danger. The sentinel finally concluded to take a shot at the alligator, thinking he might at least frighten him and probably save the darky in that way. By chance, the ball struck him in the one vulnerable spot and killed him. An ordinary musket ball will not penetrate the alligator unless striking him just back of the forearm, which the soldier's did. I afterward saw the alligator and he measured over fourteen feet in length.

As soon as our expedition was fully organized, we took up our line of march for Texas. The distance was some three or four hundred miles. The first part of our route lay through an immense belt of the finest pine timber that I had ever seen. It was at least a hundred miles in width. The country was perfectly level and grass grew among the pines most luxuriantly. Game, such as deer, was so plentiful that I frequently saw the animals run through the column on the march.

Rattlesnakes were also plentiful. On going into camp for the night, the ground would first be gone over to kill the rattlers. They were great big six-footers, too, but not so vicious as those of our country.

Ticks, too, were so plentiful that everybody was covered with them. The only way we could get rid of them was to grease or oil the person. They would embed themselves in the skin and become very annoying.

We crossed Trinity River at Burr's Ferry and, after getting into Texas, the country changed very materially. We soon began to get into the sparsely settled country and, finally, into the open rolling western country. We continued our march to Hempstead, where we went into camp and remained several weeks, probably a month.

While in camp at that point I had my first experience with an alligator. I had been in the habit of going out with a shotgun for quail and duck, which were very plentiful in that section. As I was returning one day, I discovered a large green turtle lying on the bank of a small lagoon or lake, but I was not quick enough to get a shot at him. Since green turtle steak is considered a very rare dish in that country, I made up my mind to come down next morning and secure the game. The turtle had a habit of lying in the sun, so next morning in order to make sure of my game, I took my Spencer rifle. When I got in the vicinity, I got down and crawled up to where I supposed I would find him, or at any rate where I had seen him the day before, but just as I raised the bank so I could look over, something plunged off the bank from underneath me that made a terrible commotion, about like dumping a saw log off the bank would have done.

For a moment I was frightened at what had taken place, but the next moment the back of an alligator appeared on the surface of the water. As I was ready to shoot, I did not lose much time in letting him have a round. As I did, he showed the back of his head and I "let go again" as I did whenever he showed any portion of his body. I finally got the alligator so "rattled" he undertook to crawl out on the opposite bank. With the number of shots I had fired, I supposed I had mortally wounded him so I ran around to the opposite bank to secure my game; but, just as I arrived, he opened his eyes, raised himself on his forelegs, and gave an awful "snort." About that time I was "ready" and gave him another shot that entered back of his ear and came out of his underjaw. I supposed that would finish him, but it didn't. However, I now had him so demoralized that he was in no shape to run away.

I called to some men who were nearby and, with their assistance, dragged him up to General Custer's headquarters, where he was a considerable curiosity, to the ladies especially. One of them got a broomstick to measure him to see how long he was; but, by the time she undertook to do so, the alligator had revived somewhat. Raising himself on his forearms, he again opened his eyes and gave a fearful snort. With that, the headquarter's ladies became scarce. We finally managed to dispatch him in some way or other.

By that time I had been assigned to duty on General Custer's staff and was well acquainted with him, his wife Elizabeth, and the general's father, who had come down to visit him in Texas. The old gentleman had lots of fun with us young officers and was everlastingly playing some joke or tricks off on us. One of his morning jokes was to come around early and pull us out of bed, so we always had to sleep with an eye open and a dipper of water handy.

The general's brother, Tom, was also on duty at headquarters, as was Captain James Calhoun, who married their sister, and was massacred with the brothers on the Little Big Horn, where almost the entire male portion of the family lost their lives. Mrs. Custer was a very amiable lady loved by everyone in camp. She rode with us during the entire march, through all kinds of weather, and was always in good humor and kept everybody else so.

Since the general was very fond of hunting, many nights we were out the entire night hunting for coons with Mrs. Custer always accompanying us. Our plan was to get an old darky, who had a good coon dog, and then start out (all mounted) with the darky and dog in the lead, generally followed by a darky boy. After the dogs had treed a coon, the darky boy would climb the tree and shake him out. We often got as many as two or three coons out of a single tree.

From Hempstead we continued our march to Austin,

where the command went into permanent camp. Soon after our arrival, I was ordered to Corpus Christi to make an inspection of some colored troops. Corpus Christi is the point in the Gulf of Mexico where General Zachary Taylor landed his troops in starting out in his campaign against the Mexicans, which resulted in his capture of Mexico. My route was by stage from Austin to Hempstead, by rail from there to Galveston, and by steamer from Galveston to Corpus Christi.

That was the first time I had been to sea and I will always remember how seasick I was. We had a severe storm and it mattered but little to me if the ship went down or not. We arrived safely, however, and after my inspection was completed, I took the next vessel back to Galveston. As we neared the port, we ran on a sand bar and, after several vain attempts to pull off, I offered a couple sailors five dollars if they would set me ashore, thinking I could walk into town and catch a train leaving at noon. Otherwise I should be obliged to lay [up] there over Sunday. The captain gave his permission and a boat was lowered.

As I was about to start, a couple of Jews asked and received permission to accompany me, they too wanting to go to the interior of Texas. After landing us all right, the boat put back to the ship. We started up the beach, but had gone but a short distance, when we found we were on an island. Since the body of water between us and the mainland was not great and did not appear to be deep, I concluded I would try and wade it. At any rate, I stripped off my clothes and the Jews followed. I was the tallest in the lot, so I started in ahead, the Jews following. One being quite short, it was "nip and tuck" for him to keep his head above water. We finally made the landing all right and in time to catch the train, but while we were about in the middle of the slough the ship, having got off the bar in the meantime, passed us by. Our predicament afforded considerable amusement for the passengers aboard, who gave us a rousing cheer.

In Galveston, I learned my regiment had been ordered to the Pacific Coast and that all officers on detached duty had been ordered to rejoin it. As my baggage was in Austin, I concluded to return to that point. After reporting on my inspection, General

Custer issued an order for me to join my regiment in New Orleans or elsewhere.

I returned to Galveston by the same route and from there went to New Orleans by ship. In New Orleans I learned the regiment had been shipped to Aspinwall (present-day Colón) by chartered vessel and that there was no line of vessels running regularly to that point, so the only route left for me was to proceed to New York and take the regular Pacific Mail steamship route via Aspinwall and Panama. I then took a steamboat up the Mississippi to Cairo and then rail from there to Chicago and to Johnstown, my old home again where I remained a few days. I then came on to New York by way of Williamsport, visiting my Uncle Charlie (Judge Veil) in Liberty, arriving in New York City just in time to find the regular monthly steamer had left for Aspinwall and that I should be obligated to remain there for the next thirty days.

There was then an order that officers under orders to the Pacific Coast should have an advance of $500, which I applied for and finally received. On going to the steamship office to buy my ticket, I was surprised to find it took three new one-hundred-dollar bills to pay for my passage. That, however, left me two, and I proceeded to spend them in New York. I had no difficulty in getting rid of them. In fact, I had to write home to Father and get a couple more that I had in reserve to keep me going until the steamer sailed.

The voyage from New York to Aspinwall was of eight days' length. Although it was the middle of winter when we left New York, after a few days out it commenced moderating and by the time we reached Aspinwall it was summer. The Isthmus was crossed by rail. I found the luxuriant growth of all vegetable matter and foliage was very pleasing. The black natives with their white linen dresses, clean as the snow, interested me very much as did the beautifully plumaged birds and the monkeys chattering in the large trees as the train passed.

We arrived in Panama the same day, and in the evening took ship up the coast. The voyage from Panama to San Francisco required fourteen days. On the trip up the Pacific Coast, we stopped at a number of Mexican ports—Acapulco, Mazatlán, and several others, the names of which I have forgotten. The voyage was a most delightful one, the weather warm and pleasant, the sea smooth. On the whole, it was one of the most delightful trips I ever made.

On my arrival in San Francisco, I found my regiment stationed at the Presidio near the city and a portion under orders for Arizona, for service in subduing the Apache Indians. I belonged to that portion ordered to Arizona; and, shortly after my arrival, we took a steamer down the coast to San Pedro. Our route was down the same coast I had come over, so there was but little new in that. On arrival at San Pedro, we went into camp at Drum Barracks and there fitted out for our march into the interior. The distance was some eight hundred miles over a desert and almost unknown country.

After receiving our horses, bought in California, and fitting out with the necessary transportation, we finally took up our line of march early in June. We carried thirty days' rations and forage with the command. Beef was driven along on foot. For the first hundred miles of our route, the California countryside was partially settled, mostly by cattle and horsemen and occasionally by small farms and fruit orchards.

At first water for men and animals was found at no great distance, but when we struck the California desert at San Felipe our hardships commenced. The heat was intense, almost insufferable. The country was barren sand without vegetation—no tree or brush, even, to break the heat of the sun, which reflected from the sand. Since the hills and mountains were of volcanic formation, once heated, they retained their heat so that even at night, after the sun had set, it continued insufferably hot. I remember seeing the thermometer at 100 at midnight.

Water for men and animals now became the great question in our marches. Ordinarily we found sufficient water in twenty or thirty miles of marching, but I know in some cases we had to make forty-five miles. Taking into consideration the great heat and sandy conditions of the roads, this made a very hard and tedious day's march.

At one point in crossing the desert, we were 283 feet beneath "sea level" and during that day we suffered the most. We left camp about one o'clock in the morning and pushed ahead as rapidly as possible until daylight and then until noon, still nothing but barren sand and mountains as far as the eye could reach. We carried water in barrels for animals and men, but that soon gave out.

In this manner we pushed on until nearly five o'clock in the afternoon, when all at once we saw what appeared to be a most beautiful lake surrounded by great large trees. Men picked up courage and animals apparently did the same. All pressed forward with renewed energy. We marched in this way, yet apparently not gaining on the lake, when all at once, lake, trees and all disappeared. The delusion, known as a "mirage," is often seen in the desert. I am unable to account for the delusion but it was there, sure enough. I have often since experienced the same, having on some occasions seen the most beautiful buildings rise up out of the desert and disappear in the same manner. At other times what appeared to be great forts would rise up and in a short time disappear.

After marching until nearly dark, we finally arrived at Indian Lake, where we expected to find an abundance of water and did, but it was so foul that neither man nor beast could partake of it. The animals, by this time, were almost frantic with thirst and rushed madly for the water, but one mouthful of it was sufficient. Large fish, two or three feet in length, were lying along the border of the lake in various states of decomposition, the water having become so heated by the rays of the sun that the fish could not live in it.

The lake is formed at certain seasons of the year, when the Colorado River is very high. By overflowing its banks and following waterways out into lower parts of the desert, it forms lakes. In this way, the Colorado trout follow the water out. As the river recedes, the lakes remain until the heat of the sun causes the water to evaporate or become so hot that the fish die. The usual rise of the river is caused by the melting of snow in Utah and Colorado.

Our guide informed us there was, or had been, a well some fifteen or twenty miles ahead, and that we might get good water there. Water was now a question of life and death for the command and I determined to push on after resting an hour or two. In the meantime, I had the company cooks boil some of the lake water and make coffee. I found boiling the water improved it somewhat, but at best it was a poor excuse for coffee. About midnight, we reached New River Well, let a bucket down and on drawing it up had more frogs than water in the pail, but the water was pure. I then set a detail of men bailing water and in due course we got the frogs out and the command watered. The horses had become almost frantic by this time and it was only with great difficulty that we could keep them from rushing into the well. Men with clubs had to guard them against doing so. In this way we continued our march to Fort Yuma, where we arrived about the first of July.

Fort Yuma is situated on the Colorado River. The river is quite large at this point and the command had to be ferried over by hand in a boat. The current is very rapid and scarcely anyone who falls into the river escapes, but after our dry march across the desert it appeared very beautiful. Fort Yuma was garrisoned by a company of infantry and was also a base of supplies for the troops in the territory at that time. Here we met our first Indians, the Yumas, but they were friendly and have always been so.

After crossing the river and resting a few days, we continued our march up the Gila River, following that nearly two hundred miles. Although our want of water was obviated, the heat was so intense that it was almost impossible to bear. We undertook to march at night and rest during the day, but rattlesnakes became so troublesome that we had to give that up. The fact is the sand became so hot during the day that snakes were unable to travel and had to lie by until the sun went down and the sand cooled off somewhat.

I remember one day during the march I had occasion to dismount and saw a rattler lying curled up under a little sage bush, so I took my saber and dispatched him. About that time I saw another lying under another bush, and I killed him too. I then began to look for snakes and found one under about every bush I could see. I killed thirty-seven and then got on my horse and rode off (it wasn't a very good day for snakes, either). They were of a small species called the "sidewinder," but very vicious and poisonous, more so than the larger variety.

Marching up the Gila River we frequently encountered sand storms. The day would be bright and clear, not a breath of air stirring, when we could see what appeared to be a cloud coming up. In a very short time a cloud of sand and dust and gravel, the size of peas or beans, would be carried by the force of the wind with such velocity that neither man nor beast could face it and everything would have to halt until it had passed by. I remember on several occasions we were in camp when a sand storm suddenly came upon us and ruined all our victuals that we were just about to eat. Everything would be filled with sand.

We followed the river as far as Sacaton and then struck south, toward Tucson. At Maricopa Wells we met another band of friendly Indians. In fact, we had friendly Indians all the way to Sacaton. Two tribes have always lived in that section of the territory, the Pimas and Maricopas. They have always been friendly with the whites and at war with the Apaches. They have large herds of ponies and raise crops of wheat, barley, beans, and pumpkins. Now that the government has full charge of all Indians in the territory, their prior rights to the land have been protected and no whites or settlers are allowed to encroach upon their farming land.

These Indians always retain a full year's supply of wheat on hand so that in case of a failure of crops they are sure to have sufficient to carry them over. They, however, have a very crude way of storing their crops that in our civilized country would be very risky, though in theirs it is perfectly secure. They build huts covered with thatched roofs on which they put a coat of mud and, on top of all, a lot of dirt. These are built a good deal in the shape of our old outdoor country ovens, only much larger. In order to lock the door, the Indians pile up a lot of poles so as to close up the opening—that's all—yet no one dares to touch any of the contents without the chief's consent.

The Pimas and Maricopas are a better class of Indians. They are well formed, both male and female. They have the most beautiful teeth I have ever seen, and I cannot recollect ever having seen a decayed one. They have beautiful long black hair and wear it "banged" in front. They wear no headdress, unless troubled with vermin, when they put their hair up in a certain kind of blue mud and allow it to remain for a few days. It is claimed that this kills all the "bugs," even to the "seed."

About the only clothing the bucks wear is a "G" string or

what is known as a "breech clout." That's a narrow strip of cloth, generally unbleached muslin, but from its present color, it would be hard to describe. One end is passed through the belt in front, the other passed through between the legs and over the back of the belt.

The squaws generally have a yard or two of red calico which they wrap around the loins, tucking in one end to hold it in place. Of late years, since they are being civilized somewhat, those who are able to buy cheap shawls of the most gaudy colors and use that as a wrap. The children run around as they were born until five and six years of age.

They do not use their wheat or corn for making bread, but grind it on a stone by hand into a coarse meal which they make into a kind of mush. While it is still boiling hot, all hands will dive in with their fingers, all eating from the same "olla" or pot. Meat is roasted or cooked in the fire. On special occasions, when they have a feast or some big "pow wow," they will put a dog or two in the "mush," but that's only on rare occasions. They sleep in the sand or on the earth, very much like animals. When we have an animal die, no matter if there is no Indian within twenty miles of us—to our knowledge, that is—within hours, and often in much less time, they will be on hand to carry off and eat the last morsel.

At certain seasons of the year, or after we have had a rain, a large worm makes its appearance. Where it comes from or where it disappears to no one knows, but when the worms come, then all Indians are out gathering them and all get fat. They claim them to be quite a luxury, but I don't know it for a fact, having been satisfied to take the Indians' word for it. They are something like our large caterpillar, only they have no hair or "fuzz." They feed on anything green and clean sage brush and greasewood of every particle of foliage.

As a general rule, Indians are born thieves and consider they have "carte blanche" to steal anything they can get their hands on that belongs to the whites, though I do not know of their stealing from themselves. They are also born gamblers and it is as natural for an Indian to gamble as a duck to take water. They will stake their last pony or dog, or anything else they possess, on cards.

Gambling has evidently been practiced by Indians for ages, for they have cards of their own manufacture, made out of the rawhide of some animal. Another mode of gambling the Indian has is of throwing a long pole something like our cane fishing pole. The winner is the one who can throw the pole nearest to a given point.

Resuming our march from Sacaton, where we left the Gila River, water again became our objective point for camp. While marching up the Gila, for the last two hundred miles, that in a measure had been obviated, but the quality was very inferior. Being in the summer season, the river was very low and the water very warm, often so much so as to nauseate. In order to overcome the temperature, we filled our canteens, wet the woolen covering, and then allowed it to hang in the shade and draft. In that way we cooled our water. No one who has never suffered for the want of a cool refreshing draft can realize the luxury of a good cold drink of ice water.

Our first camp after leaving Sacaton was at Blue Water Wells, an old stage station on the old Butterfield stage route. This route had been established on the Southern California overland route before the breaking out of the war and while the Apache Indians were friendly. Stage stations had been built and wells dug in many places, and Blue Water was one of them.

Leaving camp about five o'clock in the evening, we took up our line of march. The road was good and we made excellent headway, but about ten o'clock a terribly severe sand storm came up and, of course, we had to halt. After it had passed by, I thought I saw something looking like a building of some kind ahead of us and, mounting my horse, rode forward to reconnoiter. I found a small building and a man, who informed me that it was the stage station. He also informed me where the well was. After looking over the ground and selecting a camp site, I rode back and brought up the command. The station consisted of a two-room adobe house with a hallway between the two rooms and a corral, or yard, enclosed with a stockade in which to protect animals against the Indians. The only entrance was through the hallway between the two rooms.

After I put the command into camp, the Mexican in charge of the beef cattle came up and requested permission to put the remaining stock into the station yard, saying the men were tired and worn out and that it would give them an opportunity to rest. I told him all right, if the station man had no objections. He arranged that and started to drive the few remaining steers into the pen, but as they were wild California cattle they, of course, objected. "Well, all right," said the chief herder, "I'll get them in." Undoing his lasso, or lariat, from his saddle, he threw it over the horns of one of the "objecting" steers and then, riding into the hallway, endeavored to pull him in, while the other herders and a lot of soldiers tried to force the rest of the cattle in from behind, but they all objected. The herder, with the roped steer, tried his best to pull him into the hallway, but could not succeed.

The steer, in fact, gained a little on the man and his horse. Taking a run to the opposite side, the steer gained some rope way and caused the horse to lose his footing. The advantage was now decidedly in the steer's favor. At any rate, he gained such momentum that he was pulling man and horse out the hallway and around the corner of the building when, all at once, he dropped out of sight, almost dragging the man and horse with him. Finally, the rope broke and the steer was gone.

About that time the man came out of the station and told us the steer had probably gone down the well. That being the case we concluded there was no danger of his running away and, as we could not get the remaining cattle in the corral, we had to herd them.

Soon after, the military expressman came along from California riding a mule and leading another with the mail. Riding into the hallway and dismounting, he unpacked his mule that had carried the mail and then unsaddled the one he had ridden. By the time he had done so, the first mule had left the hallway to call on the other mules or, at any rate, to see what was going on. By and by, the man returned and raised a great fuss because he could not find his mule. I told him I thought the mule would turn up all right, thinking he was among our animals and not apt to stray, but I ended by telling him that we had a steer down the well and that maybe his mule had gone down to keep him company, having no idea of such being the case.

The station man told us the stage company had sunk the

well years before; but, after going down ninety feet and finding no signs of water, had abandoned it and concluded to try at another point, where they had found water at a considerably less depth. Next morning early I was up looking for the well and steer and, incidentally, for the mule. I could see by the tracks at the edge of the well that the steer was there sure enough, but could not tell as to the mule.

In the company I had a fellow by the name of Morgan, a regular daredevil, who was always ready for any kind of an enterprise. Before breakfast was over, I had decided to have him try and get the steer out, or at least see what shape he was in, but before I could broach the subject, Morgan was on hand. "It's a pity to lose so much meat," said he, suggesting we might let him down the well with the picket line and try and save the steer.

I gave the orders to assist him in making his arrangements and soon Morgan was on his way down the well. I remember watching him descend until he got down into darkness and I couldn't see him anymore. By and by the rope slacked and I heard a voice come up out of the well saying, "The steer's down here." This was followed by, "The mule's down here, too. Send down another rope." We did and, by and by, we heard Morgan call up: "Pull away on the small rope!" Morgan soon came in sight and landed. The steer was down the well sure enough, but his back was broken. The mule was there, too, but apparently all right. Morgan had the steer "roped" and said we could "haul away." All hands got hold of the big rope and commenced hauling in. By and by I could see the steer coming up and finally land. The company "butcher" was all ready for action and soon had him dressed and we "saved the meat."

The expressman then offered Morgan five dollars if he would go back down the well and rope his mule so we could draw him up also, which Morgan did. After first pulling Morgan up, all hands got hold of the big rope again and landed the mule. The expressman said he had been a little lame the night before, but he was fine when he came out of the well. The expressman then saddled him and rode him to Tucson that day, a distance of some seventy-five miles. About the first question I was asked after my arrival in Tucson was, was it a fact that the expressman's mule had been down the Blue Water Well? Although he had so reported it, the story appeared so incredible that it was doubted. It was a fact, nevertheless.

Our next day's march was to Picacho, which interpreted means a mountain peak rising out of the plain. Visible for fifty miles on either side, it was one on which Indians frequently lay watching for parties traveling on the road and many are the murders that they committed in that immediate vicinity.

From there we went to Point of Mountain, a long march but good roads, and the following day we arrived in Tucson and established Camp Lowell in the outskirts of the town. Camp Lowell was named in honor of General C. R. Lowell, killed at Cedar Creek, Virginia, on whose staff I was serving at the time.

Tucson was then about the only village in the territory. It had been a Mexican military outpost while Arizona belonged to Mexico. Buildings were all of adobe or sun-dried brick with flat mud roofs. The streets were narrow and almost the entire population were Mexicans and halfbreed Indians with a scattering of American outlaws. The town was characteristic of all frontier towns. Drinking and gambling and Mexican fandangos were "all the go," and it was rare that someone was not shot or wounded during the night. Pistols and knives were freely used on the least provocation. Saloons were open day and night, Sundays and weekdays; and, I am sorry to say, such is the case yet as far as the saloons and gambling dens are concerned.

All drinks and cigars were twenty-five cents. Wages of all kinds commanded high prices. Ordinary laborers, such as teamsters, received from $90 to $100 a month. Freight on merchandise from Yuma by wagon, then the only means of transportation, was from six to seven cents per pound. Grain, barley, or corn was worth ten cents per pound and wild hay, cut with a hoe, $60 per ton.

Tucson was then the distributing depot for military ports in southeastern Arizona; consequently train loads of supplies were constantly being received and reshipped to the different posts in that part of the territory. My company had been ordered to take station there, to give such protection to the different supply trains passing through the territory as might be necessary, because Apache Indians were operating in the immediate vicinity. I remember one occasion, soon after taking station, when Apaches stole some thirty-odd mules of Judge Hayden's train, which was camped in the outskirts of the village, and got away with them, too. I undertook to follow, and chased them so closely for the day that they had to scatter to the mountains, but having no one with me who was acquainted with the country, I gave up the chase.

Having been ordered to take the station there, we set to work to make a permanent camp. Sheds were first built to protect the horses in some measure from the rays of the sun. The poles had to be hauled some fifteen or eighteen miles. Next, sheds were put up over the men's tents, a mess house and kitchen built, and then a well dug. In that way we made ourselves as comfortable as possible.

Rather an amusing incident occurred while I was stationed there. I had several recruits sent to the company and among them a German. He could neither speak nor understand a word of English and was awkward in the bargain. The sergeant tried to use him around the stables but, as he could not understand our language, was of no service whatever and the sergeant so reported one morning with the remark that I "had better let him go." I don't remember that I told the sergeant that he should do so, but next morning the man was reported absent. Several days afterward, one of my other sergeants, who had been out escorting a supply train with a small detachment, returned and brought in the Dutchman, reporting that he found him some forty miles out with another train, so the man was reported as a deserter.

Some time after, a military court-martial was ordered of which I was a member. Among those to be tried was my Dutchman. When his case finally came up for hearing, he asked to have me sworn as an interpreter saying he was unable to speak English and that he wanted to make a statement. The president of the court granted his request and I was duly sworn to translate from German to English and "vice versa." After the evidence of the sergeant who had found him was in, I was told to tell the German to proceed with what he wished to say to the court. He commenced by saying in German (which I translated to the court) that the sergeant of the company first gave him four days' rations. Then the sergeant took him out where the whole company was in line and told him he had to run up and down in front of the company. Everyone in the company had a surcingle or a stick and, when he ran by, everybody gave him a "hell of a lick." Then, breaking out in what little English he knew, he said the sergeant told him to "skin out" and he "skinned." By that time, the court could hardly contain itself, and the Dutchman was told that would do. It is needless to say his sentence was light, but the officers had a good laugh at my expense.

Sometime during the winter of 1866 and 1867 I was ordered to Camp Grant to relieve Colonel Ilges of the 32nd Infantry. Camp Grant was located on the San Pedro River, some sixty-five miles north of Tucson. Before the Civil War, when we first occupied the territory after its acquisition from Mexico by the Gadsden Purchase, it had been Fort Breckinridge. When the war broke out, the troops were withdrawn and the territory abandoned. Some of the walls of the old adobe buildings still remained when I arrived. Colonel Ilges, who had four companies of infantry, had been ordered on my arrival to proceed to a point about one hundred and fifty miles north and establish a new post on the Verde River, afterward known as Camp McDowell.

During the fall before my arrival, the hostile Indians of the vicinity, covering nearly all the Apaches in the territory (except the tribe of Cochise, known as the Chiricahuas) had sent runners into the post and offered to surrender. They had been allowed to come in, so that when I arrived I found anywhere from fifteen hundred to two thousand Indians at the post.

The militia were issuing one pound of corn and beef per day to each Indian present, pending instructions from Washington. My company consisted of fifty-two men, two officers, and a doctor, so it will be seen I was occupying a rather precarious position for a young officer. I often wonder that we were not massacred, for the Indians were the same ones that afterward took the army in the territory twenty years to subdue.

In issuing the rations to the Indians, I would have each chief line up each member of his tribe—men, women, and children—so I could count them. After estimating how many pounds of corn and beef were due each tribe, I would then give each chief a check or ticket for the amount due.

Beef was furnished on the hoof, or alive. When we arrived at the corral or pen where the beef was kept, the whole tribe would be there. The chief would then select his man to go into the pen and lasso the number of steers due. As soon as the number were caught, as many Indians as could get hold of the rope would yank each steer out by main force and, as soon as he was outside the gate, the tribe would begin cutting it up. They would not undertake to slaughter or kill it, but would commence cutting up the live steer. The first cut would be to the hamstrings, which would let him down on his knees. Then, having him secure, the cutting commenced.

After a few issues of that kind, I refused to allow it as it was too cruel and barbarous. Thereafter I had each steer shot, which was very much to the dislike of the Indians, who appeared to delight in the barbarous butchery.

At the post I found two white men who had followed Colonel Ilges there the year before. As they had been farmers and seeing the fine farming land in the vicinity of the post and knowing the high price of corn, I conceived the idea of planting a crop of corn and did so. I raised $10,000 worth that year, which the government bought and paid for and was glad to get. The same corn was fed to the Indians.

One of the parties thought thay had done very well for the season and was willing to leave the territory, but the other was more ambitious and insisted on his partner staying and putting in another and larger crop. He finally persuaded him to do so. The ground they prepared was probably half or a mile below the post, and they were in the habit of working during the day and coming into the post with their horses during the night for security. As the men were coming in from their farm one evening, the Indians lay in ambush for them within half a mile of my quarters, killed them both, and ran off with their horses. At the same time every Indian in camp broke for the mountains. In ten minutes not an Indian was in sight. It evidently had been a preconcerted plan.

An old superannuated chief and two squaws had been out hunting at the time, evidently not knowing of what was going on in their absence. Soon after, I saw them winding their way down a steep mountain trail, leading three or four ponies laden with venison. I sent a sergeant and a couple of men to intercept them. When they brought the old chief to my quarters, I told him what had occurred and that I was going to follow the Indians and that I wanted him to go with us as a guide and show me where they lived. If he would do so, I would see that he and his squaws were taken care of; if he did not, "I would hang them up." He concluded to go, so I sent him down to the guardhouse for safekeeping and had ten days' rations issued to him the same as to the men. The rations consisted of twelve pounds of bacon, sixteen of ham as well as bread, coffee, and sugar.

When we were ready to start, about nine or ten o'clock at night, having in the meantime divided my command, half to go with me and the other half to remain in camp, I sent a man down with a horse for my Indian guide. When he reported to my quarters, I saw he had no rations and inquired of the man why he had not brought them with him. He replied that he had eaten them. In taking a look at him, I concluded he probably had for he was an altogether different-looking Indian from what I had seen a few hours before. He appeared so bloated up that I was fearful he might "bust." The sergeant said he had eaten all the bread, bacon, and sugar, but had thrown the coffee away. We generally issued a small ration of soap too, but the sergeant didn't say whether he had eaten the soap or not. I presumed he had passed on that.

Before we started I called up two men and instructed them to accompany the Indian and to kill him on the spot if he made any attempt to escape. I then had my interpreters tell the Indian what their orders were.

In that way we started out, the Indian guiding. We traveled all night down the river, up canyons, across mountains and valleys, but always on the fresh trail. At daylight we selected a nook in which we could secrete ourselves for the day. No fires were allowed so as not to make any smoke for which the Indian is always on the lookout. When darkness came we started out again and traveled that night in the same way and still on the fresh Indian trail.

When morning came we were following down a valley

leading toward the Gila River and, after selecting a little nook and secreting my command, I posted a picket on a little peak or knoll on my right, overlooking the valley and having a good view both up and down. I gave him instructions that if he discovered any Indians, to quickly slip down under cover and advise me. About ten or eleven o'clock, I heard my picket call out, "Lieutenant, Lieutenant, they're coming, a whole band of them." The fact was that he got excited and forgot his instructions when he saw a band of about twenty-five Indians coming down on our trail, the one we had marched on. As soon as he showed himself, the Indians struck for the mountain and scattered like a flock of quail. Had he carried out my instructions, I should have been able to give the Indians a dose of their own medicine as I was in good shape to ambush them.

As soon as I found we were discovered, I knew the game was up so we started out to try and find some of the party who had been following on our trail. We did get one, but the others all got away in the dense brush and high mountains. I then took up the main trail and followed that until about sundown, when I came onto a large band, but in such an inaccessible place that we could do no executing. We did manage to destroy all their camp and garrison equipage, supplies, and stuff they had been accumulating at the post, and we also captured the two horses that they had taken from the men they killed at the post when they left.

I camped near the ground that night and next day started for camp, where we arrived in due time and found everything all safe. I had made rather a risky move in dividing my small command because there were Indians enough to annihilate the whole at any time. Since the old chief had acted on the "square," I took care of him as long as I remained on at the post and my successor did the same. The Indian we caught and killed when we first discovered them coming down the valley was one I recognized the moment I saw him, as I had had him in the guardhouse at the post.

I had a train come up from Tucson with supplies and, while in camp at the post, someone stole a blacksmith's shoeing kit, with which the train was supplied. When the wagon master reported this to me, I told him I would get it. I sent for all the chiefs and through my interpreters, of whom I had to have two (one from English to Spanish, another from Spanish to Indian), I told them what had taken place. I not only wanted the "kit," but also I wanted the Indian who had stolen it.

Inside of an hour the chiefs were back with the kit and the Indian. I told the chiefs I wasn't going to have any thieves in my camp and that I wanted the Indian punished. They in turn asked me to punish him, so I sent him to the guardhouse and had him pack a heavy piece of wood in front of the guardhouse for about a day, very much to the amusement of the squaws. It was only by strict discipline, firm treatment, and never showing any fear that I think I managed to maintain my position at the camp.

I had another experience there worth relating. One day all the chiefs, a nicely dressed-up squaw (that is, dressed in paint), and the two interpreters appeared at my quarters. After I had passed the tobacco and cigarette paper and everyone had a smoke, not a word having been uttered before, one of the chiefs got up and commenced making a speech. After he had finished the interpreters took it up and, finally, I learned that the Indians thought I was a very good man, that I had treated them very well and given them plenty to eat, and that in return they wanted to make me a present of the young virgin, who was by that time standing up in front.

I don't remember whether I blushed or not, but think I did. At any rate, my speech of declination, or nonacceptance, was a rather hard one to make. I hardly remember how I got out of the scrape. Anyhow, they took the squaw back to camp with them, but the interpreters told me they were very much displeased and disappointed, the squaw especially.

One day Captain Ripley of the 32nd Infantry thought he would sidle up to Camp Grant to pay me a little visit and perhaps see my Indian squaw. Ripley, who was from Tioga County, Pennsylvania, had also risen from the ranks like myself and we got acquainted when I first came to Tucson. He started out one evening from Tucson with one man, expecting to ride through during the night, but by the time he got to Canada del Oro, daylight overtook him and he was still thirty miles from the post.

About daylight, they ran through a big band of antelope,

which were very plentiful at that time, and the captain couldn't resist the temptation of taking a shot as they ran about half a mile opposite on the side of a hill, and by chance knocked one down. They cut off the hindquarters and carried them into camp, so we had roasted antelope dinner that night.

The next day I got off a pretty good joke on the captain. I had a big herd of beef cattle for issue to the Indians and every day the officer of the guard would ride out and see that the guard was doing its duty. The captain thought he would like to go along so I told my man to bring out my horse for the captain to ride (the one I afterward accidentally shot). The captain was an infantry officer who thought he was a pretty good horseman, but when he mounted mine and started for the brush he began to wish he was at home. My old horse gave him the ride of his life. He didn't stop to go around brush or chaparral, but went over it. The captain had all he could do to hold on, but he did.

While stationed at Camp Grant, I accompanied several scouting expeditions against the Indians. General Crittenden, I remember, once organized a command to follow a large band of Indians who had captured a herd of six or seven hundred steers on the way from Texas to California. The steers had been captured on the Yuma Road, near the Picacho, spoken of before, near Blue Water Station. The Indians killed nearly all the herders and got away with the entire bunch of cattle. Lieutenant Winters of my regiment had first been sent in pursuit and overtook them, but the Indians were in such force that he had to withdraw and return to camp.

A large force was then organized and started in pursuit and again overtook the Indians not far from where Lieutenant Winters had been repulsed. The trail led us into what the Indians supposed would be inaccessible to us, but we continued following until we got down into a basin, surrounded on all sides by high mountains so steep that it was almost impossible to ascend them. After we had gotten down into the basin, the Indians showed themselves on all sides and signaled us to "come on."

General Crittenden then organized an attacking party. I had the right and front; Captain Moulton, First Cavalry, the left. As soon as we formed, which was dismounted, the "Forward" was sounded and we started up the mountain, which was covered with a dense growth of chaparral with an occasional mountain cedar. After we had advanced pretty well up the side of the mountain, the Indians opened fire on us. The first shot just missed my head, as I was a little in advance of the line.

As soon as the firing commenced, we took to cover, operating on the same tactics used by the Indians. While advancing cautiously in that way, I saw a "puff" of smoke come out of one of the cedar trees directly in my front and almost within reach of me. I could not see the Indian, but I knew there was one in the bush. Sending my men to the right under cover of a little spur that jutted out, I cautiously crept up toward where I had seen the puff of smoke and finally got close enough to be in good range. There I lay a short time to see what the Indian would do. I had but a short time to wait, as he had missed seeing my men and evidently did not know where I was. The first I knew, I saw a black head peep out of the bush and look around. Directly after that, my Indian stepped out and stood on a big rock in bold relief between me and the sky. In his hand he had an old army muzzle loader. He was near enough for me to see that he had a band of red flannel tied on the upper ramrod guard by way of an ornament.

Since I had a double-barrel shotgun and a wire cartridge with twenty buckshot in each charge, I concluded to give him one barrel and see how he liked that, holding the other in reserve. As I fired, the Indian gave a spring in the air and then settled down on all fours, but tried to rise again, so I thought I had better give him the second barrel. With that he stretched out. Before we could get to the top of the mountain, however, the Indians took to flight and carried my Indian with them. Firing, of course, was by then general along the whole line. We had but one man wounded in the skirmish.

After following the Indians for several days and losing all signs of them, we returned and endeavored to find the herd of cattle. Strange as it may seem, we were unable to do so. The Indians in some manner had so scattered the steers that we finally gave up the chase.

In returning to Camp Grant, I was sent with my command by a different route, which led me through Aravaipa Canyon. I camped for the night at the head of it in a beautiful park through which ran a beautiful stream. During the night we had an alarm and I supposed we were surely to be attacked before daylight, so I got my men up and under arms. When daylight came and no attack was made, I made a circle of the camp looking for Indian signs, which I fully expected to find, but all I found was the track of a monster bear that had come up the canyon, scented about the camp, and returned the same way he came.

After breakfast we started down the canyon. The walls were so perpendicular that the only way to get out was either to go on through or return the way we came in. At many points I estimated the walls to be six hundred feet in height. The canyon was also vary narrow, in many places not over thirty or forty feet in width. At any rate, in the middle of the day by looking up, I could see the sun, moon, and stars shining brightly.

After marching ten or fifteen miles and making a short turn in the canyon, I saw my bear—and he was a monster— coming toward us with no inclination of giving way. I had a carbine and just as he was passing on my right, not ten feet from me, I fired. The ball entered his right flank and passed forward, killing him almost instantly. He was of the kind known as the cinnamon and the largest bear I ever saw. His head was as large as that of any ox. We skinned him and packed his carcass and skin on the mule packs. He provided over four hundred pounds of meat, but it was not good. He had been an old bear and was so fat that the mules had the appearance of having had pails of oil poured over them by the time we got to camp. An Indian tanned the hide and made a beautiful robe for me.

In coming down through the canyon, we came across a great number of skeletons lying in the open. In the skull of one I picked up—why or how I came to do so, I cannot tell—I wrote my name, rank, and address. Many years later, when railroads began to look our way, a party of surveyors passed through the same route and picked up the same skull I had written my name on. Up to that time, they could not believe that any white man had ever been through the route, although one of the men who had been with me insisted that I had passed through there years before. Finding the skull with my address had confirmed his claim.

As we neared the mouth of the canyon, game began to be

plentiful. I remember I shot an immense wild turkey that weighed twenty-seven pounds when dressed. Finding General Crittenden and Mrs. Crittenden and their son John at the post, I thought it would be the proper thing to give them a dinner with my fine turkey, so I inquired of my man Cummings, who was cooking for me, if he knew how to cook a turkey. "Oh, yes!" said Cummings, "I know all about turkey." I therefore had him get up a special dinner for the next day and invited the Crittendens and all the other officers at the post to join us for turkey.

Dinner time came and so did all my guests. The turkey came on in fine shape and I was beginning to compliment Cummings (in my mind) when, as I commenced to carve and slice down some of the white meat, I discovered that Cummings had forgotten to remove the turkey's crop. About the time, my opinion of Cummings changed. If I had dared to, I should have fired him out, but I knew that would not do so I said nothing and went on carving. The crop rolled out nicely and no one discovered what the cook had forgotten to remove. Indeed, everyone spoke in the highest terms of the nice turkey we had, but after dinner was over the joke was too good to keep and I had to tell a few of the fellows.

On another occasion a large expedition in which I took part was organized against the Indians by Colonel John Green of the First Cavalry. We first organized at Tucson and then marched to Camp Grant. From there we struck out for the Apache Mountains. It was the largest expedition in which I had ever been engaged. We marched through the Indian country without finding any signs and, when our rations were about consumed, struck out for Camp Goodwin, situated on the upper Gila River, some thirty miles above the mouth of the San Carlos River, in order to replenish our supplies. The day we arrived at the post, two Indians who had been on friendly terms with the post, although belonging to the hostile group, came in and voluntarily offered to conduct us to where we could find the Indians. The commanding officer accepted their offer and gave orders to get out supplies and be in readiness to start again the next day.

I had no confidence in the Indians at the time and suggested that we better put them in the guardhouse for safekeeping, but the commanding officer thought differently and allowed them to run around camp. Next morning when ready to start, the Indians were gone, so we started without them, taking our course down the Gila River and going into camp early in the afternoon on its banks. In our command we had about a dozen friendly Indians acting as scouts, who were under the command of a full-blooded Apache named Manuel. He had been captured when a child and had grown up with the Mexicans and hated the Apaches as much as we did. The Indian scouts usually marched in advance, and in going into camp occupied the same position.

After having our camp dinner, the men were engaged in different ways. Some were in swimming, others fishing. While the men were engaged in different ways, one of the Mexican packers, of whom we had a lot with the command, was fishing probably half a mile in advance of our camp farther downstream when he discovered an Indian on the opposite bank coming down toward the river. He at once dodged back into the brush and willows growing on the bank and hurriedly made his way back to camp. I happened to see him coming and from his excited manner knew there was something up and went out to meet him, when he told me in Spanish what he had seen. I in turn told Manuel and his men. They ran down in the direction indicated by the Mexican packer, while I ran to headquarters to report to the commanding officer, who ordered me out with the company.

Riding down in the direction in which the Indian scouts had taken, I soon met them on their return and sure enough they had captured the Apache. As soon as he saw the soldiers, he made a break or an attempt to escape and as he did so, Manuel fired. The ball passed through his head, knocking him down, but it did not kill him. By the time I got there he was about to rise when someone in my command recognized him as one of the Indians who had volunteered to guide us. "Hang him," he yelled. No sooner said than a fellow was up with his picket line, with which each man is supplied in order to be able to stake his horse, and had it over the Indian's head. He threw the end of the rope over the limb of a tree we happened to be under and in less time than I can tell the story, the Indian was strung up.

The Indian was one of the friendly ones who had been at

Camp Goodwin the day before and had volunteered to show us where to find the hostiles. He was then following a large fresh trail, which we soon after found had crossed the river at that point, in order to notify them of our being in the country and to be on the lookout. Three or four years afterward, I passed that same point and the Indian was still hanging there, a perfect "mummy." The Apaches are superstitious about anything of the kind and could not be induced ever to go near the tree thereafter.

On looking to the south, we could see many fires on the side of Mount Turnbull, which our Indian scouts interpreted to mean that the Indian boys were out catching the wood rats that abound in that country and are eaten by the Indians. This meant they were unaware of our presence, which we afterward found to be a fact.

As soon as darkness came, we started out on the trail. The Indian scouts were in advance with my company next. In that way we marched over trails until daybreak, when one of the scouts came running back and reported "Indians." How many or how far in advance, I did not know, but the commanding officer ordered me to "go for them" and I started. The scouts were on foot but ran ahead rapidly. I followed with my company of about twenty-five men for probably a mile or more, when all at once I came to a deep wash. There were the Indians just getting up out of the same, where they had camped and slept—men, women, and children, at least three hundred in number.

I hardly knew who was the most surprised, myself or the Indians, but I saw that prompt action must be had before they could recover so I pitched into the band firing right and left as we charged through them. One old buck undertook to run away directly in my front. I charged after him. As I was on the point of firing, he looked back and seeing me so close with my pistol on him, turned short, wanting to surrender, but we weren't taking prisoners of that kind at that time. Since I didn't care to shoot him myself, I told the fellow behind me to fire. I must say he made a good shot, for the Indian never kicked. Just then I saw another strapping big fellow run for a rock while trying to pull his rifle from a leather or buckskin case. I knew that once behind the rock, he could knock someone of us out. My first shot took him through the leg, when he dropped his gun; yet, using his lance for a cane, he made such good time that he managed to get away.

We killed and captured quite a number, but by not knowing the situation, lost an opportunity of making a big killing. My company was the only one engaged, the others having been sent to the right and left [so that they] could not get up in time to be of service. The whole command should have followed me. We captured and destroyed all their camp outfits.

Among the captured was a little boy, seven or eight years of age. After the fight was over we went into camp and had breakfast and grazed our horses, having out a strong guard. The mountain peaks were swarming with Indians so near that we could hear them calling us names, but we knew there was no use in trying to get at them. Somehow the little boy, whom we had captured and who with others of his band was in the charge of the camp guard, managed to make his escape during the day.

We remained there until next morning. During the night we had a long trench dug in which we left a company of infantry in ambush, thinking that as soon as we left the Indians would come down from the mountains as they usually do and that the infantry would be able to give them a dose of their own medicine; but they were too smart for us, although the trench and men had been well covered with grass and brush.

We then marched from the scene of action, apparently as though starting on our return to Camp Grant. Marching down to the Gila River in open daylight we went into camp where we remained until dark, when we again resumed our march under the guidance of our friendly Indian scouts. Before daylight we went into camp in a secluded place, keeping quiet all day and not allowing any fires built. At night, we made another long march and again hid ourselves for the day. Next night, leaving our horses with a guard, we started on foot for the summit of Mount Turnbull.

During the night our scouts located the Indian camp in a narrow ravine by the braying of a jackass. Under the direction of our chief scout, Manuel, three attacking parties were organized: one above the Indian camp, another below, and the third in front overlooking the camp. In this way we waited for daylight, but the Indian dogs discovered us and aroused the camp and we had to make the attack earlier than expected. At first the Indians undertook to escape by running up the ravine, when they were met by a volley from our men stationed there. They then retreated down and ran into the lower party and met with the same reception. In this way we thoroughly demoralized the band. Had it been daylight, we should have captured or killed the whole lot. As it was, when daylight came we found forty-eight dead, large and small. We also captured a number of squaws and children. Among the children was the same boy we had captured a few days before. Two of the squaws were wounded. One was shot through the calf of the leg and the other had her arm broken, yet both walked with us nearly three hundred miles in that condition. The band was the same one we had met a few days before. We then returned to where we had our horses and afterward continued our march to our stations. I was mentioned in general orders from department headquarters for my prompt action in charging, when we first struck the band.

During the winter of 1867 I was stationed at Tubac.[3] Tubac was then a small adobe Mexican village situated in the Santa Cruz Valley, near the Mexican boundary. While Arizona and New Mexico belonged to old Mexico, it had been occupied by Mexican troops, being one of their most northern frontier posts. At the time spoken of, it was occupied by two companies of the First U.S. Cavalry and one company of the 32nd Infantry and commanded by Colonel McGarry.

One evening late in the fall, word was brought to the post by a halfbreed Indian that a train had been attacked by Indians in the Santa Rita Mountains at a point some thirty miles distant. I was ordered to proceed there with a detachment of twenty mounted men with instructions to render such assistance as might be necessary and, if possible, to follow and punish the Indians.

Leaving camp about 10:00 P.M., I rode rapidly to the point designated, where I arrived about daylight the following morning. The first discovery made was of the oxen (about sixty), all killed and lying on a space not more than an acre in extent. The oxen had evidently been rounded up by the Indians and killed with the spear. Following the road a short distance higher up the mountain, I came to the wagons and there found fourteen men bound to the wagons with chains, all burned to death. Not a living soul of the party had escaped, excepting the halfbreed who had been employed as a herder. Finding I could render no assistance to the dead, I concluded to follow the Indians and soon found their trail leading over the highest peak of the mountain. I learned from their trail that the band was a large one and that all were mounted. I followed the entire day, only halting to water my animals, and continued to march until next morning, when men and animals were so worn out that I was necessarily obliged to halt and rest a short time. The trail led over the highest and roughest mountains that I had ever been in, that being one of the characteristics of the Apaches after committing a depredation, in order to retard or delay any pursuing party.

After halting an hour or two, I again took up the trail, which was then leaving the mountains and leading down into the Santa Cruz Valley, striking it near Calabasas, only about fifteen miles above the point I had started out from. The Indians had finally taken a road leading up the valley toward a small town in Mexico called Santa Cruz. After striking the road, the Indians evidently had kept to that, for soon after our arrival on the road we found the body of a Mexican who had evidently been traveling and who had but a short time before been killed by the Indians, his body still being warm. I then knew that I was close to the Indians, and expected every moment to strike them, pressing on until nearly sundown when I was surprised to find a wagon train corralled and in park, but no Indians.

As soon as I came near, the teamsters came rushing out to meet us. They were about the most delighted lot of men I have ever met. The train I found belonged to Pennington, an old frontiersman who had been on the frontier all his life. Originally from Tennessee, in the last few years he had drifted into Arizona where I had become acquainted with him a year or more before. With the train I also found a Mr. Yerkes with whom I was also well acquainted (Mr. Yerkes's brother is now a judge in Philadelphia). They told me the Indians had just left, after having been drawn up in line, as they supposed, for an attack. The party numbered a hundred, but left suddenly in the direction of the pass in the Patagonia Mountains. The teamsters could not account for their leaving so suddenly until my party came in sight, which accounted for their rapid departure.

Unfortunately, one of their men had gone to the brow of the hill close by to see which way the Indians were going and what they were doing. He had done this against their protestations, but he had gone and a shot had been fired in that direction soon after. As he had not returned, they supposed he was killed. I rode over with my command and sure enough found the man. He had been shot through the head just as he had gained the summit and was evidently about to look over.

As my command was so entirely worn out after our long ride and the band of Indians outnumbered me at least four or five to one, and also knowing something of the country they were now heading for, I concluded "discretion to be the better part of valor" and to content myself with protecting the Pennington party and seeing them safe to camp.

On this trip I had found bodies of sixteen people murdered by these Indians and had I not reached the Pennington and Yerkes train just as I did, I should undoubtedly have numbered their party in my list. This was done by Geronimo's band of Indians.

Mr. Pennington had a large family of children, both boys and girls. Before I left the territory, with one exception (a daughter), the entire family had been murdered by the Indians. The surviving daughter, too, had at one time been captured in the same mountains where the ox train was attacked. After being outraged by the band, she had been thrown from the highest peak of the mountain and left for dead. Not satisfied with that, but after throwing her off, the Indians rolled rocks and stones down after her. After regaining consciousness (how long after, she never knew), she recognized where she was and, being acquainted with the country and knowing the nearest point she could reach friends, she struck out for what was then called Old Fort Buchanan, where she finally arrived and was cared for. She was living when I left the territory a few years since, the wife of a respected citizen of Tucson.

Pennington had been a woodsman. On arriving in Tucson and finding that lumber for building purposes was very valuable, being then worth as much as $150 per thousand board feet, was in the habit of going up to the Santa Rita Mountains where pine grew, cutting the logs and hauling them then to Tucson with his ox teams, and then sawing them with pit saws by hand (there being no sawmills in the territory at that time). The captured train had belonged to him and one of his sons-in-law by the name of Rickman.

By the way, Rickman was in Tubac when word was brought that the train had been captured. He started out with me to urge me on (as he told someone) to try and punish the Indians. After riding a day or more and two nights, as soon as we struck the road at Calabasas, my friend Rickman was missed. I found him in Tubac when we returned. He told his friends it was useless to send anyone out with that fellow (meaning me) to "push him," saying, "He's got push enough, and more than enough to suit him."

Yerkes had been in Arizona before the war broke out, or at that time, having gone there with some mining enterprise. Before our reoccupation of the territory, the Indians had stolen all their stock, burned the mills, and killed many of his men, but he always fortunately escaped. I think he is now operating mines in Mexico.

The Indians belonged to the Chiricahua Apaches, old Chief Cochise's band. Cochise was the father of Geronimo, who was afterward captured by General Miles and sent to Florida. Geronimo was in charge of the party. The Chiricahuas were one of the most bloodthirsty tribes we had in the territory.

After my return to camp, a large scouting expedition was organized under the command of Colonel McGarry. We first scouted through the Patagonia Range and then the Mule Mountains, from there through the Chiricahuas and Dragoon Mountains, but without finding Indians. In the Chiricahuas, we came near striking Cochise's band, but they discovered us before we had an opportunity of getting at them. On our return we skirted the Mexican boundary, in fact were across the line at one time. We found a great scarcity of water on this campaign and I remember we made one forced march of over fifty miles from one watering point to the other. During our march we came across a large band of wild horses that ranged in that section of the territory at the time. When we first saw them, we supposed them to be Indians. After discovering us, they came in our direction at a rapid gait. When they got within, say, a thousand yards of us, they all lined up like a company of cavalry, the leader in front. After viewing us for a while, they suddenly broke to the rear, led by their leader, and struck out for the mountains at full gallop and raising a cloud of dust. The leader appeared to be a beautiful animal, probably a stallion. The band has since been captured by the Mexicans and cowboys.

The paymaster generally came down from San Francisco about twice a year to pay off the troops stationed in the territory. Escorts would then be furnished him from one post to another. On one occasion while I was stationed at Tubac, the paymaster arrived and the command paid off. I was ordered to send an escort with him as far as Camp Wallen, our nearest post, and detailed a sergeant and ten men for that duty. The second day out, one of the men reported to the paymaster that a plan had been made by men of the escort to rob him at a certain point on the road near the Mexican boundary. One of the men weakened and informed him of their intention. The two ringleaders, finding that their plot had been discovered or reported to the paymaster, deliberately deserted and struck out for Mexico with a sergeant and couple of men in pursuit. The sergeant gave chase until the deserters reached a little town in Mexico called Santa Cruz, where the deserters defied arrest and placed themselves in the hands of the Mexican authorities and the sergeant had to return without his men.

In the meantime, a courier had been sent to the post informing the commanding officer of what had taken place. I was sent for and told to report to headquarters. I was informed, and inquired of, if I thought I could overtake and arrest them. I told the commanding officer I would do my best to do so. I was then allowed to select ten men and a good noncommissioned officer. I was furnished a Mexican interpreter and necessary funds to buy provisions and forage in Mexico and started out about five o'clock in the afternoon. Thinking the men would undertake to reach the seacoast about Guaymas (one of the men having been to sea), I concluded to make a forced march and head them off on that route and by sunrise next morning had made ninety miles and struck the road they must necessarily have passed over.

That night about ten or eleven o'clock, I halted where the town of Nogales, with a population of 3,500 to 4,000 inhabitants, is now situated. At that time there was not a white man or building within fifty miles. The point at which I struck the Santa Cruz and Guaymas road was a little Mexican village called Imuris. Through my interpreter I inquired if any American soldiers had passed the day before or within a short time and was informed that none had. In the meantime I had bought forage for my animals and concluded to remain there until toward evening before proceeding farther, having no doubt but that my men had passed the point.

Toward evening we saddled up and proceeded down the road toward Magdalena. Some ten or fifteen miles down the road we came to another little Mexican town called San Ignacio. As it was about dark, I concluded to camp there for the night. In the meantime, as a matter of courtesy to the officials, being now in a foreign country, I sent my interpreter ahead to give my compliments to the *alcalde* (who is the same as the mayor or burgess would be in our country), and say to him I should like permission to camp in his town overnight and that I had ten men and would like to buy forage and provisions. The interpreter galloped on ahead and I continued marching my regular gait. As he did not return, I continued until I reached town, permission or no permission. By the time I got fairly in, I saw the interpreter in conversation with someone and rode up and found him to be the alcalde. The interpreter informed me the alcalde was undecided about giving permission to camp with them, but as I was then in town, I presume he concluded he might as well consent as my party looked too formidable to be put out by force if we did not see fit to go peaceably. Whatever the reason, he very graciously said I could occupy the old barracks for the night. Through the interpreter I told him what supplies we wanted and, further, that I had the "cash" to pay for them. At the mention of cash, he brightened up and gave orders to some bystanders to bring what I wanted and, in a short time, I had all we needed and more, too.

After supper I sent my interpreter out again among the

people to try and find out something of the men I was after, but nothing could be learned. As there was no other route by which they could travel to reach the seacoast and as I felt certain they would strike for that, I concluded to continue my march, supposing the men of course must be ahead of me from the fact of their having so much the start. The next morning, as we saddled up and were about to leave town, I noticed a commotion among the natives and the alcalde in the lot, so I sent my interpreter to find out the trouble. He soon returned with word that the "imperials" were advancing on the town (this was at the time that Maximilian had invaded Mexico). I then rode up and inquired on what road or route the enemy was advancing and was told on the same road I intended marching myself. As this was putting a new phase on the state of affairs, I incidentally inquired of their strength and was told the advance consisted of two men. When I inquired why he did not capture them, he told me that all of his men had been pressed into service and that he had nothing but old men and boys. "Well," said I, "if you would like me to catch them for you, I'll do so." That pleased him very much.

I called for my sergeant and we rode down the road a short distance and sure enough saw two fully armed men in foreign uniform approaching. We rode on and met them, but as I got opposite I drew my revolver and made them surrender. I then took them into town and turned them over as prisoners to the alcalde. Before I was aware, a Mexican band was out and there was a great jollification. (Where that band came from on such short order, I never knew, but it was there sure enough.)

The two Frenchmen, having been disarmed in the meantime, were tied to their horses and half a dozen old men and boys put in charge of them and started for Magdalena with a letter to the prefect, who ranked next to the alcalde, saying that they had been arrested by an American officer who was on the way to his town. When I arrived there later that day, I was met outside by the prefect and a brass band. We were escorted into town in great state and quartered in the prefect's own house in quarters furnished for myself and men and treated very hospitably.

As soon as I was fairly settled, I inquired about the desert-ers, telling the prefect what had occurred. "I'll catch them," said he, giving some orders in Spanish to a fellow with a big drum who got out in front of the house and commenced beating it. In five minutes, all the men and women in town had assembled on the square in front of the house whereupon the prefect went out and told them what was wanted. He then told me to make myself comfortable. If the men were there or came in, they would be arrested. As I could see nothing better to do, I made myself at home.

After giving his orders to have the deserters arrested, I presume he concluded that with so distinguished an American officer as his guest (who had captured the advance guard of Maximilian's army), he must show him some particular atten-tion because he again called into service the fellow with the bass drum. Once again the entire population appeared in great haste, when the prefect informed them that he wanted all the town out that night for a big *baile* or dance. He wanted all to come, and so, they did.

It was the biggest Mexican dance I ever attended. I had more *cascaronies* broken over my head by Spanish señoritas than I ever had before or after. Cascaronies are eggshells filled with fine cuttings of gold and silver foil and highly perfumed. When a Spanish lady or gentleman wishes to pay anyone a particular token of respect or attention, one is broken over the guest's head and the fine cutting of foil allowed to drop on the head and hair. Mine had the appearance of being most beauti-fully gilded. I know it was several days before I could get rid of the fine-cut foil and perfumery, of which the Mexican señoritas are extravagantly fond.

That same evening I became acquainted with a Dutch Jew who had settled in Mexico and was doing business in the town. As I found he was acquainted with everybody and could speak English, I told him of my business and inquired if he had seen or knew of any American deserters having been in town. At the same time I told him there was a reward of $30 each for their apprehension and, further, that I would make it an even hun-dred dollars. I knew the money would be a big inducement to one of his nationality. He told me that he had heard of none, but that he thought he could find out as he generally knew all that was going on.

After remaining in town two days and hearing nothing of the men, I had about concluded that I must be on the wrong track and had made up my mind to strike out for Ures, the capital of the state of Sonora, thinking it possible that the men might have taken a trail across the mountains from Santa Cruz for that town. As I was about to start, my Jew came rushing in and said a Mexican was in his store who had heard of my reward offer and wanted to know if he thought I would pay the hundred dollars. I gave the Jew the hundred dollars to show to the Mexican and to tell him he would have the money as soon as the men were arrested. He soon returned and had me meet the Mexican in his store. The Mexican informed me that he had the men hidden in a cave in the mountains. From there they could look down into the town and see all that was going on. Their intention was to take the road for Guaymas that night. He was to guide them from their hiding place and put them on their right road. He further told me that the men were Catholics, that they had reported to the priest when they arrived in town, and that he had been sent out by the priest to hide them.

I soon struck a bargain with the Mexican, who agreed to bring the men to a certain point on the road that night where I was to be on hand to arrest them. After my arrangements were all perfected and perfectly understood, I had my men saddle up and in open daylight took the road leading toward home. Following that until dark, I about-faced and hurriedly marched back to town and on out to the point at which my Mexican friend had agreed to meet me with the two deserters. I watched anxiously all night, but no Mexicans or others appeared.

By daylight I was pretty mad and concluded I had been sold out by the greasy Mexican. I, however, concluded to take the road, which I followed a few miles and came to the tracks of three men, one a moccasin and the other two, shoes. I knew at once that, at any rate, I was on the right trail at last. I followed rapidly some ten miles when I lost it. Riding back a short distance, I saw where the men had turned into a field on the right side of the road. Riding across to an old adobe building and looking inside I saw three fellows lying in their blankets sound asleep. I was but a short time in dismounting, getting inside, and waking the fellows up. Sure enough, it was my men and the Mexican, too. I brought the Mexican along to town and turned him over to the prefect, reporting the circumstances. He said he would attend to his case; he drafted him on the spot and sent him to the army. I felt sorry for him afterward as he had made a very good excuse for not coming to the point designated, claiming he had lost his way in coming out of the mountain during the night and struck the road several miles farther on than he had intended. I, however, had succeeded in getting my men and saving the reward.

I rode back, but the deserters, having sold their horses, had to walk. They told me afterward that they came into town that night the prefect had given the *baile* and saw me in the crowd. They were tried by court-martial and sent to Alcatraz Island in California for a number of years.[4]

When I had made up my mind to leave Magdalena for Ures before gaining any information of the deserters, the prefect, having taken such a fancy to his American guest, gave me a letter of credit to any and all officials in the state of Sonora for any amount that I might call for. I have the letter yet. The prefect some time after paid me a visit in Tubac and, needless to say, we made it as pleasant as possible for him while he remained with us.

My success in capturing the men in Mexico and returning them to camp pleased the commanding officer so much that, soon after, he gave me another detail to arrest another deserter he had located on the Santa Cruz. In that case I was equally successful.

For some reason, I had been very fortunate in making captures of that kind. I remember the night after we received our horses in Drum Barracks, two men of my company (young boys) stole two of the best horses we had and made their escape. When roll call was held in the morning, the men were reported absent and I was instructed to pursue them. Our horses were all new to us, but I selected one for myself that appeared to be a durable animal and started out soon after breakfast. I soon found the boys' trail and leaving camp at a gallop and heading in the direction of El Monte, I took what we call a "dog trot," which is an easy trot, and kept that gait. Since the men for the first fifteen or twenty miles kept up a gallop, I knew they were wearing out their horses and that it would only be a question of time when I could run them down.

From El Monte they took the road leading toward San Bernardino, but I soon noticed that their horses were tiring and that they had come down to a slow walk. I kept up my "dog trot" to El Monte, twenty-two miles from Drum Barracks; then fifteen miles farther to San Jose; then on to Rubottoms Station, where the town of Colton now is situated; and from there to San Bernardino. Toward sundown I missed their trail and had to retrace my route a short distance, when I discovered the men had cut across the country toward the foothills lying west of the Chino Ranch. After following the trail several miles, I discovered two horses picketed up a small ravine, or canyon, and the two men lying asleep having worn out themselves and the horses. I rode up to the side of one and gave a yell that woke up the young man, who was about one of the most astonished boys I ever came across. They had ridden nearly ninety miles, which I always thought made a pretty good day's ride, considering we had green horses. The men were taken with the command to Arizona, but on account of their youth were not court-martialed. Both served out their time. One afterward cooked for my mess and was an elegant cook. The other reenlisted and was afterward killed by an accident in target practice.

The horse I had selected I afterward bought from the government, which officers had the privilege of doing at contract price, and I rode him many hundreds of miles. I became very much attached to him and never shall forget that I accidentally killed him while out gunning. He was so well broken that I frequently shot from his back and I could dismount and he would stand and wait for me or follow like a dog. When the accident happened we had started out on a scout and I, as usual, had my shotgun. As we were nearing our campground, I concluded to kill some game for supper for the mess. Seeing a rabbit in the brush on my right, I fired and killed it, dismounted, and worked my way through the brush to get my game. After turning and coming back toward my horse and when quite near him, the other barrel accidentally discharged and struck my horse in the right hip. I was so near him that the charge entered so close that it made a hole like a ball would have made and blood came out in a stream the full size of the wound. He died from the effects. I never lost a horse that I felt so sorry for, nor did I ever have another accident while gunning before or after.

Cady (one of the boys who had deserted at Drum Barracks) was cooking for our mess at Camp Crittenden after we established there. He was an extraordinarily good camp cook. Among other things in which he excelled in his "culinary art" was making pies. Pie fruit was then an expensive luxury in Arizona, costing as much as one dollar for an ordinary can. The mess occasionally indulged in such extravagances on extraordinary occasions, but nearly every time we decided to do so, our pies would be stolen. On the Fourth of July, 1869, the mess had a vote for pies. The fruit was bought and the pies made, but when dinner came, Cady as usual reported the pies gone again, so we had no pie for dinner.

The post surgeon, a member of the mess, about that time made up his mind to catch the pie thieves. The next time pies were made, he managed in some way to get a little croton oil into the pie (but unknown to Cady). Before dinner, the doctor was suddenly called for. Cady and his partner, the fellow with whom he had deserted from Drum Barracks, were reported very sick. They were said to have had an attack of cholera or some similar disease, at least a very bad attack of diarrhea. The doctor called on Cady and told him he would be all right "as soon as he quit eating so much pie." The fact was he and his old partner had been eating all the pies made for us and reporting them stolen, but we had no trouble thereafter in the pie-stealing line.

Colonel McGarry, the commanding officer of the post, had been appointed from the volunteer service, having been an officer of one of the California regiments on duty in Utah and Colorado during the war. He had been of great service in holding the Mormons in subjection and also in subduing Indians operating in that country. When not under the influence of liquor, he was a very elegant gentleman, but as he was subject to very frequent intoxication, he was a very unpleasant officer to serve under.

While yet at Tubac, I had rather a novel experience with him on one occasion. We were in the habit of having "dress parade" about sundown every day when the command would be formed on the public square. As we had been there some time, quite a number of citizens had gathered in and around the village in which we were encamped and every evening they would gather in that vicinity to witness the parade. On the evening referred to, the command was duly formed in line and waiting for the commanding officer to take his post when the "command" would be presented to him by the post adjutant to be put through the Manual of Arms.

Unfortunately, without my knowledge, the colonel was on the drunk that day. After waiting some time, he finally appeared, but in such a sad state of intoxication as to be almost unable to stand upon his feet. I recollect he wore an old slouch hat, such as we usually wore on campaigns, and his sash was about half wrapped about his waist, one end trailing behind. He finally managed to reach about his position before the command and the gathering of citizens. The adjutant, Lieutenant Winters of my company, gave the command "Present arms" and, turning, saluted and presented the command. The colonal managed to draw his sword, but then finding he was in such a shaky condition as to require a "brace," used it as a cane. Finally seeing that something was required or expected of him, he gave the command "Present arms." As the command was then already standing at a "Present arms," no one moved an arm. The colonel then repeated his command, but still no change. About that time the colonel began to grow angry and, with a strong accent on the "Present," repeated his command. Still no one moved.

About that time I concluded matters had progressed far enough and stepped in the front and to the colonel's side and told him he had better go to his quarters and that I would take command. After looking at me about a minute, he finally turned to the adjutant. "All right. Come on, Winters," he said, and started to stagger off toward his quarters. After taking a few steps and seeing Winters was not coming, he finally started alone with the remark "What in hell is the matter with you anyhow?" After putting the command through the Manual of Arms, I dismissed the men and they went to quarters.

As I was the officer next in rank, I felt it my duty to take the action I did as it was a very disgraceful exhibition for a commanding officer. I then reported the affair to General Crittenden, commanding the district, and my action was approved. I was ordered to take command of the post for the present until an officer of higher rank could arrive, and Colonel McGarry was ordered to report to district headquarters in Tucson. In the meantime, I was ordered to prefer charges against the colonel, but I personally begged of the commanding officer to be excused on the grounds that I was but a young officer, while Colonel McGarry was much older and of much higher rank. My request was granted, but General Crittenden ordered the colonel to report to department headquarters in San Francisco and reported the case to the department. After the colonel's arrival, he became so mortified at his conduct that one day soon after, while stopping in the Occidental Hotel, he committed suicide by cutting his jugular vein with his penknife.

Owing to the frequent overflow of the Santa Cruz River and the subsequent deposit of vegetable matter, the troops were all taken with malaria fever. I was about the last to be attacked and I think I had the worst case in camp. It usually came on every other day. First a person would be taken with a very severe chill, no matter how warm the day might be. Then, after shaking until you thought you would go to pieces, fever came on and you thought you would burn up. With that came intense thirst. In my case, as soon as I would take a drink of water, I would be so taken with vomiting that when the fever was on, it was one continual "take in and throw up" until the fever was gone, when I would be feeling pretty well, comparatively speaking. As I had an attack every two days, it was one day on and one day off.

Quinine was the usual remedy, and I know the doctor fed it to us by the spoonful. I took as much as eighty grams in twenty-four hours, but as I had such a continued siege of vomiting, I lost much that I took.

On account of the malaria, the post was ordered broken up and a new one established at old Fort Buchanan on the Sonoita, a small stream some sixty miles southeast of Tucson. The new camp was named in honor of Major General Thomas Crittenden, who was commanding the district of Arizona at that time. As Captain Moulton had been promoted and assigned to the command of the company I had commanded, I was appointed post quartermaster and commissary and had charge of building the post and transporting all the supplies to the new site.

After the troops and supplies had all been transported, my duties required me to visit Tucson, our depot of supplies, with requisitions for material necessary in the building of the new post. Leaving camp about midnight in an ambulance with a small escort, I intended to pass Davidson's Canyon before daylight, that being a very dangerous pass as the road led through a narrow canyon for some eight or ten miles. Indians going or coming from Mexico on marauding expeditions, as they frequently did, usually passed through on that route.

About daylight next morning, I emerged from the canyon and soon after met a Mr. Kennedy, who had been awarded the contract of supplying Camp Crittenden with hay and who was on his way to the post with several teams and a gang of men to commence work. After chatting with him a short time and cautioning him about being on the lookout for Indians while going through the pass, I pushed on to Tucson, distant some thirty-five miles.

Soon after leaving Kennedy, a large band of deer ran across the road in front of my team. As I had a Spencer rifle, I got in a couple of shots from the wagon and killed two, one rolling down the side of the hill almost under my wagon. We loaded them into the wagon and carried them to Tucson. I remember sending a saddle of one to General and Mrs. Crittenden, who was then in command of that district, and of dining with the general and his family that day. His son John, then a boy of probably sixteen, was present. He was afterward appointed Lieutenant of the Seventh Cavalry and lost his life with General Custer at the Little Big Horn.

After transacting my business in Tucson, I started on my return to Camp Crittenden. When in the vicinity of where I had passed Kennedy a few days before, my attention was attracted by a band of buzzards circling a little to the right of the road so I sent one of the escorts over to ascertain the cause. The man directly returned and reported a dead man over there. Dismounting, I walked over and, although the body was naked and much swollen, I recognized it to be that of Kennedy. We buried it as best we could with sand, piling stones on the grave to keep the wolves from it. Looking farther up the wash, I saw more buzzards circling in the same manner and, following up, found and buried all but one of Kennedy's men.

One had escaped. He carried the news to Camp Crittenden and a detachment had been sent in pursuit. They struck the trail near the head of the canyon and followed it into the Whetstone Mountains where the Indians lay in ambush. They had a spirited engagement, but were unable to dislodge the Indians and thus were obliged to give up the chase. This was the same band of Indians I had been after from Tubac. They got away with all of Kennedy's mules and supplies.

Soon after Camp Crittenden's establishment, another company of infantry was ordered to the post, making it a four-company post, two of cavalry and two of infantry. Although scouting parties were continually kept in the mountains on account of the many depredations committed by small bands of marauding Indians, I do not recollect that many Indians were killed while I was at the post.

The camp had been established on the eastern base of the Santa Rita Mountains and was much higher than at Tubac, thinking [that] the sanitary conditions would be better, but there appeared to be little improvement. The great trouble was the vast amount of decomposed vegetable matter covering almost the entire surface of the country. Being high up and near the mountains we had an abundance of rain in summer and snow in winter, but the ground never was frozen to my knowledge.

I do know we had the most terrific thunder and lightning storms I ever experienced. One day as I was walking across the parade ground, just before leaving on a scout, a horizontal streak of lightning ran across the parade ground and knocked my hat off and singed the top of my head. Next day going up a pass in the Patagonia Mountains and during a terrific rain, a streak of lightning ran along the entire command, attracted I suppose by the arms. Each and every man appeared covered with a flash of fire that ran down his wet clothes and yet no one was injured (but about twenty-five badly frightened horses struck out in as many different directions). The wet woolen clothes of the soldiers, I think, acted as a nonconductor and account for no one being injured.

Game was very plentiful in the vicinity of the post so we always had a supply of bear, blacktail deer, and antelope meat on hand. Although bears frequently came down into camp, most were taken in the mountains where we cut wood. We were in the habit of sending a detail of men up into the mountains with teams to cut pine logs and haul them to camp for building purposes. The wood cutters usually camped in the woods one night and returned the next day.

One night while a party was up after a load of logs, a black bear came into camp and got into a bean kettle that had been left standing about since breakfast. The bear evidently liked beans because he continued eating until he got to the bottom of the kettle, but by that time he had gotten his head so far inside that he could not get it out. About that time, he was discovered by the men and they had lots of fun with that bear with the camp kettle over his head. Being blinded, he did not know which way to retreat. One moment he would strike out in one direction and then, hearing a noise, would conclude to go in another, about the same as a cat will do if you blind her. We finally got tired of the fun and shot him and took him back to camp the next day.

I once had another kind of sport with the beef contractor, Mr. Hooker, who had received an order from department headquarters to deliver me two or three hundred beef cattle. About the time they were due, Hooker sent his man to me for two or three hundred pounds of salt. As we had a standing order to sell contractors any supplies they might call for, I honored his order, of course, but I could not account for his requiring that large amount of salt. Cattle in that country are not salted as in the East, as they find sufficient salt and alkali in the water and grass. Several days after, Hooker arrived in a great hurry, saying he had the cattle coming in and was anxious for me to receive them at once as he had a delivery to make in Tucson, or some other point.

The cattle soon arrived and the cause of Hooker's wanting salt was soon explained and without his telling me. The fact was, he had salted the steers well and kept them from water for a day or so before starting them into the post. As a result, they drank so much water that they were almost ready to explode. I told Hooker I was busy just then and he would have to herd them in the corral until next day when I would receive them. He blustered a good bit but, finding he could not help himself, had to comply with my orders. He and I have often since had a good laugh about the salt business. He still insists I was too smart for him, yet he considers himself a fair specimen in that way. Needless to say, the next morning the herd had the appearance of being a different bunch of cattle. Hooker is still in the cattle business and now has one of the finest cattle and horse ranches in the territory. For many years he had the contract of supplying all the beef required by troops in the territory. Government contractors in those times tried all kinds of ways of beating the government, even to salting the beef cattle and sanding the hay and grain.

About this time my man Morgan, who had gone down the well at Blue Water Station, got discharged, his term of service having expired. He was then employed as a military expressman in carrying mail to and from Tucson. One day he came to me and wanted to know if I would help him put in a crop of corn down at what was known as the Stone House. There was a fine piece of farming land there, he said.

Telling me what he thought he could make in an enterprise of the kind—as corn was still worth about ten cents per pound—he would take the chances against Indians and put in a crop, if I would help him with some money. After thinking the matter over, I told him I would help him to what he needed, if he wanted to take the chance. I also told him I thought it a very dangerous enterprise. He said he would get a good big dog or two (a watchdog), and as the little stone house was a regular little fortress, he thought he could "stand off" the Indians.

As he felt so sure of success and his ability to defend himself, I told him to go ahead. He did so and before the season was over, I had advanced him $1,200 with not a penny's worth of security but his honesty. When his crop finally was harvested—which was done without any material trouble from the Indians—and sold to the contractor, Morgan had about $2,500 cash. He paid me every dollar I had advanced him and offered to divide the profits as well, but as I had not accommodated him with a view of speculation, I refused. He then made me a present of a fine shotgun in which I took great pleasure and which I used to kill lots of game (not to mention my own horse, which I shot with the same gun, as previously related). The transaction was hardly such as would be considered good business here in Pennsylvania, where a gilt-edge note with good security and a pretty heavy rate of interest would be required, but in those times in that country we sometimes did business that way.

Major Charles E. Norris of the First U.S. Cavalry was assigned to the command of Camp Crittenden soon after its establishment. The major was a very nice old-school officer, a graduate of West Point, but he had the same failing Colonel McGarry had: he was too fond of his "toddy." My recollection is that the major had been in the Mexican War. Being a cavalry officer, he of course was somewhat partial to the cavalry and that led us to a factional quarrel that finally ended in nearly all the officers at the post leaving the service, myself among them. At that time, army regulations allowed post commanders, through a council of administration composed of a board of officers of the post, to select their own trader or post sutler. As ours was a newly established post, we were entitled to and required the service of one. Both the cavalry and infantry of the post had their favorite candidates for the coveted position, which was of considerable value and importance as a trading post.

The cavalry's candidate was an old settler who had formerly belonged to our regiment, a Mr. Hiram S. Stevens. He was afterward mayor of the town of Tucson and delegate to Congress for one or two terms. The infantry's candidate was, or had been, the quartermaster's clerk with no claims on the army for a position of the kind and, furthermore, not suited for the place. When the council of administration finally acted, the cavalry officers, by having a cavalry officer as commanding officer, were found to be in the majority and our man Stevens was duly declared elected and soon established with a fine line of trader's goods at the post. The infantry officers, of course, felt their defeat and the factional fight, instead of healing, kept growing worse and worse.

In the meantime, the term of enlistment of a large number of men in the territory was expiring and they were all concentrated at Tucson with a view of being marched to California in a body and discharged at Drum Barracks. Having been stationed at a malarial post for a long time and suffering from the effects, I was one of the officers selected to accompany the command to California with a view of bettering my health. Major Norris and Lieutenant Lewis of the 32nd Infantry, also suffering from the effects of malaria, were also detailed to accompany the command. Captain Moulton, First Cavalry, having been granted leave of absence, the cavalry force at the post was diminished by three officers, while but one infantry officer (Lieutenant Lewis) had been detailed.

The first action of the post commander—now an infantry officer—after we had left the post was to call another council of administration and oust our cavalry trader, Mr. Stevens, and appoint his man. When I returned to the post some months later, that was the shape I found things in so far as they related to the post traders. My man Morgan was still there and confidentially told me what had taken place and, further, that one of the infantry officers, a Lieutenant Ross, who was then acting as quartermaster, was interested with the post trader and together they had started a farm down on the Santa Cruz which had been pretty well supplied from the quartermaster's department.

As I was the ranking officer present and temporarily in command of the post, after thinking the matter over I concluded to close the infantry sutler store, which I did, and then issued an order detailing Lieutenant Ross, the post quartermaster, to proceed to the reported ranch on the Santa Cruz and seize all government property he might find and return it to the post. That was a pretty bitter pill for the infantry. When the lieutenant refused to obey the order, I sent for him and explained that unless he obeyed the order I should be obliged to arrest him and, if necessary, confine him to the guardhouse. He finally concluded he had better comply and did so. In a few days, he returned with a government six-mule team (the six mules having been exchanged for six condemned mules that had been sold by this same quartermaster) and a large lot of government property, such as iron and tools that could be made useful on the farm.

After their return to the post, I made a complete report to the department of my action and it created a considerable commotion as some of the infantry officers implicated had influence at department headquarters. Lieutenant Ross had been on General Ord's staff at one time during the war, and General Ord at that time was in command of the department of California to which I belonged.

Soon after my return, finding my health still very much impaired by the continued malaria (or chills as usually called) I made application for leave of sixty days, on surgeon's certificate of disability, which was granted with permission to apply to the War Department for an extension of four months. This was in the latter part of 1869.

The commanding officer gave me a four-mule spring ambulance and a small escort to accompany me as far as Tucson. For a driver I had an old soldier of my company, Ryan by name. At Tucson I met an old gentleman (whose name I have forgotten) who applied for passage with me as far as Fort Yuma, some three hundred miles distant. As I had plenty of room I was glad to give him a ride and found him a very agreeable traveling companion and very handy in camp as we did our own cooking on the road, carrying our provisions with us. We got along all right until in the vicinity of Oatman Flat, when one of our front wheels gave out and left us short a wheel some ninety miles from anywhere. If it had been a trifling break, we might have repaired it, but it was entirely to pieces.

A buckboard, carrying the mail to and from California, had by that time been put on the road, which could accommodate one passenger. As I knew it would be along next evening, I concluded to wait for its arrival in hopes that I could get out by that means as I was anxious to catch a stage leaving Fort Yuma for California. The stage made only one trip a week, so in case I failed to catch that, I should be obliged to remain at Yuma a week. That would be so much lost time out of my sixty days' leave, so I was very anxious to get there.

The buckboard finally came along but, unfortunately for me, it already had a passenger so my chances for that were gone. In the meantime, Ryan had been working up a plan which would work, provided he could get a pole long enough to make a drag to put under the hind axle. As soon as the buckboard chance was gone, Ryan struck out for the river, some four or five mile distant, with a pair of mules and an ax and during the early part of the night returned, having been successful in finding a sapling that would provide such a pole or stick as was wanted. We then went to work. Taking the front wheel off, we put the hind wheels in front, and the remaining front wheel on behind. For the other hind wheel we used the pole. By early dawn we had all things arranged and were ready to start. Our first or next point was Mohawk Station, thirty miles distant, which was made all right with the three wheels and pole, though it was a little awkward riding having the appearance of running uphill all the way.

As we got to Mohawk I discovered an old abandoned wheel lying by the side of the road, which we found fitted our axle. Although considerably larger in circumference than our broken one, we put it on as it was better than the pole anyway. In that way we started out for the next point, Mission Camp, which was kept by a fellow by the name of Reed with whom I was acquainted, who I knew had a spring wagon that I could borrow.

The distance was thirty miles again. In due time we made the camp and found Reed, who gladly loaned me his spring wagon. After resting a short time, we started for Yuma, thirty miles distant again and reached there in time to catch the stage that evening. Considering the different outfits we used and the distance of ninety miles, we made what I considered a pretty good day's drive for one team. Reed and his wife were soon after murdered by Indians or Mexicans. It was never known positively by which.

From Yuma I had a two-hundred-mile stage ride across the Colorado Desert to San Diego, where we arrived next night. The next day I caught a steamer for San Francisco, and from there I got the railroad.

The Union and Central Pacific railroads had about made connection at that time and I was one of the first through passengers by the route. At Omaha we crossed the Missouri River on ferry boats, the bridge having not yet been built. From there on home to Pennsylvania was plain sailing and I had a very enjoyable visit. I had been away from home about four years and of course Father and Mother and my brothers and sisters were much pleased. I made application while in Washington for my extension of four months and it was granted, but before the time had fully expired, I began to get tired of civilization and longed to get back to the frontier, so I started for San Francisco.

When I arrived, I reported to department headquarters for duty before my leave had fully expired. As the quartermaster's department was about to purchase horses for the troops in Arizona, I was selected as one of the officers to inspect the horses at Drum Barracks and an order was issued placing me on the board.

General Stoneman was president of the board and Lieutenant Barry of my regiment and myself were the other members. The horses were bought in open market. That is, anyone who had a good horse coming up to the requirements of the department could present him to the board, which inspected the horse. If he was satisfactory in every way, the board fixed the price the government would give and the party owning the horse could choose to take the price or not. If not, the horse was his and no harm was done. Should he accept, the horse was branded U.S. by the quartermaster, who was present, and the agreed-upon price was paid at once. I remember the limit was $125 and, as we were all interested in getting the best horses, that was about what we paid. We bought five or six hundred head and after completing our duties, I was detailed to conduct about four hundred of them to southern Arizona. I had a large forage supply train furnished me with a lot of herders or cowboys; I also had a detail of about fifteen infantry recruits to conduct to Tucson and Crittenden. The horses got through in good shape and were considered the best lot that ever came to the territory.

At Blue Water Station, I met a detail of men in charge of Lieutenant Ross to escort me through to Tucson, as I was then in Indian country again and four hundred horses would have been quite a good "bait" for old Cochise and his band, but we got through all right. In Tucson they were distributed to the different companies and I took some sixty head to Camp Crittenden.

As I am now in somewhat of a reminiscent mood, I am reminded of an occurrence at Crittenden by which I wish to show the injury that may be done another by inference without an allegation or charge by "pinching" the truth. I will show how an inference may reflect on another, when by a word of explanation the cloud reflected on a person's action would at once be cleared. I will also show that the factional fight spoken of still existed at Crittenden.

Camp Wallen, a post some twenty-five miles east of us, owing to its unhealthy state, was ordered abandoned. As ours was the nearest post, all the supplies were ordered shipped to our post. Among the lot was an exceedingly large quantity of corn. As I was quartermaster at Crittenden, I had received my own full supply plus the additional lot from Wallen, which was badly damaged by having been wet. During my absence on leave, an officer sent down from San Francisco on a tour of inspection arrived at our post and saw the large amount of corn on hand (all of which was worth ten cents per pound). When he inquired who had received such a large and unnecessary quantity, he was informed "Lieutenant Veil" and that was all.

Had the circumstances connected with the lot on hand been explained, I have no doubt but that it would have been satisfactory to him, if he was fair minded. But the simple information that Lieutenant Veil had received so large a quantity left the impression that I might have been in collusion with the contractor (as many were). The result was that I was reported to department headquarters and came near being called before a court of inquiry, but on making a simple explanation the whole cloud was cleared and no blame attached.

The officer who gave the information to the inspector was my Lieutenant Ross, whom I had sent after the government property on the Santa Cruz. He took that way of paying me back. It was many years before I became aware of how the misunderstanding had arisen.

About this time, in order to get our ring broken up and stop our factional fight, my company was ordered to Camp McDowell situated in central Arizona on the Verde River, about two hundred miles distant from Crittenden. Other companies of the post were ordered to other points and, in fact, a general change of station took place. I was glad to get away from the outfit. It had been the first and only time I had been engaged in an affair of that kind, but the fight had been forced upon me and was not of my seeking.

I have since found that an old infantry captain, Whipple by name, was at the bottom of the whole affair. He was of that class of fellows who delighted to get others into trouble of that kind and yet was smart enough to keep out of it himself. Whipple was continually coming around our quarters and telling what Veil or Winters or some others were saying and then getting us to make some reply, which he would at once make his business to carry to the interested party and then get him, in return, to make some remark that he would manage to get to our ears.

Before my company left Camp McDowell, Mr. Stevens and his partner, Sam Hughes, made me a present of one of the finest saddle horses I ever rode.[5] We have ever since been warm friends. Mr. Hughes still resides in Tucson and is now one of the wealthy gentlemen of that ancient town. Stevens was sent to Congress as delegate from our territory and served as such for several terms. He also became wealthy, but a year or two since became despondent and partly lost his mind. Coming into town one day from his cattle range, he attempted to murder his wife by shooting her and then, turning his pistol, blew his own brains out. He was one of the last men I am acquainted with who I should think would be guilty of committing such a crime. The only excuse that I can find for his action is that he became insane.

He was by no means the only one. Judging from the large number of men who resided in the territory in the early days with whom I was acquainted and who ended their lives by their own hands, it would appear to me that the effect of the climate and the excitement incident to their early life must have had some demoralizing effect on their minds. Mr. J. H. Toole, another intimate friend of mine, at one time mayor of Tucson and afterward a banker largely interested in Tucson committed suicide by shooting as did Colonel Kaney, an old gentleman in Prescott, [and] Tom Gates of Fort Yuma; [also] Fitzgerald of Mojave, who took chloroform and died in my house in Phoenix on his return from the territorial legislature; Colonel McGarry, who cut his throat with a penknife; Colonel Morrow, U.S. paymaster, who placed the muzzle of his pistol in his mouth and blew the top of his head off in one of the hotels in San Francisco; Lieutenant Small of my regiment, who dressed himself in full uniform and then lay down on his bed and ended his life with chloroform. Others who died by the pistol were Collins, Seeling, and Herrick of Phoenix and a number of others whose names I cannot recollect.

My company arrived at McDowell in due course of time and, with our arrival, also made that a four-company post: two companies of First Cavalry and two companies of infantry. In command was Colonel George B. Sanford, First Cavalry, a very nice and agreeable gentleman and a good officer. He had served during the war of the Rebellion and I was therefore acquainted with him. On our arrival he appointed me post adjutant, quartermaster, and commissary, so that I had plenty of work and no time to get into squabbles with other officers even had I been so inclined. The change was very agreeable to me, but having the executive duties of the post, it gave me no opportunity to go out on scouts, which I should have preferred.

I found there a very pleasant lot of officers and men. The only objection was that the post was surrounded by hills and mountains, which made it rather close and very warm in summer. I have seen the thermometer register 100 in my quarters at ten o'clock at night. One did not have occasion for much heavy bedding at a time like that. I think it must have been fully as warm at our post as the one at which the old soldier died when, after getting down to Purgatory, he found it so cool he had to send back for his blankets. The soldiers tell that story in Fort Yuma, which is said to be the hottest post in the United States.

Troops were kept in the field from McDowell almost continuously. Colonel Sanford, being young and active, was out the greater part of the time. The mountains and country north of the Gila and Salt rivers were mostly covered, as they were all infested with Apaches. A number of Indians were killed while I was at the post, but as my duty required me to stay in and look after the departments of which I was the head, I had no opportunity, as I thought, of distinguishing myself by killing Indians. While my duties were pleasant and kept me engaged, I would have preferred to be in the field, could I have had my choice.

This was in 1870. By that time prospectors and emigrants had begun to flock into the territory to prospect for mines and locate homes. Mines of gold, silver, and copper were discovered and considerable excitement was created thereby. Labor soon became high, as were prices of all kinds of goods and provisions. Labor of all and any kind commanded from $90 to $100 a month. Coffee and sugar were worth 50 cents per pound, flour $15 per hundred pounds. In the meantime, soldiers were getting but $13 per month and soon became dissatisfied, wanting an opportunity of either prospecting for gold and silver or getting the big wages that could be had.

The result was that desertions became very common. After the paymaster had paid our troops in the fall, about every morning at roll call, the report would be "two men absent" from G or C Troop or from one or the other of the infantry companies. Parties would be sent in pursuit, but none would be apprehended.

In this way the force of the post was being decimated or reduced until one morning when the usual report was made by the First Sergeant of my company—"two men absent again." On reporting this to Colonel Sanford, he inquired if I could not make it convenient to go into pursuit, saying he would assist in my duties and see that everything was kept going all right if I would go. I told him I should be glad to get out for a little exercise, so he told me to take whatever I wanted. He hoped that I should be able to apprehend them because, if the desertions continued, we should soon be without a command.

After breakfast, I had two men of my company saddle their horses and also the post guide, a Mexican named Salazar. I started out riding the animal presented me by Stevens and Hughes. As there was but one road to and from the post, I naturally followed that as the men must take that road or soon come to it even should they strike out across country.

The men had left on foot, as we kept the horses under such guard that it was impossible to get away with a horse. Continuing on the road to the crossing of Salt River, some eighteen or twenty miles from the post and finding no sign of men having traveled the road, I halted. At this point the road diverged. One fork led to California by the Wickenburg and Ehrenberg route, the other by Maricopa Wells to Yuma and from there to California. As this was the route we had marched in by, if the men were trying to leave the territory, I felt confident it would be the one they would select.

I then instructed Salazar to follow that road until he overtook a Mexican supply train that had been to the post with supplies, thinking the men might have gotten into the wagons and were leaving by that way. I told him to cautiously look through the train and, if the men were there, say he was going to Maricopa Wells, which would throw them off their guard, and to continue with them. I would then follow at night and arrest them. If they were not with the train and he found no signs or tracks of them, he was to return to where I was and I would know they must be on the other route, and I would take that.

After waiting until dark and the Mexican not returning, having had ample time to do so, I concluded my men were there so I had my horses saddled and we started out at a stiff gait. After crossing Salt River, I accidentally got into a blind road leading off southwest. As it was level country without any landmarks to go by and dark, I did not discover my error until I had traveled some fifteen miles and came to where some parties had dug a well or rather started to dig one. Then I knew I was on the wrong route to Maricopa Wells. Being acquainted with the country and selecting a point of mountain I could see in the bright night, I started across country knowing that the road lay between that mountain and the point I was at. I finally struck the Maricopa road and followed that until daylight, when I struck the Gila River near what was known as Morgan's Station.

As I arrived, Morgan was getting out of bed. Everybody sleeps outdoors around there on account of the heat and generally on the roof to keep away from rattlers and other venomous snakes and reptiles. I inquired of Morgan, with whom I was acquainted, if he had seen any men passing his place the day before or during the night. He answered he had not. I then inquired about Salazar and he said he had not seen him either. By that time I began to have doubts as to whether Morgan was telling the truth.

Just then an old Indian chief with whom I was acquainted and to whom I frequently issued rations at McDowell came up. He, of course, shook hands as friendly Indians do, and I inquired of him in Spanish if he had seen any soldiers lately. "Yes," he replied, "two down the river a little while ago." Saying he could show me the tracks, I accepted his offer and told him to do so. He then struck down the riverbank on a run. I put my horse to a gallop, but the Indian easily kept ahead of me. After going about two miles, he suddenly halted and pointed to the ground. Sure enough, there were the tracks. As I saw they were made by government shoes or boots, I felt I was near my men.

The tracks led down to and into the river. I followed, supposing, of course, that the men would cross directly to the opposite side. When I reached the other bank, however, I could not find where they had come out. I then thought they were probably trying to play smart to have me lose their trail and that they would come out lower down, so I rode downstream watching the bank to find their trail. After following quite a distance and not finding them, I concluded they had probably gone up, so I rode out onto the opposite bank and turned to ride up the river.

I had ridden but a short distance when I came to two barefoot tracks that had started downstream and then turned and gone back up. They were so freshly made that the tracks were wet. I followed a short distance when the tracks led into a patch of arrow weed growing on the bank of the river. Arrow weeds grow very rank, about three feet high, and offer good cover.

Following the trail but a short distance, I was surprised by two men's heads "bobbing" up out of the weeds. The men had carbines in their hands and one opened fire on me. The sudden appearance of the men, however, had frightened my horse. In an instant he had whirled, but so quickly that the fellow missed me. As my horse whirled, I concluded it was about time to draw my pistol and get ready for business, as I saw I had a fight on my hands.

As I got around again, I saw my man had his carbine about ready for action again and the other fellow was following me with his, trying to get an aim. I fired a "snap-shot." Fortunately, I killed one and mortally wounded the other. The fellow who had fired fell dead in his tracks, but the other one still held on to his carbine. I had him covered with my pistol and ordered him to surrender, not knowing that he had been wounded. If he had made the least move, I would have fired again.

After I repeatedly called on him to drop his carbine and surrender, he finally said he was hit. With that he sank to the ground and died within an hour. They were the men I was after, but I did not recognize them. Both had had heavy beards and rather long hair before leaving the post, but now they had their beards shaved off and hair cut short.

I have often thought of the intelligence displayed by my horse. She had whirled in a complete circle, apparently on her hind feet, and as she again faced the men she appeared to realize that I was in close quarters and that she must hold "steady." I could feel her trembling under me with excitement yet holding as steady as she could under the circumstances.

That was about as close quarters as I was ever in. I had ridden to within ten feet of the men before they raised up so it was close range. My pistol shot is the only one I am aware of that killed two persons at one discharge. To this day I prize the old "shooting iron" greatly, for I think it saved my life.

Now comes the sequel to my story and accounts for my Mexican not reporting to me as instructed. After following the road on which I had sent him, probably twenty miles, and not overtaking the wagons, he was carelessly riding along when the two men saw him coming and lay in ambush for him. As he came opposite, both opened on him with their carbines. They fired so close that they put several balls through his clothes and frightened the Mexican so badly that he struck out across country and did not draw rein until he reached the post, where he reported what happened to Colonel Sanford and claimed I certainly would be killed. On my return, in fact, I met a detail of men coming to look after me, probably to bury me if necessary, but that put a stop to desertions at the post.

I asked for a court of inquiry, which was ordered and assembled and which complimented me for my prompt action. I often think I got out of that fight pretty lucky considering the men were lying in ambush for me and that I got so close before they fired, but I always think their time had come and mine had not. I afterward learned the men had sworn before leaving camp they would never be taken alive and would kill any party who came in pursuit, but of that I was not aware at the time.

I continued on duty at Camp McDowell until February 1871, when Congress passed an act to reduce the army from forty-five regiments of infantry to twenty-five and the cavalry to nine regiments. The same act allowed officers who might wish to leave the army the privilege of doing so with a year's extra pay and traveling allowance to their home. I took advantage of the act, receiving my extra pay and traveling allowance to my home. I bade good-bye to the army, but not without many regrets as I had many friends and trust I have continued to hold the friendship of those yet living. At this late day, however, I see I made a great mistake in leaving as I did and should have remained, though we do not always know what may be for our best interest.

To show in what estimation I was held by my commanding officer, I copy a letter sent me soon after leaving the post.

Camp McDowell, A. T.
April 5, 1871

Brvt. Maj. C. H. Veil
Dear Sir,

Since your departure from this post and from the Service, I have been intending to write you a short note for the purpose of thanking you for the assistance you have always so cheerfully rendered me while under my command, and also for the highly efficient manner in which you have performed the many and responsible duties which have fallen to your share.

A constant press of work has heretofore hindered me from carrying out my intentions, but I avail myself of the present opportunity to do so. It has been my fortune to meet you at long intervals of time, and under widely varying circumstances but that the admiration I conceived for the gallantry and spirit of the boy seven or eight years ago, has been confirmed and heightened by the sterling and honorable qualities of the man.

I need hardly tell you that as an officer of the Army and comrade of the "Old First" I regret your loss. You know that better than I can express it but in regard to your future, you will allow me to wish you every success. I know it will be richly earned, and I think it will be sure.

With the most sincere respect, I am your friend,

George B. Sanford,
Captain First Cavalry

3. Arizona Anecdotes, 1871–1891

As I had never been to the northern part of the territory and as I had some business in Prescott with a party to whom I had loaned some money, I joined a group going there. Prescott is situated in the mountains at an altitude of about five thousand feet above sea level. The climate was altogether different from anything I had been in in the territory. Pine timber grows in the immediate vicinity, so that it was much like our eastern country. Snow, too, falls in winter so that is much like our climate in Pennsylvania, only not so cold in winter, more of a temperate climate. The buildings are all of lumber, which was a great contrast to what we had in the southern part of the territory. In short, I was much pleased with Prescott and its inhabitants, who were all Americans.

On leaving McDowell, I had made no disposition of the horse that had been presented to me by Stevens and Hughes. Not wanting to sell her, I left her with Captain Sanford for future disposition. While in Prescott, one of the gentlemen who had accompanied me, Mr. Joseph Collingwood of Florence, made me a proposition to give me a deed of ten acres of land he owned in Los Angeles City, then a town of about twenty or twenty-five thousand inhabitants, if I would give him an order on Captain Sanford for the horse, saying he would take the best of care of her and that nobody should use her but himself. Furthermore, if I ever wanted to buy her back, I should have the privilege of doing so. I accepted his offer and gave him an order for the mare and, in due course of time, he sent me a deed for the land, which I saw was as represented and situated within the city limits. (As I am writing "my recollections" in a chronological order or as they occurred, I think I shall defer termination of the land matter until later.)

After remaining in Prescott a week we started on our return. I intended to accompany my friends as far as Wickenburg and there take stage for California, then fully intending to return to my native state, but "man proposes and God disposes" as the old adage goes and that was certainly verified in my case. The incident and transaction that occurred at Wickenburg on our arrival demonstrates how a trivial affair may change the entire course of one's plans and, in fact, the lifetime.

When we arrived in Wickenburg and had gone into camp, we found a Jew from Tucson by the name of Lazard with whom I was acquainted who was on his way to Prescott with two large ox trains of corn for sale (about 200,000 pounds). After supper Lazard proposed to sell me the corn saying he was hard pressed for money. If I would advance him $4,000, he said, he would deliver the corn at Prescott at the rate of five cents per pound and I could then pay him the balance.

While in Prescott I had visited Fort Whipple, which is a military post just outside, and incidentally learned the department was short of grain and that the contract price was $7.25 per hundred pounds. Since Lazard was so persistent in having me make him the advance and my friends with me were recommending me to enter into the arrangement, assuring me there was no chance of a loss and a big chance of a speculation, I finally entered into a contract with the Jew to deliver the corn in Prescott at five cents per pound and advanced him the $4,000 which I had with me. With the ox trains in the meantime being "en route," I then caught the stage and returned to Prescott to dispose, or contract, the sale of my corn.

On my arrival there I learned the contractors for supplying Whipple were Prescott businessmen who had been expecting to buy the very corn I had bought to fill their contract. I also learned there was a scarcity of forage in the northern part of the territory. I soon saw I was master of the corn situation and would at least have no trouble in disposing of what I had to sell.

The contractors also quickly saw that I had the best of the deal and began to make offers, but I was in no haste to sell until they finally became so alarmed at the situation that they offered to allow me to turn the entire lot into the post at contract price ($7.25 per hundred pounds), which I accepted and they paid me for. That transaction, which consumed about ten days' time, netted me a profit of about $5,000, counting the difference between coin and currency, and was the incident that changed all my plans and whole course of my subsequently eventful life in the territory where I resided for twenty years thereafter.

That was twenty-six years ago. I was that much younger than I now am, and I fear it had the effect of making me think I was a born speculator (instead of a soldier) and that Arizona, instead of Pennsylvania, was the field for my future operations. At any rate, I concluded to remain and cast my lot with the pioneers then flocking into the territory, though I have always since believed that I came to a wrong conclusion at the time.

Had I returned to my native state and judiciously invested the money I had made and saved, I might today be in very different financial circumstances. At any rate I might have had an enjoyable life in a civilized country, whereas I passed the prime of my life on the frontier endeavoring to open up and develop the territory. While I had none of the comforts or pleasures of a civilized life, I have the satisfaction of knowing that where I located there were not then half a dozen adobe buildings and not a single family of whites at the time, yet the capital of the territory is now located there with a population of fifteen thousand inhabitants, five or six churches, three school buildings that will do credit to any town of its size in the eastern states, electric cars, electric lights, gas and water works, and railroads and telegraphic connection with the outer world. With all that, I take some satisfaction in knowing that I was one of the pioneers of the country, who helped develop the desert and make it possible to sustain the population that now exists. Where orchards of oranges, lemons, figs, peaches, apricots, and grapes are growing and where alfalfa and grain fields extend as far as the eye can reach, these results were all made possible and accomplished by the pioneers of the territory and by the diversion of the water of Salt River for irrigating purposes. I assisted and took an active part in all these enterprises.

One of the gentlemen who had accompanied me to Prescott was W. B. Hellings, the post trader or sutler at Camp McDowell, who soon after made me a proposition to go into business with him in contracting with the government for supplies of hay and grain. He had some contracts previous to the time spoken of and on his representations that we might do a good and profitable business, I concluded to do so. Bids for the supplying of all posts in the territory were soon after asked for and we made a proposal of the whole lot and were the successful, or lowest, bidder for about $7.20 per hundred pounds for grain. The posts were McDowell, Whipple, Verde, and Hualpai. Our first contracts were for the supply of hay and grain. The hay furnished was all wild and cut with hoes. The grain was corn, which by that time was being grown in the territory. Wheat and some barley were also being grown by the friendly Indians on the Maricopa and Pima Indian reservations in the vicinity of Maricopa Wells. Our prices were good and the first year realized us a very good profit.

In the meantime, as all flour for use in the territory was being transported from California and Old and New Mexico, my partner had commenced erecting a steam flour mill near what is now the capital of the territory (Phoenix). Seeing that the cost was much greater than he had anticipated, he proposed that I go into partnership with him in that also, which I did. Before we had the mill ready to operate, however, all our money was gone and we were in debt besides. The cost of freight alone on the machinery which was bought in San Francisco was some $17,000 in gold coin, to say nothing of the cost of machinery itself. Lumber had to be hauled from Prescott and cost $150 per thousand. Labor was also very high with the millwright being paid $10 per day and board. Coffee, sugar, and bacon were 50 cents per pound.

The building was two stories in height and built of adobe, but as it had a shingle roof (the first in that section of the territory) considerable lumber was required. We finally started up and soon had such an income that our debts were soon paid and our invested money returned to us almost before we were aware of it. Flour, which was nothing more than ground wheat with the bran taken out, was sold at the mill at $10 per hundred pounds. We were then making money so fast that I supposed we would certainly be millionaires.

Still having the hay and grain contracts for the military posts, our next move was to get contracts to supply the government with flour also, and we were successful, getting about $22 to $25 per barrel. Freight, of course, had to be deducted from this. About this time, however, the corn crop turned out to be a failure and we were meeting with big losses in that way. In other words, what we were making by milling was being lost in our hay and grain contracts.

In addition to this, a big mining excitement had sprung up in the Bradshaw Mountains near Prescott and we invested in that, too. I put $5,000 in one hundred feet of the Tiger Mine, of which ten tons of ore from the surface had been shipped to San Francisco and sold for over $13,000. I thought I was very lucky in my purchase and felt under many obligations to the two particular friends who, as a matter of accommodation, let me have fifty feet each off their claim for $2,500 apiece, thinking they would have enough to make themselves rich anyway. Besides, they thought I was a pretty good fellow and wanted me interested with them.

I often since wished they had not had such a kindly feeling for me. Soon after going to work in a systematic way to develop the mine, I had an assessment of $675 made for my share (and paid it, too) instead of getting out rock that could be sold at the rate of $13,000 per ten-ton lots. When the second assessment came around I declined to stand in with the boys, but they went on on their "own hook" and kept on doing so until a quarter of a million dollars was expended on the Tiger Mine and the mill they put up. That was all I ever saw of my original $5,000 and the $675 assessment I paid afterward.

That gave mining a "black eye" with me and I never made or lost a dollar in that way thereafter. Once I did beat a mining deal out of $300 and I always considered that clear gain. I had acquired an interest in the Grey Eagle Mine, a location near the Tiger, that had cost me little or nothing upon arriving in Prescott. Long after, a party of mining sharpers had acquired a bond of the other interested parties and were waiting for and expecting me to sign the same, of course, but I refused to do so unless they paid me $300 and they did. I guess that mine is still there, too, for I never knew or heard of any shipments of ore or bullion from the Grey Eagle Mine.

In the meantime we had also opened a general frontier assortment store at the mill. All such goods as went to make up a frontier store were kept, whiskey and wine among the rest. Emigrants commenced coming in and locating and farming commenced.

Planting of wheat was especially encouraged by our firm. Bona-fide settlers who were willing to work and open up the country were assisted or, in other words, supplied with necessaries of life and seed wheat. When harvest came on, we had to provide harvesting machinery such as headers and threshers, all of which we had to supply with men and provisions. When harvest came, then everything was "rushing." Wheat was the currency of the valley and all bills contracted by the settlers during the season were paid at that time.

The customary price of wheat at the thresher was three cents per pound, or $1.80 per bushel, but in that country everything goes by weight (even today). As we did the cutting, which was rated at $2.50 per acre, and the threshing, at 15 cents per hundred, all of which first came out of the crops, we generally had the crop and sometimes it would not cover the amount of credit the settler had from us even though the land yielded anywhere from twenty-five to fifty bushels per acre and even more.

We had also opened a flour depot at Prescott to supply the Prescott market and surrounding mines. It was my part to attend the northern, or Prescott, end of our business and I had considerable traveling to do, which was by private conveyance. As the Indians still continued marauding and depredating, it was very dangerous. We usually at that time made all our drives by night and lay in by day.

One day while at the mill looking out for that part of our extensive business, one of the clerks of the store came to the office, which was in another part of the building, and reported that Jack Swilling was on another "drunk" and that he was sending for large quantities of liquor.[1] I told him not to give him any more. Supposing that would be sufficient, I noticed the clerk hesitate some time before leaving, but as I gave no further order, he finally left. Some time after, remembering his action, I began to wonder what might have been the cause of his delay and finally got up and went into the store. I saw that all the clerks appeared to be agitated, but I said nothing and walked through and out of the front door.

About that time I saw a fellow with a big broad-brimmed hat, long hair, belt with pistol and knife, and a shotgun on his shoulder turning the corner and coming toward the store. Although I had never met Jack Swilling, who was a noted desperado of the country, I knew him at once and in an instant made up my mind I was, as I supposed, "in for a fight." I had no arms and Jack was by that time so close I had no opportunity to get to any. I stood my ground and waited for developments. In the meantime, I made up my plan of action, which was to tackle him at close quarters in case he made a hostile demonstration.

As he approached I said, "How-de-do?" By that time, Jack was pretty close and he replied by asking, "Are you Major Veil?" I at once replied yes. "Well," said he, "did you give orders not to give me any more whiskey?" As by that time he was close enough that I thought I could reach him, without any hesitancy and while watching every move and looking him straight in the eye, I replied, "Yes, and you're Jack Swilling, ain't you? They say you're a bad man when you get drunk. The boys said you were on the 'tear' and I thought you'd better sober up."

Jack looked at me about a minute while I tried to keep up a bold front and finally he weakened. "Well," said he, "that's so. I know I'm a pretty bad man when I get drunk. I guess I'll go home and sober up, but won't you let me have a little something mild to 'sober off' on?" I told Jack to come in and asked the boys to give Jack a bottle of sherry. He went home and sobered up and ever after that, when Jack got on a spree, he would come to me and give me his weapons, saying, "I am a bad man and keep these until I get sober." In after years, I have known him to give me the last mess of beans in the camp kettle, when I knew his children needed them. He had been the terror of that part of the territory and had committed many murders, but had I not faced him as I did, or if I had turned my back or tried to escape when he came to the store, the chances are he would have opened fire and shot me in my tracks. Meeting him as I did, however, gave me the "best" of him, as stated, and ever after that I could do as I pleased with him.

Jack Swilling was finally sent to the territorial prison on suspicion of being connected in a stage robbery, but I do not believe he would steal, although the circumstantial evidence was rather against him. The fact was, a stage had been robbed near Wickenburg and a horse with a peculiarly fitted shoe had been tracked from Swilling's camp in the mountains to the place of robbery and then returned. It was found on his range and belonged to Jack, but that might be accounted for because horses free-ran on the range and often were not seen or used for weeks or months even, so some other party might have ridden the horse to the scene of the robbery. Jack died in the penitentiary while awaiting trial.

By the time I am now speaking of, the Apaches had in a measure been subdued and the government decided to put them on reservations and feed them, thinking it more economical than to fight them. We were called on to supply the established reservations with flour. As we had the only mill in the territory, we had a monopoly of the trade and could almost command our own price. Reservations had been established at Camp Date Creek, Camp Verde, and San Carlos. For all of them we received orders for flour, and at the usual price of about $25 per barrel.

I remember that in the early part of 1874, we received an order for 200,000 pounds (1,000 barrels) to be delivered to San Carlos. We had had heavy rains that spring and the crossings of the Salt River and Gila were not fordable, so we established temporary ferries in order to cross, both for flour and the large teams. The mules could swim, but not so with the wagons and flour. The large wagons had all to be taken apart and carried over in the boats. After all had crossed and been on the road some time, I followed in a buggy. The distance was about three hundred miles. Our route took us by Tucson. When I reached that point, I ran across my man Morgan again and employed him to go with me to San Carlos. The route from Tucson was still considered dangerous as Cochise, the old Chiricahua chief, had left San Carlos where his tribe had been placed. He refused to remain there, saying it was too warm and that his people had always been accustomed to the mountains, and so he went out.[2]

After making the trip to San Carlos I found that the Gila River on which the reservation is located was still too high to ford and we had to build rafts and cross the flour that way, the reservation being on the opposite side. On delivery I received receipts, or vouchers, for the amount of $25,000. When I arrived in Tucson on my way home, I found letters saying another 100,000 pounds (500 barrels) had been ordered to be delivered to Cochise's band somewhere in the vicinity of Apache Pass in the Chiricahua Mountains. The flour was en route by train and I had better go on ahead and make arrangements as to its delivery. I immediately started out to find Cochise and his band. I finally located him in what was known as the "Pinery" in the hills of the Chiricahua Mountains, some twenty-five miles south of the pass. When I arrived in his camp, the Indians surrounded my outfit and they were about as savage a lot as I had ever seen. I felt somewhat nervous, but had sense enough not to say so.

I soon found there an old frontiersman by the name of Tom Jeffords, whose quarters were in a small log cabin.[3] Jeffords had been placed in charge of the party by General Howard of the army, who had been sent out by the department to treat with Cochise, and the old Indian had insisted that Jeffords should have charge of the supplies. Jeffords had the reputation of having been in collusion with the Indians during our troubles and of supplying them with ammunition.

As soon as I arrived, Jeffords wanted to know if I had anything to drink. As I had been told that if I wanted to do any business with him I must be sure to provide something of the kind, I was prepared. I handed him a jug and a tin cup and he helped himself. He then poured out a cupful and handed that to Chief Cochise, who was standing by attended by a couple of his squaws. Cochise, by the way, was one of the finest specimens of an Indian that I have ever seen, straight as an arrow and about six feet tall, not a spare ounce of flesh, and very dignified in his manner. The chief drained the cup without water and I began to think I would make my stay in camp as short as possible or, in other words, get away before the liquor had a chance to operate.

Jeffords, however, insisted upon having me feed my team

and stay for dinner, and about then someone called, "Dinner!" Jeffords again helped himself to my whiskey and poured out another cup for the chief, who took it, and we went into dinner. The chief accompanied us, taking a seat at the camp table with the rest of us. The liquor did not appear to have had the least effect and I noticed he used a knife and fork with as much ease as any of us. The only peculiarity I noticed was that he filled his coffee cup about half full of sugar, so that it must have been a regular syrup. His two squaws stood by him, helping him to what he might want, but not helping themselves to anything, at least not while we were present. Our bill of fare was not very elaborate—bacon, beans, bread, and coffee is what it consisted of.

I soon had my arrangements perfected for the delivery of the flour and left camp feeling lucky to think I had saved my scalp, as there were hundreds of savage Indians surrounding us and not more than half a dozen whites were in our party. Before getting away, however, Jeffords repeated the "dose" of whiskey to the Indian chief and himself, probably thinking it would be some time before he might have another opportunity.

Cochise was the father of Geronimo, who, after his father's death, succeeded him. They were the same Indians that afterward required the combined force in the territory under such skilled Indian fighters as Generals Crook and Miles almost a year to subdue. After their final capture they were sent to Florida and placed in a fortress.[4]

By the time I arrived home in Phoenix I had made a long and tedious trip of some seven hundred miles, all through Indian territory. In a number of cases, it was as far as sixty miles from one station to another and not a soul would be seen between stations.

In making our drives through the country at that time we had many narrow escapes. I know that in making one trip from Phoenix to Prescott, I barely escaped. It was our custom in making a drive of that kind to leave home about five o'clock in the evening and aim to reach Wickenburg, which was a small town that had grown up around a mining camp, before daylight. We would remain there, which was about sixty-five miles distant from Phoenix, and rest during the day. The following night we drove to Skull Valley (another station where we again remained for the day), and then drove on into Prescott some thirty-five miles farther. The whole distance from Phoenix to Prescott by the traveled route was 150 miles.

On this occasion I did not leave home as early as usual, being detained by business of some kind until dark, when my man brought out my team (a span of black broncos). Armed with a shotgun and pistol, a can of water, and a bottle of whiskey, I finally started. After driving until break of day I found myself just entering the Hassayampa Wash, about the most dangerous part of the route and fifteen miles short of where I had intended to be by daylight (Wickenburg).

As I drove into the wash I overtook two frontiersmen who had been down to Phoenix for supplies. They were driving a two-horse team and leading a saddled animal in the rear of the wagon. I had long been acquainted with both of them. The one had been in my employ at the mill and the other lived at Wickenburg. Following along in the rear of their wagon a short distance and chatting with them as we drove, some presentiment of evil or danger appeared to take possession of me. The more I thought of the matter, the more impressed I was that I had better proceed. I finally drove to the side of the wagon and remarked to Swain, the name of one of the men, that I did not like the idea of driving through the pass by day. I thought I should drive on by myself, I told him, as he could not travel as fast as I with his loaded wagon. Swain replied by saying he thought it was all right as he had not seen any Indian signs, but I could not overcome the presentiment that had taken hold of me. After passing the boy my bottle and giving them an "eye opener," I gave my horse the whip and drove by and on into Wickenburg, where I arrived all right. The next night I drove on to Skull Valley and Prescott without any further incident, but the stage following me to Prescott the next day brought word that Swain and his partner had been found massacred by the Indians within a quarter of a mile where I passed them. Their graves mark the spot today. I have often since passed by, but never without a thought of how near I came to being numbered in the long list of Apache murders of Arizona pioneers.

The point on which the massacre occurred was in perfectly

open ground, so the Indians could not have reached it without being seen by the men and giving them a chance of defending themselves. The only way in which I can account for their being caught in the trap, therefore, is that the Indians were already there in ambush when I passed. They knew that if they attacked me, it would give the other party a chance of escaping or making a fight, and as there were three horses and two men in the other party, the Indians must have concluded to allow me to pass and take the largest game.

On another occasion I had business at Camp McDowell, which was only thirty-eight miles from the mill, but we had to make the usual night drive. Toward evening of the day mentioned, two fellows who were farming in the reservation at McDowell drove up to the mill. One was named Toorney. As I was acquainted with them, as in fact I was with almost everyone in the territory at that time, we had a little chat. I inquired if they were going home and told them I was going up to McDowell, too, and proposed they should wait awhile and I would accompany them. As I was again delayed by business, my friends finally got tired of waiting and said they would drive on. Since I drove faster than they anyway, I could overtake them.

By and by I got through with my business and started out, it being dark by that time. After driving about eighteen miles, I came to Whitlow's Station on Salt River. The station was then kept for the accommodation of travelers and was supplied with forage and such. Whitlow had not gone to bed yet and, as my team watered, I chatted with him and inquired how long it had been since Toorney and his partner had passed. "Not long," he said. I would overtake them before I got to the divide, considered the most dangerous part of the route, which was where the road crossed a low range of mountains running down to Salt River. So after passing my bottle to Whitlow, I started out.

I don't wish to impress the reader with the idea that we were all a lot of drunkards out in the territory. It was the custom of the country that everybody have whiskey in the house and on the road—on the road more especially as a medicine, an antidote in case of a rattlesnake bite.

I drove at a rapid gait and as I was about nearing the summit, my horses all at once gave a spring to the right and went off the road, racing through brush and over rocks, etc., so that I can hardly see today how I managed to get through without a breakdown or being thrown out. I finally got them circled and round into the road again, but beyond the point at which they had been frightened, and then drove on to McDowell, not losing much time on the road either. My impression, of course, was that Indians were in the immediate vicinity.

The next morning, hearing someone at the post inquiring for Toorney, I told them he had come up the night before ahead of me and must now be up at the farm. As the party wanted to see him, he went up to the farm but found that Toorney had not returned and so reported to the commanding officer. I then told of my horses having been frightened the night before and suggested that all might not be right or that they might have met with an accident. The commanding officer sent a detail of men down the road, who in due course of time returned and reported Toorney and his partner dead and lying in the road at the point my horses had become frightened. I have no doubt, judging from the time they had passed the station ahead of me, that the Indians must have been rifling their bodies and outfit at the very time my horses became frightened.

In returning that day I saw where the Indians had lain in ambush. It was so near the road that they could reach them with their spears; both men and their horses had been killed in that way. I never could account for the Indians not having run the horses off, unless, their being so near the post, the Indians were afraid the troops would be better able to follow their trail. Possibly they had no need of supplies, as only a small portion of the horse meat had been carried away. Perhaps my coming up the road frightened them away. At any rate, I considered that a pretty close shave.

On another occasion I had business at Camp Verde, it being one of the posts we had the contract to supply with hay and grain. I had to visit the post, which was situated some fifty miles from Prescott. The first thirty-five miles of the route was considered comparatively safe, and we usually drove that by day and the balance by night.

Since the government had established a sawmill and kept a guard at that point, we would feed and remain there until after dark and then drive on into the post. On the occasion referred to, Lieutenant Rheem of one of the infantry regiments stationed at Prescott concluded to ride down with me. We left camp early in the morning and, after driving about ten miles, met a courier coming into Fort Whipple. He informed us that Indians that morning had run off all stock at Bower's Ranch in Agua Fria Valley, which was on our route, and that when he had left there the cowboys and herders were having a fight with them and he was going to the post for reinforcements.

My friend Rheem wanted to return, but as I had important business at the post, I concluded to drive on and did so, arriving at the sawmill without encountering the Indians. When we arrived at that point, we went into camp and fed and rested the animals. We there found the beef contractor and a number of men who were also en route to Verde. With them was a sergeant of the post who had been at Prescott on furlough. After talking the matter over as to our chances of getting through, I concluded to drive on that night, much to the displeasure of the balance of the party, who argued I should wait until morning and go in with them, that our party would then be sufficiently strong to get through all right. On the other hand, my argument was that we knew Indians were in our immediate vicinity and that they would know we were on the road and have time to get ahead of us and select an ambush. In short, I thought our chances were much better to push on that night. They, however, refused to go and I hitched up and pulled out with my friend Rheem who also much preferred to remain but, as he was in my company, he could not help but accompany me.

We had driven but a short distance before I became aware that Indians were in the immediate vicinity. My horses became very restless and excited and I knew they smelled the Indians, so I let them run full out. We got through all right, but one of the horses fell dead ten minutes after we reached the post.

Next forenoon, one of the beef contractor's party got into the post with word that the Indians had attacked their party as they were coming down what was known as the Hog Back. Several of their party had been killed and others wounded, and they were still fighting the Indians when he got away. The commanding officer sent out a company, "post haste," but the

Indians saw their dust and struck out for the mountains. Two men of the beef contractor's party and the sergeant had been killed; the contractor and several others were wounded. If I had remained with them at the sawmill that night, I should at any rate have been in the fight and probably killed or wounded. I have always thought it was my better judgment, or knowledge, of Indians that kept me out of that scrape.

At this time Indian depredations were almost a daily occurrence in the territory. Stagecoaches and freight trains were being attacked and emigrants and prospectors murdered almost daily.

On one occasion, I had been to Prescott by stage and intended remaining until the next week's stage for my return, but upon learning that passengers were booked for that trip, I concluded to return by the same stage I had come in on in preference to being overcrowded. On leaving Prescott I found I had a fellow passenger by the name of Adams, also bound for Phoenix. On our way down Adams told me he had made up his mind to leave the territory for California. He said he had family in San Francisco that he had not seen for several years. He had failed in business there, but someone in the liquor business there had given him credit to a stock of liquor which he had brought to Arizona and disposed, making about $10,000 on his venture. Having some unsettled accounts in Phoenix, he was going down there to settle up and then come back to Wickenburg to catch the next week's stage to California. He now had money enough to again start out in business in California and was going there to live with his family.

After getting to Phoenix, Adams collected his bills and started back for Wickenburg where he met the stage for California. There were ten passengers and the driver, making a total of eleven persons in the stage. They left Wickenburg in the early evening, all in good spirits—telling stories and singing songs—but had driven only about six miles when Indians lying in ambush fired a volley into the stage, killing nine out of the eleven and wounding one (a lady) of the remaining two. Adams was killed as was Professor Loring and a party sent out by the government.[5]

The lady and her friend were the only ones that escaped.

The lady, with whom I was personally acquainted, was shot through the arm. She was taken to Camp Date Creek, where her wound was treated by the medical officer.

In that one attack the red devils captured nearly $50,000. The lady had $17,000 in currency in a handbag which was captured as was also Adams's $10,000. Among the killed was an old jeweler from Prescott who also had quite a large sum with him. The culprits were undoubtedly Indians who were supposed to be on the reservation at the very time and were receiving the government rations.

At that time we had no banks in the territory, so large amounts of money had to be carried on the person or sent through the open mails. No money order post office existed then, and I know that I often sent thousands of dollars in currency from Prescott, which was our largest moneyed town, to Phoenix, where we required the ready currency in our daily business transactions. Our payment from the government was in quartermaster and commissary checks on the assistant treasurer in San Francisco. The Prescott merchants, who had remittances to make to San Francisco, were always anxious to get these checks and when our payday for supplies came round, they would cash our checks and, in that way, be kept supplied with currency.

I remember on one occasion sending $5,000 in one lot in open mail to Phoenix. I wrapped it in a bundle in newspapers, tying it well with twine. Putting on sufficient stamps to carry the bundle through, I threw it into the mailbox in the post office late at night and it arrived all right. In fact, I do not recollect of ever losing a single dollar that way.

Our careless and reckless way of doing business even followed to the States when I returned in 1874. At this late day I can hardly excuse myself for the extremely foolish thing I did on one occasion while in Harrisburg (this state). I had some $15,000 in currency received from the sale of some Indian vouchers in New York, which we had cashed at one of the banks. Instead of asking for an exchange or a draft, I got paid in currency, which I carried to Johnstown and from there back to Harrisburg, intending to use the money in Canton. When I arrived in Harrisburg, I concluded to remain there a day or so and, after being assigned a room, happened to think of my currency, which I had wrapped up in a newspaper package in my trunk. I took the package down to the office clerk of the hotel (The U.S. near the depot) and handed it to him for safekeeping.

After remaining in the city for a few days, I concluded to continue on my way to Canton, so I went to the office, paid my bill, and asked for my package. The clerk, being the day clerk and not the one to whom I had given it, inquired what it was. I told him it was a money package and also to whom I had given it. He looked through the safe and found it gone. About that time I began to feel a little nervous and began to want my package pretty bad. The clerk then called the proprietor, who soon made his appearance and wanted to know what the trouble was. I stated the case to him and then he, too, began a search of the safe. As the doors were open, I could see the package was gone and told him so, stating the amount it contained. He looked me over and, I imagine, began to wonder what kind of lunatic or imposter he had to deal with. After looking through the safe again and also the desk, he finally picked up a package and threw it on the desk and inquired if that was it. I recognized it at once, and tearing off the wrapping of newspaper, exposed my greenbacks. The proprietor took a good look at me, no doubt thinking that at some future time he might need to identify me as a thief or swindler of some kind.

In looking back over my checkered business career, I often think there are some excuses for my failures and foolish way of doing business. It must be remembered I was nothing but a boy when I entered the army and had had no education or business experience before that time. In the army, where I spent ten years, I had had no experience of that kind, other than that every man's word was good as his bond. If I wanted fifty or a hundred dollars and any officer had it, it was freely given, no note asked, and promptly paid. When I left the army and became associated with businessmen, I found that way of doing business would not do. A banker in Phoenix once told me that the way to do business was to do it as though you thought everybody was a damned rascal.

While I think of it, I must tell what became of my ten acres of land in Los Angeles that I got in exchange for my horse.

Within a year or so thereafter I met in Prescott a gentleman from Los Angeles who hunted me up, saying he understood I had some land in Los Angeles and wanted to know if I cared to sell it. As I did not then need any money I said no. "Well," said he, "I'll give you $4,000 for it or give me the refusal when you do want to sell."

When he said $4,000, I was surprised, but did not say so to him. As I had not placed any value on that land up to that time, I thought I had probably better look after my interest. Soon after, an acquaintance of mine was going to Los Angeles, and I requested him to look it up and see if there weren't some taxes to pay. Soon after, I had a letter from him enclosing the tax receipts that he had paid for me—that is, he paid the county and state taxes. I sent him the money he had advanced, supposing all was right, and so he paid the taxes for several years for me.

In 1875 someone sent me a marked copy of a city newspaper showing that my land had been advertised and sold for taxes. As I had the tax receipts, as I supposed, in my pocket, I paid but little attention to it, believing it was some mistake, but as a matter of fact it was correct. The county and state taxes had been paid but not the city taxes and, since I was a nonresident and my address was not known to the city collector, the land was advertised and sold. Under the California laws at that time, I had no chance of redemption and lost it.

I later went to the city to see if there might not be some chance of recovering it, but the best attorney in the city, Frank Ganahl, said there would be no use in spending good money in trying to get it back. Had I succeeded in keeping that land and letting it lie for, say, twenty years, it would have made me a rich man.

The horse I had traded for the land I bought again, giving Collingwood $375 for her. I kept her as long as she lived.

I have a few other land matters that I think I must relate. I became convinced in the early days that the fine agricultural land lying in the Salt Run Valley must certainly become very valuable and at once set about acquiring title to all I could, both by purchase and by right of presumption under the homestead and desert land acts, all of which the government allowed one to acquire under the several acts of Congress.

The first story concerns a tract of 160 acres lying due east of the mill quarter section that I bought off Jack Swilling, the old outlaw whom I have spoken of, and filed on under my homestead privilege. He had on it a large adobe house sixty by ninety feet, with halls and rooms innumerable, so I did not have to build, as the law required.

Before I had perfected my title, an old widow lady and her family of boys, some of them full grown, came into the valley and camped out under a tree for a while. One day she sent one of her boys up to the mill wanting to know what rent I would charge her for the use of a portion of the house for the winter. I told the boy I would not charge her anything, that she was welcome to the use of as much room as she wanted, and that I was glad to be able to accommodate her, so she and the family moved in.

Toward spring my herder, who was in the habit of pasturing our stock on the place, part being planted to alfalfa, reported one day that the "old woman" had ordered him off the property. I thought there must be some mistake and told him to take them back. When the same report was brought back, I got into the buggy and drove up to find what the trouble was.

When I told the old lady what the man had reported she replied, "Well, I'm a lonely old widow woman and have a big family. You've got plenty other land. I've been here and here I'm going to stay. Possession is nine points of the law and I want you to keep off the place."

"Well, now," I replied, "I gave you possession here without any charge. I want you distinctly to understand this is my place. I want you to get off and at once."

That afternoon, when I was in Phoenix I saw my lawyer and told him all the circumstances as to how she gotten possession. "Well," said he, "I guess we will get rid of her. Go back with a witness and order her off. If she don't go, I'll get her off."

Taking my miller up with me, I told her I had brought a witness with me and was ordering her off in his presence. "Well, Mr. Veil," said she, "I've prayed to the Lord and he has told me to stay here. In the presence of your witness, I'll tell you, I'm going to stay and I want you to get off my place."

To cut my story short, I had to go to law. When my case

came up in court and I had stated how she got possession, calling her son to verify how his mother had sent him up to get my permission, that ended the matter, although I had to pay the jury fee of $48 to get the verdict (the law in Arizona). I got judgment against her (and have it on record yet).

That's the way I got rid of her—well, not quite. I had an adjoining 160 acres which I had bought but upon which I had not as yet a valid title. She moved onto that and put up a little "shack" or cheap house. I let her alone there, for I knew she had the best of me. Along about seeding time, however, when I wanted to plant the place to wheat she sent her boy over again wanting to know how much I would give her to get off. I gave her $100 worth of provisions to get rid of her.

That was one case. I have another. After I had exhausted all my rights of entry, there remained a quarter section (160 acres) that I wanted to fill out my holdings. I then would have a strip one mile wide and three miles long, all level as a plow and as rich a soil as could be found in the world. As the quarter section was open and I was anxious to get hold of it, I persuaded a young Swede who was working for me to file on it. As an inducement, I gave him a team and all the farming implements, seed, and water he needed to put in a crop of wheat, of which I was to have one half for what I had furnished. He went to work, put in the crop, and wound up by selling me the wheat. As the half amounted to over a thousand dollars, he had done pretty well for the season's work. In the meantime, he had made his proof and paid his $1.25 per acre, the government price, and got title to the land.

About that time I was ready to buy and he to sell. He wanted $500 and I offered him $300, which he refused. When a day or two afterward, I found he was trying to sell it in town, I thought I had better close the deal or somebody else would buy it. I then raised my offer $100, got it, and had the deed made in my wife's name.

In that way the land lay for probably ten years. Once or twice I had it sown to grain, but no improvements were put on the place. One day my wife had been out calling on some neighbor, and when she came home wanted to know if I had sold her ranch. I said of course not. "Well," said she, "someone has a lot of lumber on it and has commenced building a house." I thought there must be some mistake but to make sure, got into the buggy with her (and the rifle) and we drove down. Sure enough, there was a big pile of lumber, and the foundation sills laid on posts.

It made me so angry that without taking a second thought I jumped out of the buggy and gathered up a few armfuls of straw, of which there was plenty close by, carried it to the lumber pile, and out with my matches and "touched it off." In that dry country there was no trouble in getting a fire started. I then sat down in the buggy and watched it burn up. Although no one was in sight, a few days afterward I was in town and the district attorney said a fellow had been trying to have me arrested for burning his lumber.

I did not know who the man was until some time afterward, when I met a pretty tough-looking customer on the street who inquired if I was going to pay him for his lumber. I told him I was glad to make his acquaintance, that I had been wanting to know the scoundrel who had put the lumber on my premises, and that when I wanted any more I would let him know. I wound up by telling him that I had a good old army rifle and plenty of ammunition and that if I ever caught him on the premises again, I would make a "sifter" out of him. That was the last claim he made for his lumber.

Probably within a year, in going to town one day, I found a nice wooden house, complete, about fourteen by sixteen, with clapboard roof, and locked door on the same place—put up during the night, probably, in sections. At any rate, there it was and I hadn't ordered it. So back to the ranch I went. I had the Mexican boy hitch up the hay wagon, taking some crowbars and picks along, and down to the farm we drove. We first pried off the roof and put it on the wagon, then the sides, and loaded them, too. Inside the house we found a carpenter's tool chest full of tools. We put that on, too. Then I sent the team home and I drove on into town to try and find out who had put up the house.

After some inquiry I found a carpenter who had done it. As he was a pretty nice kind of fellow, I was much surprised and went to find him and learn what he meant. He said he had made inquiry at the land office and it had reported the quarter section as "open," that is, not filed upon, and he thought he might as well have it as anyone. I assured him I had the title, not only from the man who had made the proof, but the government patent as well, and that if he would come up, I would show it to him so as to satisfy him. He finally said he didn't want any trouble, but supposed I would pay him for the lumber. As I was having a good bit of trouble about that ranch, I declined, and kept the tools, too. That was the last of him.

Since he had told me the land office was reporting the land "open," I went there to make inquiry and found it to be a fact. When land is filed on, it is the custom of the land office to note in the township plot, "Such and such quarter filed on," or some such proof made. By some error of the agent, or some clerk, that had been omitted in this case and that had caused me all the trouble on that quarter section.

Now, I guess, it would be in order to tell what became of that land. We held it until the latter 1880s by which time what was known as the California land boom took place and began to reach Arizona. Several tracts of land outside of Phoenix were bought and subdivided and a street railroad put in operation. The car track was extended out through the subdivision and in our direction and I began to think things were probably coming my way again (they had been going the other for some time). When I went home, seeing what was being done, I said to my wife that things began to look favorable to get something out of that piece of land and we must put a price on it. "Well, what do you think we can get for it?" said she. My price was $5,000. She said I must be getting crazy and laughed.

Several weeks afterward I found they had contracted for another 160 acres, leaving but one between ours and the one they were then at work on. When I went home, I told my wife again and wound up by saying we must raise the price to $10,000. She replied by saying she was afraid I had probably had a little something to drink that day, but I assured her things were all right again and coming our way.

Within a week of that time a couple of gentlemen came driving up to our land. As they drew up in front of our house, I recognized them as the "promoters" or "land boomers" who were laying out the new addition to the Phoenix street railway, and I knew something was "up."

After visiting a little while, one remarked, "Major, you've got a piece of land down here in front of the asylum. Do you want to sell it?"

"That belongs to my wife," said I. "Well, Mrs. Veil," said he, "do you want to sell it?" That was getting her into pretty close quarters, so she turned it by saying, "The major always tends to my business."

I told Sherman, the name of the spokesman, "We don't want to sell yet. We have a fixed price, probably higher than you care to pay, but by and by, if you need it, we can fix you out."

Inside of ten days they were back and ready to talk business. "Well, Mrs. Veil, what's your price on that land?"

"A hundred dollars an acre," was my prompt reply. When my wife heard that, I thought she would faint.

"Whew!" said Sherman. "Nothing small about you. Why that's sixteen thousand dollars."

"Yes," said I, "that is what I would figure it."

"Well, how about payments?"

"Oh, well," said I, "I guess we can arrange that—a quarter cash, balance your own time, one and two years. How would that strike you?"

"Well, are you going to town today?" I said yes we were thinking of driving in that evening.

"Well," said he, "come to the office."

After they had gone, my wife began to want to know what I meant by the price I had named and to wonder if it were possible they would think of paying such an enormous price for something that had not cost us $500. I assured her it was "coming all right," and when you had things coming your way the way to do was to press your luck. When we went to town, I went round to their office and their lawyer had already drawn up the agreements: $16,000 with $4,000 cash down, which we get then and there, the balance to run for one and two years, with interest on the deferred payment at eighteen percent per annum, no deed to be made until payment. That ended the day's doings.

At the end of the first six months the interest was paid. The next six months it was defaulted. In short, the boom had collapsed and no more was paid until the contract matured, when we brought suit. As the parties were responsible, they made proposition to pay $10,000 which we accepted and received in twenty-dollar gold pieces. All in all, the little land deal paid pretty well for the original investment.

I had another tract which I took up under the Desert Land Act, 160 acres, which cost $1.25 per acre to make proof. In the course of time, the territory decided to build a territorial insane asylum, and as Phoenix, or rather Maricopa County was the most centrally located county, the board of commissioners decided on our county. When the commission came down to select the site, I offered my quarter section and they accepted it for $3,200, paid for in territorial bonds.

My original hobby of acquiring the land was all right in one way. The soil in the valley is as fine as can be found anywhere, but in order to cultivate crops, it requires irrigation. With water a continual crop can be growing, but that was the great trouble. There was too much good land and not enough water. Water was abundant when we first commenced cultivating, but as soon as people found what the soil would do, emigrants began to flock in. As a result, more land was farmed than there was water to irrigate.

One party after another would come in and locate water canals above those we had at first taken out. As a result, those first located were cut out with the later ones taking the water. The first settlers then resorted to the courts to protect their priority water rights, and when I left the territory in 1891 we were all at law and still are today. The government now has taken hold of the matter and is building what is known as the Roosevelt water storage reservoir on Salt River, some sixty-five miles above Phoenix. When completed, it will obviate all the trouble, and water will be in sufficient quantity to irrigate all the lands of the valley the year round. Not only that, but the water will be utilized to furnish electrical power, both for electric lights and all kinds of motive power.

In certain seasons of the year water is in abundance, but it is just at the time when little is required. At the very time water is needed there is a scarcity. However, with the storage dam and big lake that it will form, an abundance can be preserved and on hand for the entire year. Then the Salt River Valley will bloom like a rose and all the land I once owned will be worth what I thought it would many years ago. A hundred dollars an acre will then be a small price; I expect to see lots of it sell for a thousand an acre.

Among my various business enterprises and operations while in the territory, I had another: raising hogs. While in the army at Camp Tubac, my first sergeant one day told me there was a Dutchman who had a few hogs he wanted to sell and suggested that it would be a good speculation for the company to buy them. We had sufficient surplus corn that the horses did not eat to fatten the hogs and, as we could buy them cheap, they would not only afford the men fresh pork and sausage but we could sell pork enough to pay for them in the course of time. Not only that, we could create what was called a "company fund" to buy extras for the company mess. The only trouble was that, at the time, we had no company fund on hand with which to buy the hogs.

After thinking the matter over, I told the sergeant I would advance the money and that he should go ahead and buy them, which he did, and the venture turned out all right. The company had fresh pork, sausage, head cheese, and such, yet sold enough to outside parties to make up what the original cost had been and accumulated a fund in the bargain. We still had a stock of hogs on hand when I left the post. The fact was, the feed cost us nothing, as we had an abundance of extra feed left from the horses, and the hogs still kept increasing as fast as we were butchering them.

While I was at the mill in 1874, a rancher—a Dutchman, too—with a couple of hundred hogs and nothing to feed them came to me one day and offered to sell them cheap, so I bought them. Since we had an abundance of mill feed on hand and they appeared to do so well, I thought I might as well go into the hog business all the way, so I bought up all the hogs in the valley at that time, about six hundred head, and started fattening hogs. When my partner came home he was thunderstruck. "What in the world are you going to do with all those hogs?" he asked. "Why," said I, "fatten and butcher them, of course. Pork and lard is worth twenty-five cents per pound and readily sold at that."

We had as fine a lot of hogs to butcher and case as ever I saw, but it made a lot of work and expense before the job was finished, yet it was a money maker. I remember we sold the government a couple of hundred barrels, at fifty dollars per barrel, and they were glad to get it, for our pork was fresh and far superior to what they had shipped in from California, but this is only introductory to my real hog story.

Along in the latter 1880s, when I had plenty of land and not much of anything else, I was living up on the big ranch I had bought off Jack Swilling, which afterward was known as Major Veil's Hog Ranch, when I got to studying up some plan to "raise the wind" again. Everything had gone wrong from some reason or other. I was at my "wits' end" to know what to get at and happened to think of the hog business that I had been in before. The more I thought of it, the better it appeared. I had plenty of alfalfa, which hogs thrive and get fat on. I had, besides, a big stock of wheat that wasn't worth the threshing at the time, supply and demand making the price. Whenever we had any more wheat or barley, which were the grain crops, than were required for home consumption, the surplus was absolutely of no value and that was the condition that year. I got to talking to my wife about the matter and she, too, fell in with the idea. "But how will you get the money to buy the hogs?" was her query. "Oh, well," I said, "you sign a note with me in the morning, and I'll raise the money."

The next morning I started to town and going down I passed by a rancher who had twenty-seven big, black sows all coming in shortly. I struck a bargain with him for the lot, to be delivered at once, and then went on to town to raise the money.

As I was getting home, I passed the rancher with the sows on their way up, where in due course they arrived. I told him to drive them into what we called the corral, that is, the stockyard, in which I had my big stack of unthreshed wheat. As I had a large pond or artificial lake of water adjoining, I thought that it, with the wheat and water and shade trees growing around, would make a fine place for my "piggies," and so it did.

The old sows took to the wheat stack at once and, after they had a feed and drink and wallowed in the pond, they appeared perfectly satisfied and at home. The rancher assured me I need not worry myself about their leaving. He knew and he was right. I paid him and everybody appeared satisfied, hogs and all.

In a short time thereafter, in going to look at my hogs, I discovered one of the sows had pigs—ten of the nicest, plump, little all-black piggies. I at once began to calculate the value of my increase. In a short time they all had pigs. Averaging ten to the sow, I had 270 pigs for a starter. As I had paid $10 per head for the sows, I estimated my pigs when grown would be worth the same, so I thought I was on the right road again and that pigs would bring me out.

Almost before I was aware of it, my sows came in with another batch of pigs, averaging about the same number. Not only that, but also my little sow pigs began to get pigs. By that time, as they were all black, the ranch began to get black with hogs and pigs.

In the meantime, they were getting away with my wheat stack and alfalfa. After they had cleaned up one alfalfa field, they cleaned up another. By that time the wheat stack was gone and the hogs began to get hungry. I had taken the precaution to put what we call hog-tight barbed wire fencing around my alfalfa patches to confine them to that, but a hungry old sow is hard to confine. The first thing I was aware of, an old sow had found a way into an adjoining barley field and about the next thing I knew the whole batch was harvesting the barley.

When that was "cleaned up," they took to the next field, which was wheat, and that went the same way. After they had cleaned up and harvested all the grain (and the piglets were still coming), I began to think it was about time to begin selling some of my stock, but nobody wanted to buy.

I had an orchard and vineyard loaded with fruit, enclosed I supposed with a hog-tight fence, but one day an old sow found a way in. The others no sooner saw her than all began to march around the fence, looking for the place she got in. They found it and almost as quick as I can tell it, the orchard was black with hogs. The first thing they did was to follow up each row of grapevines—the grapes were just about ripening—and clean up all the grapes.

Then they took to the peach trees. First they ate all they could reach. Then an old sow would stand up on her hind feet, her forefeet up in the branches, reaching for all she could get while her pigs ate the peaches off the limbs she would be bending down with her weight.

I had six dogs, but the infernal hogs had gotten so hungry and saucy that, instead of the dogs running off the hogs, the hogs ran off the dogs. In fact, the hogs had got them so demoralized that the dogs wouldn't leave the house.

My wife had a hobby of raising chickens, ducks, and turkeys, and she had little coops for the young chicks. The first thing we knew, the old sows were eating them as fast as they came out of the coop. They got so smart they would stand around the corner of the coop and wait. As a chick made its appearance, the hog would make one gulp and down went the chick.

After the hogs had eaten everything I had on my ranch, they struck out for my neighbors'. The first thing I was aware of, one of my neighbor's boys would be over to say there were a lot of my hogs over in their field and that "Dad" wanted me to come and get them, so I would send a boy or man over to drive them home.

That boy had hardly gone before another would come from the other side of my ranch saying, "Dad says there are a lot of your hogs over in our sorghum and if you don't come and get them, he'll shoot them."

"All right," said I to that one, "tell him to shoot," as the hogs by that time were getting me demoralized (as well as the dogs). I made up my mind that as they had eaten up everything I had (and were still coming), I must get rid of them and then sell them to the butchers, but everybody else had gotten hogs by that time, the market was supplied, and there was no demand.

Judge Hayden had a mill up at Tempe, some six miles above me; I thought I might persuade him to buy some hogs. I met him about that time and proposed to sell him my stock. "Why," said he, "you've got a pretty big stock. What do you ask for them?"

"Make your own price," said I, "only I want to sell the lot."

"Well," said he, "I'll give you a dollar a head."

"All right," was my answer, "come and get them." I think if he had said fifty cents apiece I would have taken it.

Next day he sent down a lot of men and boys and they

commenced rounding and gathering them up. The judge wanted to know how many there were or how we could count them. As I had no place big enough to run them into, I told him to drive them home, where he had several big yards, and he could count them there and I would take his word for it. He was to pay the money to a Mr. Goldman in Phoenix, from whom I had borrowed the money to buy them.

Several days afterward I was in town and Goldman inquired if I had sold my hogs, saying Judge Hayden had left $1,350 for my account, so I suppose he had that many hogs. I don't know that I ever was as much relieved as I was when I saw the band, about a mile in length and all black, winding its way up the road and away from Major Veil's Hog Ranch.

In the lot were two litters of seventeen that had, as is often the case, taken to roaming or associating by themselves. After they had got about a mile from home, they suddenly made up their mind to stay with me and started back for home. The judge said, "Let them go, we've got enough."

Several days afterward, when I saw him and informed him of the fact, he said he had enough and more, too. It took so much to feed those hogs he didn't know what to do. At any rate he wouldn't have the balance.

I had by that time fully made up my mind to go out of the hog business and meeting a friend of mine, I said, "Mr. Shaw, I've got a few hogs left. Don't you want them?" When he asked the price, I told him I would make him a present of them. He said that was very kind and would send his boys up for them the next day, and so he did, but the hogs had made up their mind that they had been born and raised there and there they would remain. After running themselves almost to death, the boys had to give up the job and let them stay.

Next day Mr. Shaw came up himself with the boys, dogs, and other help, but after they had run themselves down, they too gave up the job, so I had seventeen hogs left in my hands and they were annoying me, too. They got so wild, they would keep under cover during the day and only come out at night, when they damaged my fields.

About that time some Mexicans who had been in my employ came to the ranch. Knowing that I was going out of the hog business, they wanted to know what I would charge them for a hog. I told them to go out and help themselves to whatever they wanted, which pleased them very much. They thanked me very kindly in Spanish, telling me I was a very good *patrón*, and then started off to get their hog. They had the same experience that Shaw had had, however. Finally one of them came to the house and said the hogs were very wild. Wouldn't I shoot one for them? Yes, I said, and told them to drive them out from cover. Meanwhile, I picked up my army rifle and a handful of cartridges and started down for the point I knew they would break from. While the Mexicans were beating down along the corral where the hogs were under cover, I took my station.

I had barely gotten there when I saw one come out of the brush, stop a moment on seeing me, and then start to run across the fields toward other cover. As he got about opposite me, I let drive and knocked him over like a jack rabbit. I hardly had time to put in a cartridge when another put in an appearance, and went through the same performance. As he got about opposite me, down he went, like his predecessor.

In that way the band ran across the field and, as they did, I knocked down five, all the cartridges I had. The Mexicans, who now had plenty of fresh pork, were delighted, and I was rid of five anyway. That about ended the hog business, but there is a little sequel to the story that I now must tell.

About that time, a branch railroad was being built from Phoenix to the Southern Pacific Railroad. Our being off the main line of the road, it did not benefit the town much, so the people of the town and county petitioned the territorial legislature for permission to give $200,000 in county bonds running for twenty years and bearing ten percent interest as a bonus to anyone who would build a branch road to intersect with the main line. It wasn't long until a party (the Southern Pacific Railroad Company) accepted the proposition and went to work on the road.

The line of the road ran along my property line for one and a half miles. Everybody was granting or giving the right-of-way free of cost, but when they came to me—finding they wanted to run on my side of the line, taking sixty-six feet off me, and nothing off my adjoining neighbors—I refused to grant the way.

I said if they wanted me to give half, or thirty-three feet, I would do so, but if they wanted me to give all, I wanted $100 an acre for whatever land they took. They refused to do so and went to court to have appraisers appointed, which I knew they could do.

The appraisers awarded me $650, which I agreed to accept, but before this was paid, the graders, a large gang of men and teams, probably a hundred all told, reached my lines. I had notified them not to come on my land without my permission, but as soon as the award was made, the man in charge of the teams and men started to come onto my land and go to work grading. He, in fact, had gotten there before I saw them.

As soon as I did, I started for the gang with a rifle to enforce my orders, if necessary. As the dogs generally followed me wherever I went—the hogs were now off the ranch and it was safe for them to leave the house again—they followed along, six all told.

As it happened the Mexicans for whom I had shot the hogs were employed with that railroad gang. Knowing there had been some dispute between the railroad company and me, and seeing me with the gun and the dogs, and probably thinking I might use the gun, they got demoralized. The Mexicans began shouting, "Run, boys, run, he shoots like hell. He shot five hogs, poof, poof, poof." They jumped onto the scraper mule teams and started to run, which demoralized the whole gang, and so I cleared the ground.

The fact is, I know, as the old lady on the ranch told me, that "possession is nine points in the law." I was determined to—and did—hold the ground until the $650 was paid into court. If I had allowed them to go ahead, I would probably be lawing them yet, but I held them to the strict letter of the law and made them settle.

As a matter of fact, they did try to have me arrested, but when the district attorney inquired what I had done—had I shot anyone or threatened to shoot anyone?—all they could say was that I came out with the gun and dogs and their men were afraid to come onto the ground for fear that I might shoot.

The district attorney said he told the superintendent of the road that there was no use fooling with me. They couldn't "bamboozle" or "bulldoze" me, so they might as well go according to the letter of the law, which was what I was holding them to.

Well now, my hog story has grown rather long, and I must think of something else to write of. I think it will be dogs because I had a good many while I was in the territory and the post. One I call to mind was a big greyhound General Crittenden gave me when he left the territory. Not long after, I got another of the same breed. They made a fine hunting team.

Our greatest amusement was hunting "coyotes," a small species of prairie wolf that abounded out there. Our usual custom was to go out on horseback and when we "jumped" a coyote we would take after him full speed. The dogs were fast and could soon overtake the wolf. As they did so, one would put on a "full head of steam" and run up and knock him over. Before he could get up, the other would have him by the throat. The other would then "tackle" him in the small of the back and, in that way, they would worry him to death. We usually saved the "brushes" (tails) of the wolf to keep tally of the number we had caught.

One day I was out alone when we jumped an extraordinarily large one. They put after him as usual, I following. It wasn't long before they had him down and were worrying him in the usual way when I got up, but he was a plucky and tough old wolf. Although one had him by the throat and the other in the small of the back, I could see the wolf's eyes flashing and he wasn't near dead. After harassing him in that way for some time, one of the dogs let go his hold and started to trot off, thinking I suppose that the wolf was done for, but as he left I could see the wolf following him with his eyes. As soon as the dog had got far enough to give him a chance, he made a spring for the other dog. If I hadn't been there, the coyote would have whipped the remaining dog, but I had dismounted and between kicking him whenever I got a chance and finally getting him so far exhausted that I got a chance to use my revolver, I got in a shot and saved his brush. It was some time before I could get a chance to get in a shot without hitting the dog.

We caught jack rabbits in about the same way, only when the dogs caught up with one of those, instead of catching him on the ground, the first dog would run up and catch and throw him up in the air with his nose and the other would catch him before he would light. These two were about the only dogs I had while in the army, but afterward I had a lot of others.

While living up at Prescott, I had another greyhound, which used to follow me wherever I went. Among the other places I used to go at that time was to see a girl and, of course, the dog went, too. In fact, he got so well acquainted with my girl that when he met her on the street, as he sometimes did, he would not hesitate to run up to her, jump up, put his forefeet on her shoulders, and try and kiss her. He evidently thought as much of my girl as I did, and the boys used to laugh and say it was easy to see whose girl she was.

Down at Phoenix one day a fellow came along by the mill wanting to sell me a big brindle English bulldog. He said he was going to California and couldn't take the dog along and would take a sack of flour for him, that he needed the flour more than the dog, and that he was an elegant watchdog, etc. In order to get rid of the man, I finally said, "All right, tie him up there and take your flour."

For a day or two none of us dared go near him as he was such a savage-looking animal. We fed him by throwing his food to him, and watered him by putting the water in a pan and then pushing the pan up to the dog so he could reach it.

I finally mustered up courage and got within reach of him. As he made no belligerent demonstration, I finally let him loose. From that time on he took to me. Wherever I went, he went, too, and he was what the man recommended him to be, one of the finest watchdogs I ever had.

Among other things, he took to retrieving when I went duck shooting. No matter where I might shoot a duck he would always land him. Sometimes I would knock down half a dozen, yet he always got them all. He would even dive after a wounded duck. I have stood on the bank and seen the dog go after the duck under water. He would invariably get him and bring him to shore. But the old dog finally took sick and died.

On the ranch we were bothered with the wolves and lynx which were after poultry and young animals. We were in the habit of putting out poison on their runways and getting them in that way. When I did so, I usually shut the dogs up in the evening. Then, tucking my strychnine in little particles of fresh meat, I would place them on their trails by putting a piece of poisoned meat on a little stake and sticking that in the ground, keeping tally of how many pieces I had planted. The next morning before the dogs were let out, I would go out on my trail and any particles that had not been taken were removed.

One evening I was putting out a lot of it, having first shut up the dogs, but just as I was about to place my last poison, my best dog made his appearance. He had followed my trail and taken up every particle I had placed. That was the end of him. I never was so sorry for a dumb animal in my life.

Shortly before this we had considerable of a flood in the river and some of the headgates in the irrigating canal had been washed out. As I was down on the bank of the canal that passed through my place, I found that a long plank used in one of the gates had floated down and was resting partly on the bank and partly in the water. Thinking I would save the plank, as lumber was valuable, I took hold of one end of the plank and turned it on edge with a view of dragging it out farther to keep it from floating off. As I did so, I uncovered a very large rattlesnake coiled up under the plank. The moment the dog saw the snake—without an instant's hesitation—he made a dive for the snake, caught it, dove into the canal and under water, and then came out on the opposite side, still holding and shaking and killing the snake. That was animal instinct.

Mr. Kaly, a banker in Phoenix and a friend of mine, wanted a watchdog. He sent to San Francisco and had one sent down by express. He was a cross between a St. Bernard and Newfoundland, a great big black fellow that looked like a big bear, but Kaly found he was too savage for him in town. One day he wanted to know if I didn't want "old Maje," as he called him, saying he would make a fine ranch dog for me. By the time I got home I found Mrs. Kaly had driven up and brought Maje along.

The dog did not appear to know at first if he had better let me stop in or not, but I finally made friends with him and like all the others, wherever I went, Maje went, too. Among the places he followed me at first was to the corral where I milked a cow we kept for the family milk. I used to attend to her morning and evening. She had a calf tied up in the corral and was always at hand at the bars in the morning to be let in and milked.

This particular morning, I started out to milk the cow and Maje followed along in my wake. As soon as I let down the bars, the cow came in and, seeing old Maje, started for him on the jump. Maje undertook to stand his ground, but the next thing he knew he was up in the air about twenty-five feet, the old cow having caught him with her horns and tossed him up for at least that distance. He landed on his back with a thud and a grunt. Acting very "sheepish," he then started for the house, not on a run but a deliberate walk, looking back occasionally to see if the old cow was coming. That was the last time old Maje followed me to milk the cow. After that he would sit on the bank outside the corral and watch.

Among Maje's other traits, he considered it his duty to whip every strange dog that came on the ranch and he could do it, too. The only way I could break his hold once he got one was to get a stick in his big collar and then turn and twist it until I choked off his wind.

Strangers also learned to stay away from him. One day after going to town, we were coming up the lane alongside a lot of cottonwoods that I had planted and had grown to good-size trees, when we noticed old Maje sitting under one and looking up into it. I remarked Maje had "something up a tree." As we drove up, I found he had a big old Indian up there and was holding him, too. The Indian began to make "sign language" mighty fast. I called off Maje and the Indian appeared mighty glad to get away. I don't think he ever bothered me after that.

Another time I came home and my wife said the stock herder had not come in to dinner. I looked out to see Maje down in one of the fields under a tree, with the Mexican in it, holding him there.

During the last few years I was in Arizona I had five dogs, four large ones and one small one. They all had certain places to sleep and watch during the night. Old Maje's place was at the post door, another at the rear, one at each side, and the little one anywhere and everywhere. He was always the first to give the alarm if a wolf or lynx came round, and the moment he gave his little "ki yi" all were up and on the jump.

After I had gotten up in the morning, which was always early, the dogs would start out on a hunt (on their own hook).

The old shepherd was the leader, Maje next. After they had started, the shepherd would look back and see that all were following. If anyone was missing, she would give a "yelp" and the missing one would soon make his appearance. Sometimes they would be gone until noon, depending on what luck they would have. They often returned with from one to as many as three big jack rabbits of a morning's hunt.

I don't know if they brought them in for us or not, but I often think it was for me to roast or broil the rabbits for them. As I did, I found they liked broiled jack rabbit much better than raw. It amused me to see them stand around and watch me skin the rabbits and then put them on the coals to cook. As they were about done they would begin to "smack their lips" and "yow yow." After the rabbits were broiled I would portion them out in equal parts, the dogs standing by, but they would never attempt to take any until I said so.

I was often amused at their sagacity in hunting rabbits, for they appeared to have an understanding, or plan, of hunting. When they started out across a field, they would be two or three abreast with an interval of a couple of rods between them. As soon as one or the other would jump a rabbit, one of the dogs would put after him as hard as he could go, while the others would start off to the right and left, evidently knowing that the rabbit would run, as is their custom, either to the right or left. As soon as he did, the one on that angle would take up the chase and be the pursuer. In that way they would soon tire out the game and capture it. If any of the boys read this far I think they will now have had enough of dog stories and I will close the subject.

While we were out on a scout in southeastern Arizona, the boys ran down a nice little white-tail fawn (deer) and carried it several hundred miles horseback. When we got back to camp, they gave it to me and it followed me almost everywhere I went. It was always on hand at meal times and ate and drank almost everything or anything we offered it. I used to give it roast beef with mustard, which it appeared to relish very much. It would drink coffee and tea and was particularly fond of tobacco. At meal time it was always at my elbow waiting. If I wasn't prompt enough in giving it something, it would nudge my elbow and look up into my face with its beautiful big eyes. If I didn't pay attention to the first notice, it would give me a good big one that I had to take notice of.

At the time I had a set of three rooms for quarters, the first for a sleeping room, the next for a dining room. In order to get into the dining room, one had to go through my sleeping room and the kitchen in the adjoining one. For some reason the deer took a notion to sleep in the dining room. I would run it out time and time again, when it would wait and watch to see if I had gone to bed. As soon as I had, it would dodge into my room and on into the dining room, where it would remain until morning.

In the doorway between my room and the dining room I had a big bearskin robe, the skin of the big bear I had killed coming down the Aravaipa Canyon. Every morning as the deer would start out, it would get on the bearskin and stop to drop his "pills," and all the boots and shoes I could throw at him would have no effect. He just waited until he was ready, then cocked up his white tail and out the door he went. That would be the last of him until breakfast, when he was promptly on hand.

He took great pride in following me around on Sunday morning inspection. As I would go up and down the company front examining and inspecting the men, the deer would follow, evidently eyeing and inspecting each man as I did. The men would often have all they could do to keep from laughing at his peculiar antics. As soon as the inspection was over he would trot on ahead to my quarters and get in the shade and wait for me to get there.

At the mill ranch I got hold of another deer that also became a great pet, but she was rather a nuisance in nipping all the fresh buds and shoots on any foliage we had growing. After growing up she disappeared and was gone for a week or ten days, when she again returned, the most forlorn and dilapidated deer you ever saw, almost starved, full of cactus thorns, and scarred up in every way. By and by she got filled out again and began to look herself. In due course of time she began to show she was going to have a fawn of her own, but about that time some neighbor's vicious dogs ran her into the canal and caught and killed her, and that was the last of that pet.

Now I think I ought to quit. These reminiscences are getting pretty "long-drawn out" and I wonder if anybody will ever read them. I have one other little story that I think I shall record. The subject is a remarkable one and that's my "old pipe."

When I was a "chunk of a boy" about twelve or fourteen years old, I had a hankering desire to try to smoke (like most boys). One day I got hold of a couple of my dad's "stogies," of which he had a box, and meeting Andy Kunkle I proposed, "Let's have a smoke."

"But," said he, "where can we get the cigars?"

"Oh, I've got them, come on!" So we went down to the creek, just about the present bridge crossing Little Paint Creek in the village, and there we got a shady place, put our feet in the creek, and lit up and got our smoke going. It was the first time I had tried it.

It went first rate for a little while and we made a big smoke, but I soon began to have some very peculiar feeling, although I didn't say anything to Andy. But this feeling kept growing worse and worse until I finally said, "Andy, I'm not feeling well." About that time, Andy felt the same way and before much longer we were two as sick boys as you ever saw. I lost dinner and breakfast, too, and so did Andy. We finally managed to get under the bridge and there we lay—for how long I never knew—but I thought I was going to die sure. Well, that cured me of wanting to smoke.

It was only in the latter years of the war that I undertook to do so again and that was "medicinally." I had several snags in my teeth that bothered me. Every time I took a little cold, the snags would ulcerate and cause me trouble, so much so that often I could not sleep.

When we were on the march to join General Grant before Petersburg, just before the close of the war, we had to camp in a house on the line of our march, our wagon being stuck in the mud, and as we had been exposed to the rain and cold, I had a bad time with my snags. We were all lying around on the floor in a big room, everybody asleep but me. I had such a jaw ache that I couldn't sleep and was annoying everybody else in the room. The doctor finally said, "Veil, why don't you smoke a little; it might help you." As there was some tobacco and some clay pipes on the mantel in our room, I got up and filled one and got it going and as a matter of fact, it did relieve the pain. It allowed me to get some sleep, and it did not make me sick as my first trial had.

Next morning my jaw was still growling a little, so I took another smoke. The result was it relieved me for good and I never had any trouble with my snags after that, I presume from the fact that I have kept smoking ever since. Now I'll get back to the pipe.

When I arrived in San Francisco, St. Patrick's Day 1866, I saw some nice Meerschaum pipes in a show window and went in and bought one, paying ten dollars for it. The bowl was rather a high one and I afterward cut it down. I smoked that pipe out and through Arizona and on all occasions—on the march, in camp, and on scouts. Then, when out hunting near Camp Lowell once, I lost it, but not long after saw a quartermaster employee smoking my pipe. On inquiring where he got it, he said he had bought it off a Mexican who had bought it off an Indian. "Well," said I, "that's my pipe." As he had given the Mexican two dollars for it, I gave him two dollars and got my pipe again.

After that we were out on a big scout in the Apache Mountains and one day while on the trail, I lost my pipe again. That night after we had gone into camp, one of the Mexican packers came in and handed me my pipe, saying he had found it on the trail, so I had it back again.

When I came home on a visit in 1869, my pipe with me of course, my father took a fancy to it, so I gave it to him and bought another. Next time I came home, I had one that had a silver top or cover that took Dad's eye and he proposed to change, so I got my first pipe back again and he got my new one. I then went back to Arizona, pipe along, of course.

The next time I lost it was while driving across country from Phoenix to Florence, sixty-five miles. We were making a night drive in the buggy and I had a habit, after having a smoke, of laying my pipe on the back of the buggy seat until I wanted it again. After riding along some distance, I reached for my pipe and found it gone. It had dropped out some way.

During the night I met a couple of Mexicans on horseback going to Phoenix. I told them of my loss and, further, in case they found it, to leave it at my place and tell the lady to give them five dollars. About the first thing my wife said, or wanted to know, when I came home was if I had sent two Mexicans for five dollars. At any rate, she said, they had come with the pipe and demanded five dollars. Since they had my pipe, she supposed that was a sign that I wanted them to have the money, so she gave it to them.

My partner and I were going duck shooting one morning on horseback and, as we got near the river, we saw a big flock of geese come sailing up the river looking for a place to light. We halted and waited until they did so. As we knew the lay of the land, we tied our horses and crept up to the bank overlooking the point and blazed away. He got two; I killed one and wounded another. The wounded one at once put for the brush to get cover and I went after him, wading the river and running him down.

After securing our geese and trying them on our horses, I thought, as we had made a pretty good start, it was time to "take a smoke" and reached for my pipe, but it was gone. I knew I had it just before we saw the geese, so I took my trails up to the point where I had caught my wounded goose, but no pipe was there. I then thought I might have lost it in crossing the river. As I knew it would float, I thought there might be a chance of finding it at a headgate in an irrigating canal, probably a half mile below, and rode down to the gate. Sure enough, there was my pipe bobbing up and down against the gate.

Next time I lost the old pipe was in a hay field on what was known as Major Veil's Hog Ranch. I had a couple of men running mowing machines and one was having trouble with his, so I went down to determine the trouble. After looking it over and making a couple of changes, I got in the seat and started up to see how it would operate. After cutting a round and finding out it worked all right, I put the man aboard and started to take a smoke, but my pipe was gone. I knew I had had it when I was "monkeying" with the machine, so I followed around the whole piece of land, kicking over the cut grass, but couldn't find it. I then thought that in raking up we might do so and had all the hay men on the lookout for it, but without success.

I now thought my pipe was gone for good, but next year, a tramp came along wanting work while we were haying, so I sent him down to help the boys "cock up" the hay. When he came in at noon he handed me the bowl of my old pipe, remarking that it must have been a "pretty good pipe some day." The stem had rotted out of it. Nothing was left but the bowl. Now that's my pipe story. If anyone can beat that, go ahead.

I know this stuff is not worth writing, much less reading, but it helps kill time and that's what I have been doing for the last six weeks, so I'll quit—for the time being anyway.

I had intended to close my reminiscences, but have thought of a few more incidents that I must record. One day while I was engaged in milling, an old Dutchman with his bundle of blankets on his back came to where I was sitting in front of the office, and wanted to know if I was the boss. I told him I was. "Well," said he, "have you got any work? I'm busted and hungry and wish you would give me a job." I did not need any more help at that time, but thought I would give him a meal anyway. As it wasn't quite dinner time yet, I told him he might go over to the woodpile and exercise himself a little until the bell rang. He went over without any remarks and took hold with a will. By and by the bell rang, and the mill boys filed over to dinner. The Dutchman had his eye on what was going on and fell in with the lot. After I had my dinner, I noticed the Dutchman at the woodpile again, chopping wood like a good fellow, and I supposed he wanted to make good for his dinner; but he kept to working and along toward evening I called him over to where I was and asked him what he could do.

"Oh," said he, "I can do anything, but I'm a butcher *und* want work."

"Well," said I, "we butcher a sheep about every other day. When the boy comes in this evening with the flock, you can butcher one."

Soon after, the boy brought the sheep in, and Jake (that was his name) struck for the corral. That evening I noticed we had as fine a slaughtered sheep as you could find in a city market, all "scarred" or "scored" as the fancy butchers do to decorate their mutton. I said to myself I must try and find something for Jake to do—and did. He remained with me a long time and was a very useful man about the place.

He could turn his hand to anything and was very willing to

do so, but he evidently was not very bright. We had sent to California for some grapevines and had a little vineyard. The grapes were just beginning to turn and ripen, when the little linnets (a small bird we had there, something like our English sparrows) took to eating the grapes as fast as they turned. I kept shooting and shooting, trying to kill them or drive them away, but it appeared as though the more I shot the thicker the linnets got, and they were getting all the grapes.

When in Phoenix one day and telling someone about my problem, he said, "Why don't you poison them? Take a melon, cut it in half, and sprinkle some strychnine over it. Then drive a couple of posts in the vineyard and put the pieces of the poisoned watermelon on them. The birds will all go for that."

It struck me as a good idea, so as soon as I went home I got a big melon, cut it in half, put poison on as directed, and planted the pieces in the vineyard. I then stepped to one side and waited to see what the birds would do. They at once took to the melon in preference to the grapes. They would peck and take a few bits, then apparently think there was something wrong, but by and by they would take another few mouthfuls. By the time they had made up their minds something was wrong and start to fly away, they more than likely fell before they had gone very far. In this way I was making much better headway in getting rid of the birds than by shooting them, when I happened to think some of the mill hands might be out that way and take a cut of the poisoned watermelon, so I went to the mill and notified all the men of what I had done.

During the afternoon, I made several trips to see how my birds and grapes were getting along. When I reached the last one, I saw my man Jake taking a slice off with a big butcher knife just as I came in view.

"Drop it, Jake, drop it!" I cried. "You didn't eat any, did you?"

"No," said he. "Why?"

"That's poisoned," said I. "Didn't I tell you? You're sure you didn't eat any?" I questioned him further, but he persisted that he had not and walked off.

A little while after, my wife and partner and I were sitting in the hallway, when in walked Jake, about the most forlorn-looking picture of a man I ever saw. As he neared us he said, "Well, Major, I dink I got to die. Oh!" Then down he went to the floor, every muscle apparently quivering, just as a person or animal does who has taken strychnine.

My impression, of course, was that he had gotten a dose of the bird poison. My first thought was of oil, and he took a bottle. Then my wife came up with a dipper of black coffee and the cook with a big spoonful of lard, all of which Jake manfully took. Meanwhile, a man had jumped on a horse, bareback, and raced for the doctor, whom he luckily found at home.

While waiting for the doctor, we had carried Jake, every muscle quivering and jerking, into a big room and laid him down to die, as I supposed. By and by the doctor came, and I met him at the door. "Well, Major," said he, "what's the matter?"

"Well," said I, explaining the circumstances, "I suppose I've poisoned a man." By that time the doctor had reached Jake, whom he looked at a moment and then gave him a slight kick, telling him to get up and get out. Jake did as he was ordered, and that was all there was to it. The fact was just this: After thinking the matter over, Jake evidently thought that he probably had eaten some, and I believe, if left alone absolutely, he would have died from fright. Thereafter, if Jake got a little "frisky" with the boys, all they had to say was "poison" and he would shut up.

One day a seedy, genteel-looking fellow came up and introduced himself as a minister, saying he was tired and hungry and wondering if he could get a "bite to eat." I said, "Certainly, sit down and rest. It's pretty near dinner time and I'll fix you out." When the bell rang and the mill men came over, I took him into the dining room and gave him a seat, to which he had no sooner stuck than he commenced reaching with both hands for anything and everything in sight until he had his plate loaded. Then you should have seen him shovel in the food. The men, in fact, stopped to watch him at it. He kept both hands going until the plate was emptied, when he filled another, but finally got enough.

After he quit, he came out to where I was and said, "My friend, I'm very tired. Would you have any objection to my taking a little rest?" We had a spare room with a nice cot in it, so

I took him to that and told him to rest himself. That was the last I saw of the preacher until the supper bell rang. Then he promptly made his appearance, rubbing his hands and remarking that he guessed he'd have a little supper, too, and in he went. I said nothing. The China cook, though, after dinner said to me, "Him John belly hungry. Him John belly full." (Everybody is a John with a Chinaman.) What he meant to say was that the man was very hungry and thought he was now well filled up. I think the preacher would have held his own with the old Indian chief who ate the ten days' ration at Camp Grant.

After supper, without saying anything to anyone, he went back to his cot and I did not see him again until the breakfast bell rang. Then he was promptly on hand again; after breakfast, he went back to the cot.

By that time, I had made up my mind he had had enough of my good grub and that he should change his boarding house, but I said nothing until the bell rang for dinner, when I made it my business to be on hand at the dining room door. As he came out, smilingly rubbing his hands and remarking that he guessed he'd have some dinner, I interrupted him with the remark that I guessed he'd get it somewhere else. Never in all my life did I see the expression of keen and pleasant expectation expressed on one's face so suddenly change to one of sad disappointment. Without a word of good-bye or thanks, he took up his hat and that was the last I saw of my preacher fake. I heard afterward that he had been down below town where they had been holding a camp meeting and tried to palm himself off for a preacher, but that they had run him off.

I had been over to Globe City one day. In returning I came across the Pinal Mountains on horseback as far as the King Mine, as that was a short cut, but it could not be made by wagon or buggy. From the King Mine, there was a buckboard running that I had expected to ride home. At the mine, however, I ran across a preacher from Phoenix who was apparently glad to see me and inquired how I came to be there. I told him the circumstances and, further, that I was going home in the morning by the buckboard. "Oh," said he, "ride with me. I've got a good two-horse rig, and will be proud to have you ride with me."

The sisters had put up lots of provisions for him and he

insisted on my accepting his offer, so I did. I wanted to know if there wasn't something I could get in the way of food for the road, but he said no, we had plenty, although I might get a can or two of "blackberries." So I went over to the store and bought a couple of cans for the preacher.

Next morning he was promptly on hand with his rig, and he had a real good one, so off we started. The distance was sixty-five miles, but for about fifty, there was no water so we had to carry drinking and coffee water with us. About noon the preacher said, "Now, Major, whenever you are hungry we will stop and feed the horses and have dinner." Very soon I saw a nice camping place with wood and grass, so I said, "There, Parson, is a nice camping ground." In he turned and jumped out. "Now," said he, "I'll take care of the horses, and you make the coffee. You'll find everything in the box." So I did, plenty of everything and more, too.

After I got my fire going, the coffee made, the blanket spread out, and the table set on that, I called the parson. He had been working on the horses all the time. The first thing he did on halting was to jerk off his coat and put on a jumper that he had. Then he unharnessed the horses, got out the curry comb and brush, and was taking elegant care of them until I called him to dinner, when over he came. "Why," said he. "You've got a fine layout. I always make it a rule to give thanks for what I am about to partake." With that he dropped down on his knees and made a good long prayer. I stood by waiting for him to finish, which he finally did.

No sooner had he said "Amen" than he began to pitch in, and I wish you could have seen him eat. The fake preacher I had at the mill would have been a "second." I lit my pipe and had my smoke, while the parson was still at work. Finally, he came to the can of blackberries I had opened but had not tested. He "topped off" by eating the entire two-pound can.

When he finished this he remarked, "I always make it a rule to give thanks for what I have had." With that he dropped down on his knees and did so. No sooner had he said "Amen," however, than up he jumped, grabbed the curry comb and brush, and back to work on the horses he went.

He carried me home in good shape all the same, but some

time after that I lost my good opinion of the parson. I had some men ploughing a field alongside the main road leading to town and Saturday evening at quitting time, instead of bringing their plows home, they left them alongside the road—plows, double-trees, etc., etc.

Sunday morning, as I was driving to town, I caught up with a man on foot and found it to be my parson friend. I said, "Good morning, Parson, are you going to town? If so, jump in and ride." I noticed the parson did not appear himself and wondered what the trouble could be. He ordinarily was very talkative, but this morning he had nothing to say. I really had enjoyed my ride over from the King Mine with him, and I couldn't understand why he was so quiet.

Finally, after a long silence he said, "Major, as I was coming down the road, I found a clevis that I supposed belongs to you and thought I would save it." At the same time he produced the article from his back coat pocket. The fact was, the parson had stolen the clevis off one of my plows and was fearful that I had seen him. I had seen him about where the plows had been left, but did not know that he was picking up clevises, and I am convinced it was his guilty conscience that was working on him which caused his inquietude.

One day as I drove into Phoenix, I saw a crowd of men in an open hallway. After I tied up my team, I went in to see about the excitement. They said a strange man had fallen off the roof where he had been sleeping (everybody slept on the roof then, at least everybody who had a house), and that he had about killed himself. As I got inside the hall, I saw a man lying in a cot and thought the face looked familiar. As I drew nearer, I recognized the man as an old army friend of the First Cavalry, Lieutenant Barry. I at once sent for the doctor and had Barry removed to our house.[6]

After a while he got well and remained with me for some time. Barry was the officer who had found the blackberry brandy or wine the day Lee surrendered and brought us the jug while we were on the line of battle. As I have before stated, it was the custom of the country for everybody to keep whiskey on the premises, and I have acknowledged mine was no exception to the rule. Barry was fond of my whiskey and every time I went away from home, he would get a little "shine on." In fact, he got more than I wanted to stand good for, not only because I thought he was taking more than was necessary or good for him, but because it was expensive. So one day when I was going away, thinking I would fix Barry so he would not be quite so jubilant when I returned, I took precaution to take the whiskey demijohn and push it up the throat of the chimney. It was warm in those parts. In fact, as the fireplace was but seldom used, I thought that would be the most unlikely place for him to look for the jug. I drove off thinking I had done a good joke on Barry. When I came home, however, I found Barry with his heels cocked up on the porch post and a bigger "shine" on than usual and laughing all over. "Oh, Major," said he, "no use to hide it. I can smell it." I guess he could, at that, for anyone who could find blackberry wine or brandy in Virginia after four years of war and the country having been run over by both armies must have had a good smeller. I never tried to hide the whiskey from Barry after that.

Poor old boy, I wonder what has become of him. He left the army shortly before I did. In coming along by the Picacho Mountains, near the Blue Water Well, where the mule and steer went down the well, Indians attacked. They killed a number of the party and captured all of Barry's goods and baggage. That was while he and his wife were leaving the territory, after he had left the army.

Since Barry was with me some time and had been of service to me, I gave him a hundred dollars and he left for San Francisco. I never heard from him from that time to this.

Now I have nearly exhausted my Arizona reminiscences and recollections. I can think of one, though, that may be of interest and that's the early discovery of gold in the territory.

In the early days, that's along about 1861 to 1864, Indians would come to California's eastern boundary to trade and sometimes they brought nuggets of gold. The traders tried to find out how or where they got them, but without avail. Finally a party of prospectors decided to follow the Indian trail, to try and find where the Arizona Indians got the gold.

There were four old frontiersmen as prospectors in the party: Jack Swilling (the outlaw); A. H. Peebles, a prospector and a saloon man; Joe Fugit, a gambler and prospector; and Darrell Duppa, an illegitimate son of an English nobleman. (I became personally acquainted with all of them afterward.) They employed a Mexican trailer to accompany the party, and started out on the trail of Indians, who had been in trading. When they got into Arizona, in the vicinity of Wickenburg, or rather what was known afterward as Wickenburg, they camped one night at the base of a mountain. During the night, the Indians stole all their animals, and next morning they found themselves "afoot" and a long way from home.

After holding a council of war, they concluded to follow the Indian trail and try and recover their animals. The trail led around the base of the mountain, which they followed all day. Toward evening, as they did not overtake the Indians, they concluded to give up the chase.

The Mexican trailer said the camp, or where they had camped the night before when the animals were stolen, was directly west of where they then were. The shortest way to reach the camp would be by tramping over the mountain, but it appeared so high the Americans would not undertake to climb it and decided to take the "back track."

The Mexican guide refused to follow them and struck out alone across the mountain. When he reached the summit, he found a flat top and something on the surface that fluttered. On examination he found it to be gold nuggets, exposed by the action of the weather so they lay on the surface. Picking up what he readily could, he struck down the opposite side of the mountain for where they had made camp the night before, which he reached long before the others. When they arrived and saw his discovery, they were not long in reaching the top of the mountain, where they picked up about $40,000 in pure gold. Some of the nuggets were of the size of hen's eggs. Some were in long strips, where the melted gold had run into crevices or cracks in rocks. In some places, the gold was the thickness of a knife blade; in some one-fourth of an inch in thickness. The formation must have been volcanic, for the gold had evidently been upheaved when in a molten state and then deposited in those shapes where it lay for ages. They gathered what they could easily pick up and struck out for California.

As soon as the discovery became known in California, daring prospectors at once began flocking to Arizona. Jack Swilling and his party returned and the mountain on which the gold had been discovered was overrun. Tunnels were run into it, shafts were sunk, but no lode could be found. To this day, parties are at work in that immediate vicinity. A great deal of gold had been found, but owing to the scarcity of water, it is only at certain seasons of the year that the ground can be worked. On extraordinary occasions, such as a wet season, considerable gold is found. The last nugget I saw found in the immediate vicinity was in 1890 and was worth about $96. The surrounding country is all gold-bearing to a greater or lesser extent, so there is a possibility of some rich mine yet being discovered.

The discovery of Rich Hill, as it was referred to, led to the locating of Phoenix and the settling of the Salt River Valley. Jack Swilling returned with another party to the mountain and from there drifted down to the Salt River Valley. He was one of the first to discover that the country had once been under cultivation from finding the ruins of canals that had been in use at some former time.

Henry Wickenburg, a German, came to the territory about that time. In prospecting through the Indian country, he saw a black mountain peak rising up out on the desert, some fifteen miles west of where Wickenburg now stands, and on investigating found it rich in gold. He afterward got some eastern parties interested, and they put up the first gold quartz mill in the territory. The mill had to be built at Wickenburg because there was no water any nearer to the mine. The quartz was hauled in by large teams and many encounters with Indians were had in that immediate vicinity. Building the mill at that point led to the location of the town or village of Wickenburg.

Henry Wickenburg located the town site, a portion of which was susceptible of cultivation by taking water out of the Hassayampa River for irrigation. The last time I saw the old man was to appraise the damages done him by a flood caused by the breaking of the Walnut Grove Water Storage Company's dam, which went out after an extraordinary rain and caused much damage and the loss of seventy-five lives. The citizens on the line of the creek who were damaged endeavored to hold the company liable for damages, but failed.

The Silver King Mine was discovered in a very remarkable way. General Stoneman, while in command of the District of Arizona had established what he called a "picket post," which was an outlying post from which the Indian trails and movements could be watched and from which scouting parties could be sent out. In crossing the Pinal Mountains, which were very steep to ascend, the saddle of one of the soldiers on such a scout slipped and he had to stop and fix the cinch or girth. The command, in the meantime, continued on its march. As he was arranging his saddle, he overturned some rock that to him had a very peculiar look, so he picked up a piece and put it in his saddle bag.

The man soon after was discharged from the army. On his way out of the territory, he passed through what afterward became the village of Florence. In it were a number of prospectors who knew something of quartz. He exhibited what he had found and the men at once pronounced it rich silver ore.

He told them he had found it while out on a scout and promised to guide them to the point at which he had found the rock after he had made a visit to his home, but he never returned. After waiting a long time, a party of four was made up and started out on the trail the soldiers had made in making their scout and they actually found the float rock, as it is called, from which the soldier had found a piece. After following that, they located the mine which turned out to be wonderfully rich. Millions of silver bars were taken from the mine. It made them all rich men.

I have seen some of the rock. Pieces that would probably weigh five hundred pounds, after being cracked or crushed with sledgehammers, could not be parted without cutting the threads or seams of native silver with cold chisels.

The Tombstone discovery was another remarkable one. Ed Schieffelin, who had passed through the territory with a government expedition in the latter fifties, had noticed the peculiar formation and become impressed with the idea that it must contain "mineral." After hearing of the discoveries made in the territory, he undertook to get back to the territory along in the eighties and prospect the country he had noticed many years before. He was "hard up" and could only get as far as Mojave, a trading post on the Colorado River when he was swamped or, in other words, "busted." There he met a man by the name of Gird, whom he got interested in him and furnished him what is called a "grubstake." In Arizona parlance that meant Gird gave him a supply of provisions to last, say, three or six months, with the understanding that the party who gets the stake makes the party furnishing the provisions an equal partner in any discoveries that are made.

In that way Schieffelin got over to Tucson, where he tried to make up a party to go out to the section of the territory he had in mind, but as Geronimo, the noted Indian chief who lately died at Fort Sill, was then on the war path, no one could be induced to go with him. Whenever he broached the subject, he was "turned down." They all said it would be utterly impossible to go into that section at that time, with the Indians out as they were. Finally, Schieffelin said he was going even if he went alone. "Well," said they, "you'll find a tombstone if you do." He went anyhow and found—and located—the richest silver mine ever discovered in Arizona, and he named it Tombstone.

After working the mine for some time, he sold his interest for $1,300,000 in cash. Gird, the man who had furnished him the "grubstake," got $650,000 for his investment. This is an Arizona story, but an absolutely true one.

I had scouted and hunted Indians over the same identical country, long before. I even camped on the very ground where the town of Tombstone is now located. The discovery of the mines brought about the building of a town of some four thousand inhabitants. After working the mines for many years, water was struck in such quantity that they had to be abandoned, but of late years wealthy California people have taken hold of the mines again. They are installing the largest pumping plants in the United States with a view of draining the mines. The ore is there. If the water can be controlled, lots of silver will be produced.

And now a word as to what became of Ed Schieffelin. First he deposited his $650,000 in California banks, then he struck out for Alaska. When he got up there, he reached the Yukon River, but could not ascend it for want of a boat, so he returned to San Francisco and had a boat built in sections, which he had shipped to that territory and put together on arrival. Then he ascended the river for many hundreds of miles, but did not discover gold in any paying quantities, so he returned to San Francisco and took to prospecting in California. He died all alone in a cabin out in the mountains. Gird, his partner, bought the China Ranch in Southern California and put up a sugar beet mill, having all the ranch planted to sugar beets, and was making money last I heard.

The China Ranch was a part of the country in which I caught my first two deserters, the ones who had deserted from Drum Barracks in 1866. At that time it was barren wasteland as was, in fact, almost all of that section of country lying between Drum Barracks and San Bernardino. At that time, there was but one ranch house—where a Mexican had a few cattle—between Drum Barracks and Los Angeles. It was known as the Domingues Cattle Ranch. Later, on discovery of artesian water, every acre was put under cultivation and now the land "blooms like a rose" the entire year. Every acre is worth a thousand dollars or more.

In looking back, it is most wonderfully surprising to me to see the remarkable changes that have taken place in the territory from the time of my arrival in 1866 to the time of my leaving in 1891. When I got there—an area in extent the equal of the states of Pennsylvania, New York, Maryland, and New Jersey—it was almost unknown territory inhabited almost entirely by the most savage tribes of Indians known. The only mail we had was that carried by a military expressman once a month. To get a letter East and a reply required sixty days. I have seen first the "buckboard," then the stage making weekly trips, then the daily mail by stage. Next came the military telegraph, when we could send a ten-word message to the East for $1.25; then the Southern Pacific Railroad came through the southern part of the territory followed by the Atlantic and Pacific crossing the northern part; afterward connection was made by the two via Phoenix. Then the town of Phoenix grew up where not a residence had been before within a distance of two hundred miles. Today it has fifteen thousand inhabitants, rich churches, schoolhouses, electric street railways, water works, electrical lights, and all the modern improvements. Where not a spear of grass would grow without irrigation, you now see wheat and barley and alfalfa fields, almost as far as the eye can reach and fruits of all kinds—oranges, lemons, peaches, grapes, figs. By last year's Chamber of Commerce reports, I see Phoenix alone shipped 127 cars of oranges and nearly a thousand cars of cantaloupes.

To have seen all these improvements made and know that I have had a hand in bringing the changes about or making them possible is a source of gratification to me almost equal to that of being able to say I was one of the "boys" who helped to preserve the Union.

$Notes$

INTRODUCTION

1. These letters, which evidently are no longer extant, were cited in Edward J. Nichols, *Toward Gettysburg: A Biography of General John F. Reynolds* (University Park: Pennsylvania State University Press, 1958).

1. PERSONAL RECOLLECTIONS AND REMINISCENCES OF THE CIVIL WAR

1. Brigadier General John Cleveland Robinson, a division commander in the V Corps, placed himself in the forefront of his reluctant troops at Laurel Hill and was severely wounded in the knee. Although his leg was amputated, he remained in the army until 1869. He later was awarded the Congressional Medal of Honor for his actions that day. Ezra J. Warner, *Generals in Blue: Lives of the Union Commanders* (Baton Rouge: Louisiana State University Press, 1964), pp. 407–408.

2. Captain Samuel McKee, a West Point graduate, was wounded at Cold Harbor on May 31, 1864, and died the next day. His commanding officer, Brigadier General Wesley Merritt, described him as a "pure, unaffected, modest man, a chivalrous, educated, accomplished soldier, he fell at the post of honor doing his duty as but few could, and died a true American soldier with warm words of patriotism and valor on his lips." *War of the Rebellion: Official Records of the Union and Confederate Armies,* 128 vols. (Washington, D.C., 1880–1901) (Report 194), I, vol. 36, p. 849.

3. This incident occurred September 24, 1864. Lieutenant Charles McMaster was mortally wounded after being taken prisoner by two of Mosby's men. He did not die until October 15, however. Although the atrocities on both sides in this incident are well documented, there is some confusion regarding the number of men captured and then executed. Theodore F. Rodenbough, *From Everglade to Canyon with the Second Dragoons* (New York: D. Van Nostrand, 1875), states that thirteen prisoners were hanged (pp. 358–59), but Jeffrey D. Wert, *Mosby's Rangers* (New York: Simon & Schuster, 1990), indicates that only six men were captured, two of whom were hanged; the others were shot. He also indicates that several Union generals witnessed the executions (pp. 211–20).

4. Captain Thomas Drummond was killed in action at Five Forks, Virginia, on April 1, 1865. Francis B. Heitman, *Historical Register and Dictionary of the United States Army,* vol. 1 (Washington, D.C., 1903), p. 384.

2. ARIZONA ADVENTURES, 1865-1871

1. Forsythe's brigade was part of a two-division force under the overall command of General Wesley Merritt. It was part of General Custer's division, which formed in Alexandria, Louisiana. The two divisions were to move out separately with Merritt commanding the first column and Custer the second. Their mission was to clear out Confederate guerrillas in Texas and to restore order in the state.

2. The "mutiny" to which Veil refers concerned an officer on Custer's staff intensely disliked by his men. They not only threatened him, but several signed a petition demanding his resignation. On Custer's orders all but one of the petitioners—a sergeant—apologized and were restored to duty. The sergeant was court-martialed and sentenced to death, a sentence—as Veil describes—that Custer commuted at the last moment. The trooper who was executed that day had not participated in the supposed mutiny; he had been a deserter. Lawrence A. Frost, *The Custer Album: A Pictorial Biography of General George A. Custer* (New York: Bonanza Books, 1984), pp. 70–71.

3. Veil and his company, consisting of one officer and thirty-eight men, departed Camp Grant for Camp Tubac on May 10, 1867, and arrived on May 23, having traveled 120 miles. According to the Regimental Returns for Camp Tubac, which are in the National Archives, the post was established on May 27 with a complement of 107 men from Company C, First Cavalry, and Company K, 32nd Infantry, and five officers. Tubac was formerly an old Mexican post containing a presidio of two adobe buildings, corrals, and a small piece of land.

4. According to Regimental Returns, three men—not two as Veil remembers—deserted on May 21, 1867: Privates William I. Doyle, Francis Dougherty, and Isaac Wheeler. The following day Veil and ten men started in pursuit. Veil returned to Tubac on June 10, having apprehended the three deserters in Magdalena, Mexico. The rest of the detail and the prisoners did not return until June 21, the delay no doubt the result of the men having to walk, as Veil recalls.

5. Sam Hughes (1829–1917), considered the dean of Arizona pioneers, was born in Wales and arrived in Tucson in 1858. A successful businessman, he formed a partnership with Hiram S. Stevens and A. Lazard and went into the mining, mercantile, and beef businesses. Stevens (1832–1893) later killed himself over despondency caused by his failing business interests. Four days after his death, the firm of Hughes, Stevens, and Company was attached by its creditors. Frank C. Lockwood, "Who Was Who in Arizona," Tucson *Star*, Dec. 1, 1940.

3. ARIZONA ANECDOTES, 1871-1891

1. Jack Swilling (1830–1878), a veteran of the war with Mexico, is credited with developing the first irrigation canals for Phoenix, an idea evidently inspired by seeing the evidence of pre-Columbian Indian canals in the area. Swilling, a noted public figure who worked at times as a miner, farmer, postmaster, and justice of the peace, also had a dark side. Pain from a bullet he carried from a shooting in 1854 caused him to become a morphine addict. He was at times violent and unpredictable, and he was an excessive drinker. In 1878 he and two companions were arrested for robbing a stage. Although charges against his companions were later dropped and he was exonerated, Swilling had meanwhile died in jail awaiting his trial. *Arizona Heritage: A Commemorative Portrait Collection,* courtesy Arizona Historical Foundation, Arizona State University, Tempe, Arizona.

2. Cochise, leader of the Chiricahua Apaches during the time Veil served in Arizona Territory, was born about 1824 and died in 1874. For a detailed account of Cochise and the troubles with the Apaches in the Southwest after the Civil War, see Dan L. Thrapp, *The Conquest of Apacheria* (Norman: University of Oklahoma Press, 1967).

3. Thomas Jefferson Jeffords (1831–1914), reputedly one of the few white men that Chiricahua Apache leader Cochise trusted, was a Civil War veteran, trader, and rancher who spent much of his life in Arizona. He agreed to serve as Indian agent for the Chiricahuas when Cochise agreed to accept a reservation. Jeffords remained the Chiricahua agent until 1876. *Arizona Range,* Feb. 27, 1914.

4. Geronimo (1829–1909) succeeded to the leadership of the militant Chiricahuas upon the death of Cochise. Despite his violent life, he lived to a ripe old age and died of exposure after falling out of his buckboard. His capture in 1886 marked the end of the Indian wars. Robert M. Utley, *The Indian Frontier of the American West, 1846–1890* (Albuquerque: University of New Mexico Press, 1984), pp. 196–97.

5. This incident is known as the Loring, or Wickenburg, Massacre. Early on November 5, 1871, the Wickenburg stagecoach, carrying eight passengers, was attacked. Six passengers were killed outright and another died later of wounds. Among the passengers were three members of the George M. Wheeler surveying expedition, including the writer Frederick W. Loring of Massachusetts. Although never proven, it was assumed the attack was made by Apaches from the nearby Date Creek Reservation. Dan L. Thrapp, *The Conquest of Apacheria* (University of Oklahoma Press, 1967), p. 105.

6. After leaving Arizona, John Barry relocated in Washington, D.C., where he died of pneumonia and "stricture of the oesophagus" on February 2, 1880, at age forty-two. According to his Invalid Pension File (190811) in the National Archives, he suffered so severely from rheumatism that his limbs had to be contracted to fit into his coffin. Barry, who had been born in Ireland, was mustered out of military service on January 1, 1871, the same day as his friend Veil.

Index